# REUNION

## JUDGING
## THE
## FAMILY COURT

MARY W MAXWELL, LLB

ISBN:  978-0-9807627-6-1




Key words
Reunion, Protective parent, The Family Court Survey, Fixated Persons Investigation Unit, *Rilak v Tsocas*, Truth Commission, parental alienation, Senator Nancy Schaefer, Russell Pridgeon, Dunblane massacre, Tim Minogue, Parent Responsibility Contract, Franca Arena, Beaumont children, Freda Briggs, George Potkonyak, Maurice Kriss, citizen's arrest, Fiona Barnett, Ghislaine Maxwell, Kieran Le Plastrier, chit


Author's websites: ProsecutionForTreason.com,
   MaxwellforSenate.com, and MaryWMaxwell.com

Author's email: MaxwellMaryLLB@gmail.com



Front cover: Dr Russell Pridgeon, giving his historic speech in front of courthouse, Brisbane, April 5, 2019

*To the innocents*

*and to innocence*

Peter Lewis (1940-2015), Speaker of the House in the South Australian Parliament:

I [was] bringing some of the people who had made the allegations to the point where they might pluck up enough courage and confidence and swear the truth of those allegations, enabling them to be more carefully investigated.

But they were being 'bumped off'– that is, murdered and viciously assaulted – quicker than I could get them to write down their allegations.

The most outrageous thing of all [is] the related and organised activities of those pedophiles in high public office – that is, the judiciary, the senior ranks of human services portfolios, some police and MPs, across the nation....

Canada's Prime Minister Stephen Harper, June 11, 2008:

We realize that by separating children from parents, we undermined [that child's] ability to parent, and sowed the seeds for generations to follow and we apologize for having done this.

# South Australia Supreme Court Schedule of Fees

General Fees as at July 1, 2018 (www. courts.sa.gov.au):

On filing an application for disclosure of documents before the commencement of a proceeding: $429.00

On filing to commence a proceeding in the Supreme Court: $2526.00

On filing a summons for permission to appeal: $429.00
On filing a notice of appeal for which permission to appeal is required: $2,097.00

**On setting a date for trial:  $2526.00**

**Copying**:  For a copy of a document: $4.90 per page (other than a copy of evidence).
For copy of evidence -- per Page in electronic form $8.10.   Per Page in hard-copy form $10.40

**For copy of reasons for judgment:  $8.10 per page** [wow]

Trial fee -- For each day or part of a day on which the trial is heard by the Court    $2,526.00

For opening Court (or Court remaining open) after hours for urgent hearing:  **$1,169.00 per hour or part of an hour.**
[Emphasis added]

**What ever happened to the Magna Charta, of 1215 AD:**

"We have also granted to all freemen of our kingdom, all the underwritten liberties, to be had and held by them and their heirs ... forever…. **To no one will we sell, to no one will we refuse or delay, right or justice.**"

# Preface

Who would believe that Family Law courts are corrupt? Who would believe that governments of US, Australia, UK, and Canada steal children and get away with it?

Almost certainly it's a global racket. We must end it.

The way I came into this odd story was through a beautiful member of the McIntyre family of Adelaide, Rachel Vaughan. Her father, Max McIntyre, died in 2017 at age 89. He was quite a terrible human being. He was employed by a powerful pedophile ring and did any murders they ordered.

This book isn't about those murders, nor is it about child sexual abuse. Granted, it's set against a background of an existing pedo-and-trafficking system (which is global and therefore our judges are probably under foreign instruction!) but there won't be nitty-gritty here about sex.

My concentration is on the law. We need our law. Our law is fabulous -- when it is not being perverted. This book says 'Legal kidnap' is *illegal*. Today judges take your kids away without so much as a by-your-leave. They even order the removal of a baby from the hospital on the day it's born.

"Unjust!" you cry." "*Outrageous!* I'll fix that guy's wagon." No, you won't because there is a tight system to lock you out of the civil courts, and to legally prevent you from exposing your plight via the media. It really outdoes Kafka.

The second half of the book is about solutions. Once you have become aware that "legal kidnapping" by the courts is taking place, and you realize it is criminal, you can crack down on the miscreants. Prosecuting them and suing them to within an inch of their wallet is possible. But so is getting the children reunited with family.

Perhaps some readers picking up this book do not know of the disrespect with which many a parent has been treated by so-called child-protection agencies. I will briefly state it now. To my amazement I have heard from mothers that they are allowed only *supervised* visits with their darling children – usually once a week or a fortnight, located at a governmental place where the interaction of kids and parents is watched through a two-way mirror.

There, I said it. Did you faint on the floor? Good. Many parents have been broken by this persecution. I am not talking about a parent who has choked her child – we would all approve of supervised visits. I am talking about a parent who, say, let dirty dishes pile up at home. Is that the state's business? They claim it is. (Faint again.)

I can tell you more. The parent may be instructed not to hug her child during the "visit," or say "I love you," or even give him a gift. We know this instruction is wrong on the face of it. Also, she, the mum, will be asked to prove over and over that she's not a mental case. (Remember, this is for "dishes.")

Note: the same can happen to a father. Family Law is the great equalizer.

For reasons of my slightly odd research background, I know a lot about the efforts to change our culture that have been undertaken for decades, clandestinely. So I "get it" re the supervised visit nonsense. It is part of a so-called experiment to see how far a person can hold out against frustration, confusion, and humiliation. (Remember Abu Ghraib?)

But *I'm not having it.* We need to stop all such cruelty. It's time to terminate the whole gig. I think it is the judiciary that needs to be held to account. They are, in the end, the kidnappers. We ought to stop honoring kidnappers, do you agree?

Nevertheless, reunion is the goal in this book. Punishing the bad guys has its place, but only a secondary place. I seem to write a lot of books about how to punish bad officials. This is not the career I want! I'd like to kick aside my PhD in Politics and study the lilies of the field.

All right. Time to jump onto the case. Please join me!

Note: This book incorporates articles that I published at GumshoeNews.com, which is based in Melbourne. So when I say "in this country" I mean Australia. I was born and raised in US. My Bachelor's degree is from Emmanuel College, Boston; my law degree is from University of Adelaide, with part of it completed in Germany.

Mary W Maxwell, LLB                    February 28, 2019


UPDATE: I originally provided a Net copy of the February 2019 edition of this book. Some may have it on file. It was called "Reunion and Family Law." Now I've changed the subtitle to "Judging the Family Court." This version contains a Foreword by a Mum and an Afterword by a sagacious GP, and late-breaking stuff on the Jeffery Epstein case. I've also added to the appendices new writings by Fiona Barnett, an eye-opener by autism doctor Andrew Wakefield, and helpful court cases here and abroad.

August 16, 2019

## CONTENTS



10

<h1 style="text-align:center">Court Rulings Cited in This Book</h1>

<u>**FOREWORD**</u> -- by Mrs [Redacted]

I suppose my story might a typical one. It started with me reporting abuse, then being whisked off to hospital for a mental health assessment. Thereafter was a roller coaster ride through investigations, Family Court, and Youth Court.

The corruption seeps in like bacteria over stale yogurt, and the department that supposedly exists to protect children, took my daughter away. Incredibly, they claim it is for the *good of the child*. After nine months I sent a letter (one of many) to the social worker supervising my child. I wrote:

"Over the last 9 months I have been trying arrange a meeting with you to discuss my daughter's situation. I had wanted to talk about the misleading reports submitted to Court, but was deflected at every turn. I was trying to bring to your attention the facts and the truth. … You are keeping my daughter against her will. Do you ever consider the stress on her?

"The CPS never investigated any of my abuse allegations, including photos of my daughter's injuries. No words can describe my despair and anger -- as I know that you have seen official reports substantiating past abuse by the man. Your department kept that out of court, never informing the judge.

"Without investigations being done, the social workers are putting this child in a high-risk situation and jeopardizing her safety, her development, and her very life.

"Every daughter needs a loving mother, but maybe you don't believe that love has anything to do with a child's wellbeing. Can you imagine the humiliation of a child going to school and having to explain why her mum no longer looks after her, and that everyone is calling her mother dangerous and crazy. It is emotional abuse of the child.

"Your reports and notes are filled with lies and deliberate deletions. Where are you getting your information from? Your documents (supposedly written by yourself) do not match the reports in the system, and then your summaries are so far from what actually happened. Is someone else writing the reports on your behalf?" [End of letter to social worker]

The worst day of my life was when social workers took my daughter away. The second worst day was when I had to see my daughter "under supervision," with rules and boundaries. That's when one understands that the government has turned a citizen into a slave. At least a criminal is punished for doing something wrong. I was punished for doing something right.

Now my friends tell me that Mary W Maxwell has produced a book, attempting to reunite children with their parents. I am so ready for the reunion. My beautiful child is ready. I want to mention her admirable strength. She was told at age 7 by the perpetrator that if she spoke she may be killed. She spoke up.

She has been called by the pedo's "a 14-million dollar girl." Oh really? Her value to the world is much greater than that. And why do these persons think it's their right to "cash" her?

As far as I know – and here I am listening to Don Rufty in America who runs a "civil rights movement" – the only answer to the cruelty and corruption is publicity. Rufty says "The highest court in the land is the court of public opinion."

That means I need any reader of this book to join with me and the thousands of other affected parents – plus any kind soul – in facing, straight on, the powerful criminals who think our babies are commodities. And who think they can buy off, or scare off, everyone in sight.

No, they can't. My daughter is proof of that.

# PART ONE

# "LEGAL" KIDNAP IS ILLEGAL

> **Kidnapping.** Division 9, sec 39 (1) A person who takes or detains another person, without the other person's consent — (a) with the intention of holding the other person to ransom or as a hostage; or (b) with the intention of committing an indictable offence against [him] or a third person, is guilty of an offence. [Maximum penalty: (a) for a basic offence—imprisonment for 20 years]
>
> -- Criminal Law Consolidation Act, 1935, South Australia

# 1. Introduction to the Plan for Reunion

*Citizens of the Czech Republic in Prague protest child-stealing in Norway!*

What an amazing situation!  In Australia – and elsewhere – there are courts making *sinister decisions* to remove a child from one or both of its parents.

If you walked into the courtroom and were a naive citizen, you may not see at first what is going on.  It looks like a normal, decent place.  There are clerks and lawyers, probably a security guard, a sober judge, a gavel. Plenty of paper files.

No doubt there are some cases where the court is doing the right thing for children. OK, but his book isn't about those cases. It is about "judicial kidnap." Many judges pull a kid out of a perfectly good home and send him or her to reside with a pedophile. That is to say, the courts are part and parcel of the well-known tragedy of child-trafficking.

Yes it's true and it's time we stopped being too shy to say so.

**Outside Influences.** It is the theory of this book (easily proven) that the impetus is coming from outside. Some say child-sex is money-driven and indeed financial incentives do play a part. But that is not the big engine driving it all. The big engine is a power grab in which the powerful few want to remove whatever gives us personal strength, such as our family ties. They prefer a nation of scared weaklings.

They have been trying for decades to attack ordinary sources of strength, such as nationalism, marital covenants, and religion. Please consider the hypothesis that the Catholic scandal (pedophile priests) did not come about because a number of men had an irrepressible urge to sexually abuse children. Rather their indulging in this behavior was *engineered.*

Here in Part One, I will lay out as many parts of the problem of "Judicial Kidnap," as I know of. We will see how arrangements have been made by legislators, by police departments, by media, and others to bring about this truly fantastic situation of stealing children. Part Two will analyze it.

This book's Part Three, "Operation Crackdown," offers solutions. It will be easy enough to kick the bad system over, as we now see how it works. Various chapters will recommend the full range of lawful methods: you can indict, sue, defrock, enjoin, negotiate, etc. As for the aforementioned outside influences, we'll need to look beyond the courts to "The Bigger Picture" – that is the task of Part Four.

**Reunion Chits Now Available!**

This book recommends that we adopt the goal of reunion. A large number of kids today want relief from a harmful pedophile parent and to be reunited with the other parent. It is absolutely do-able. What possible basis could there be for saying the reunion can't happen?

Citizens can get together and examine a case brought by a "Protective parent." That is the term used in this book for the parent who is trying to get his or her child back from a parent who is causing harm. I suggest that a group of citizens write up all the improper activity of the court in the particular case.

The next step is to produce, if appropriate, a "chit." A chit is something like a voucher or a coupon. It will be a valuable instrument, a legal instrument, for rescuing a child.

**Kansas.** Here is an idea cooked up by sensible people in Kansas, USA – see douglascountyks.org. They've started a Citizen Review Board to overcome the problems of bad decisions by judges or child protection services. Quote:

"There are currently five Citizen Review Boards – CRBs -- which meet monthly. Potential volunteers must submit a written application and go through a screening procedure.

"All must complete training requirements set forth by the Kansas Supreme Court before they can be sworn in by the Chief Judge to review cases. CRB volunteers are assigned to review *child in need of care* cases and to report in writing to the presiding judge.

"Volunteers meet as a group once a month and interview *families and service providers* and then deliberate in private before sharing their recommendations orally with the people in attendance. The presiding judge can use the CRB recommendations to make his/her own court orders."

Simple but brilliant! Why not get your state to endorse such a thing? Even without 'permission' of government you can act. Are you worried this would be subversive? Stop worrying. Society owns the law. Chits will be discussed in Chapter 30.

In the last two months I've traveled in Queensland, New South Wales, and South Australia, interviewing Protective parents. You'd be amazed at the similarity of stories. No need to read about Lena [pseudonym] if you already know the routine, but if you are a newcomer (Welcome! Welcome!) please accept, tentatively, that the following is "standard":

**Lena's Story:** At 25, I was glad to be introduced, by a mutual friend, to the charming Francois, complete with French accent. The dating relationship lasted six years off and on. We never married or even lived together. Francois started to perform what I am now told is "gas-lighting" to lower my self-esteem (which was low anyway).
After I fell pregnant, he said such things as "I never touched you." I am grateful to nurses at hospital for advising me not to put his name on the birth certificate; it was left open. The bottom line of my story is that the baby, Ben, was given to Francois by a court at age 5. Yes.

That was 8 ago and I am still trying very hard to get him back. One of my biggest sadnesses is that people look at me funny and whisper "There must be more to it." But there isn't.
Francois used violence and threats. I fled with the baby to my cousin's house. Later I made the mistake of recontacting Francois, thinking he should share the joy of having a child. He already had an older daughter, Marie, and I treated her as my step-child, naturally. She still calls me Mumma.

At first, Francois behaved OK, but later he kidnapped Ben. I went to police and luckily they found Ben and brought him back to me.  They told me if the dad's name had been on the birth certificate they would not have been able to do so.

At age 6 my son Ben start to complain about going to visit dad. He refused to speak to him. Worryingly, he told me that he – age 6 -- was planning to injure or even kill his dad using kitchen weapons. By now I was in a relationship with a new partner and was about to give birth to my son Shane. Francois broke into my house and said "I'm going to destroy you and your family in court and see to it you never see Ben again."

I was required to go to Mandatory Mediation and was told I might go to jail (!!!). Francois had written to my employer, my friends and neighbors with lies about my mental health and my ability to raise kids. The wrongly named "Department of Child Safety" began to investigate on his behalf, searching for something that could trigger the removal of Ben. For example, they went to Ben's Daycare Center to record him, asking if Mum goes out and leaves him alone. Of course Ben said No.

The police *colluded with* Francois to take Ben. Yes! They'd been unable to find a reason to get a safety order -- but that did not stop them from removing my child. At this point I was made out to be the baddy. Francois had learned how to involve such government departments as commissioners, Parliamentarians, child protection people, persuading some of them that Ben should be removed from me immediately and permanently.

**Court Experience.** The next five years were shockers for me. The threats of jail, allegations of coaching, enmeshment, parentification, and extremism – made me think Francois's prediction would eventuate. Two persons connected to the court – an ICL and a Report Writer -- acted against me 100%.

One ICL (Independent Children's Lawyer) yelled, swore, and threatened **to have Ben sent to foster care** if I didn't sign the "consent" orders he was pushing. Also, a Family Court report writer clearly supported Francois and didn't believe any of my reports of domestic violence by him. But, to me, it was the judge who was the most shocking. He ordered me not to see *–not to even speak to* -- my beloved first-born again.

I assure you I presented with a clean bill of mental health, perpetrated no domestic violence, did not neglect or harm the child in any way mentally, physically, or emotionally.

So what was the reason for such an order? When Ben was 5 years old, he finally broke down and told me why he so desperately didn't want to go back to see his dad. Ben confessed that his father had been sexually abusing him ever since he could remember. Ben had been threatened. He also said dad instructed *him* to kill both me and Shane (his little half-brother).

I did get "permission" years later to visit my child in a "supervised setting." This occurred at a "contact centre" where the environment is totally unnatural and tends to damage the bond between mother and child. And the child thinks the separation has been *his* fault! (By the way, Ben loves his brother Shane of course and misses him – and vice versa.)

After 18 months, Ben had become trusting of the staff at the contact centre and one day while I'm in the loo, he began to open up about what his dad does to his "privates." As any mother would do, I went to the nearest police station. There I found that a cop may lie, to cover up the fact.

The police officer attempted to coach Ben to say that his dad was **only washing him**, despite the abuse reportedly occurring on the couch in the living room without soap, water or towels. Shortly after this, Ben is handed back to Francois. At trial:

1. I was not allowed witnesses. 2. I was denied a chance to show the police's 93A interview with Ben (it "went missing"). 3. Medical evidence of Ben's damaged genitals was *not allowed*, and 4. I was not allowed to present affidavits by my relatives that said they'd been threatened by the child protection police to not assist me. As far as I know that is not even done in the trial of a criminal suspect. Anyway I am grateful that I still have my younger boy. I took a polygraph to prove my "innocence." But the word goes around that I am delusional. Do you believe me?

***Comment:*** I more or less interrogated Lena and I believe her. The folks who whisper "There must be more to it" haven't experienced the untrammeled power of a court. Similar things have occurred to thousands of unlucky families in Australia. It is an urgent matter and we must tackle it together.

**Academic Study of 27 Cases**. (All hands on deck! Please help!) by Joyanna Silberg and Stephanie Dallam, in the JOURNAL OF CUSTODY, July 2, 2019, Abstract [Bolding added]:

… The goal of this case series was to determine **why family courts may place children with a parent that the child alleges abused them rather than with the non-offending parent**. We focused on "turned around cases" involving allegations of child abuse that were at first viewed as false and later judged to be valid. **The average time a child spent in the court ordered custody of an abusive parent was 3.2 years**. In all cases we uncovered the father was the abusive parent and the mother sought to protect their child. Results revealed that initially courts were highly suspicious of mothers' motives for **being concerned** with abuse. [!!]

These mothers were often treated poorly and **two-thirds of the mothers were pathologized by the court for advocating for the safety of their children**. Judges who initially ordered children into custody or visitation with abusive parents relied mainly on reports by custody evaluators and guardians ad litem who mistakenly accused mothers of attempting to alienate their children from the father or having **coached** the child to falsely report abuse. As a result, 59% of perpetrators were given sole custody and the rest were given joint custody or unsupervised visitation. **After failing to be protected in the custody determination, 88% of children reported new incidents of abuse**. The abuse often became increasingly severe and the children's health frequently deteriorated. The main reason that cases turned around was because protective parents were able to present compelling evidence of the abuse and **back the evidence up with reports by mental health professionals** who had specific expertise in child abuse Since completing this study, we have been made aware of four cases in which **mothers were the alleged abusers** and the **father was accused** of parental alienation after attempting to protect their children from further abuse. [All hands needed on deck for this!]

# 2. Four Whistle Blowers of Family Law

*(L) Don Rufty, North Carolina     (R) Bill Windsor, Georgia*

We need all the heroes we can get. Two such heroes are Don Rufty, owner of a small newspaper, and Bill Windsor who invented the Lawless America series on Youtube. Each of the two men had a personal grievance – harassment by a court. But soon they branched out to help any fellow sufferers.

Rufty in the US blames judges for the Family Court prob-lems. He says he put community pressure on the judges of Mecklenburg County, NC by newspaper publicity -- and that it worked! Rufty says he turned the judges into angels. Great!

As for Bill Windsor, he drove his car around 48 of the 50 states making videos of people who had been treated horribly by courts. This included criminal and civil matters but he honed in on family law. For his trouble he has been jailed twice. Note: *so far*, no one has been punished for wrongly punishing Bill Windsor like that.  But it will come to pass.

## Senator Nancy Schaefer

In the past, Protective parents were unaware there was a large racket. Today organizations such as Exiled Parents and forced-adoption.com hold rallies and send emails. A leading light in this movement was Senator Nancy Schaefer (1936-2010) of the state of Georgia. Her constituents had told her about the problem. She held a meeting in a library, attended by fifty Protective parents, with more queued up outside.

*The late Senator Nancy Schaefer of Georgia*

Nancy observed that persons who lose their kids are "dazed and glazed"; they have no idea what to do. As a legislator, she proposed that **if there is a threat of having one's child removed, a jury must make that decision**. But Senator Nancy Schaefer is no longer alive. The allegation is that her husband, Bruce Schaefer, supposedly shot his wife in the head and then shot himself in the chest, in a suicide pact. Lies! Clearly both of them were murdered. A woman on a mission does not choose to quit this world. A man who loves his wife does not put a bullet through her brain.

In a Youtube video, Schaefer wisely concluded her speech by quoting the Old Testament: Proverbs: 31:8 – **"Speak up for those who cannot speak up for themselves."**

Carol Woods of the UK is another heroic whistle blower. As a child-protection social worker, she saw a lot. While working for a local authority, the Lancashire Council, UK, Ms Woods blew the whistle and got the usual round of punishments for it. Another patriot. Yay!

You can find her talk with Brian Gerrish at UKcolumn.org, which has a very good Youtube channel. The following is from her speech, *paraphrased* by me.

## Carol Woods' Story

In my work, I [Carol] had cases including 4 disturbed boys who lived in a group home. And I had a depressed mum with a baby and was asked to falsify records against her so the state could take the baby. I refused and so gave the required 2 months' notice of resignation, but I later rescinded that.

The council wanted to take, speedily, a huge piece of land on which lived many persons-in-care and 46 staff. I told them there was a requirement to give consideration as to what would happen – who would look after the kids and what new employment could the 46 staff get?

*Carol Woods, UK whistle blower*

Two of the boys on that land burglarized a home causing death by heart attack of the resident. I call it "corporate manslaughter," and pinned it on the council for uprooting the boys. Council then tried to show that they hadn't yet made the decision to take the land. This began in 2003 and led to years of harassment. I got isolated as my family and friends were bought off or scared off. Also I voluntarily stayed away from associates so they wouldn't also be targeted. Living in a cul de sac I saw big cars park in front of my house for, say, an hour. At night they'd shine their high beams into my house.

Mike Todd, Chief Constable of Manchester, tried to help me, but he died mysteriously. They came after me to arrest me for "failure to attend" which is meaningless. In order to build a case against me they invented a fake lady named *Mrs* Wood*se*. (I am *Ms* Wood*s*.) She is said to be a smoker and drinker; I do not smoke or drink.

Also at work the bosses gave me too many cases to handle and insulted my appearance, even saying I walk too self-confidently! They made not-very-veiled threats. Once they smashed my windows and drilled holes in my walls.

I have referred to the aforementioned stolen baby as "an ordered baby." The mum had not done anything wrong but some family must have wanted a baby. They simply put into the mum's file that she had done bad things.

Their main coup was to get me incarcerated in a mental hospital three times, once for 3 months. Each time no one told my family what happened; they reported me as missing. I wasn't allowed to receive phone calls or visitors.

At one point I moved into the district of Norman Baker, MP, as he had said David Kelly's death (Iraq weapons) was not suicide. He tried to ask questions for me in Parliament. What saved me in the end was publicity.     – End of paraphrase

That's wonderful news. People got involved when they heard what was going on. *They stuck up for Carol.* Please tell as many people as you can about these things. I think it's fair to say that where we have whistle blowers getting punished by government – instead of thanked and celebrated – the problem they are dealing with should be taken seriously on that basis alone!

Now see a spoof that whistle blower Don Rufty wrote. His speech seems to sum up the problem of bad judges. Rufty put it up as a Youtube video:

**Don Rufty Role-playing a Family Court Judge (fictional)**

"I am the honorable Judge Roy Bean. I will be presiding over the destruction of your family. The course of your trial will be very lengthy. These cases will be conducted on a kangaroo court basis. During the upcoming months I will be violating your rights left and right….

"I prefer for you to be as compliant as possible with all of my directives. I have backup – the sheriff's deputies are here to do all of my bidding. They will not actually be enforcing the law, they will be enforcing my orders.

"They violate the law as part and parcel of our family court racket. Do not mention or reveal to anyone what takes place here. I am putting you under a gag order. In the event of appeal, the judges over me will condone everything that I do.

"Our aim is to extract as much money as possible from you. By dragging it out, it will help you become accustomed to not having your children. By the way, the attorney you hired will be colluding with myself and with the CPS workers. You will become a pauper. You will not have a chance.

"And don't mention "constitutionality." I don't allow that in my courtroom. There will be no rights to a jury trial; you will not be allowed to defend yourself. Also there will be no adherence to due process. If I were to allow that, it would be crystal clear from the record that we have no case to stand on against you.

"The years ahead will be very stressful. Some of you moms and dads will commit suicide. I don't encourage that, but it happens.   All rise.

# 3. Visits, Parental Alienation, Responsibility Contracts

*Ministers for Child Protection, as at March 2019: Top row: Rachel Sanderson SA, Jacquie Petsuma Tas, Simone McGurk WA. Bottom row: Di Farmer Qld, Luke Donnellan Vic, Pru Goward NSW*

The average Australian has no idea of what goes on in the "Contact Centers" of their state's alleged child-protection agencies. It's humiliating. It could well be that *the point of the exercise* is to find out how much bashing a parent can take.

This book claims that the state wants to hand children over to an abusing parent. That person may even be a *convicted* pedophile. Note: it's incorrect to assume it's a mum versus a dad. We know of cases where the offending parent is *female*.

## PAS – Parental Alienation Syndrome

However, this chapter focuses on Protective *mothers*, to highlight the bizarreness of a mother being given the "right" to have a 2-hour weekly "visitation" with her offspring, in a "supervised" setting -- despite there never having been any charge against her. Oh wait, she does have an accusation against her. Standardly the state accuses her of *turning her child against its father*. This is called parental alienation.

"Parental Alienation Syndrome," or PAS, is a fake diagnosis. Granted, many divorcing husband and wives let their kids know they are angry with or disgusted with the other parent. Kids are usually aware of their parents' bad habits even in non-divorce cases. But do mums make up a sex-abuse story and then coach the kid on it? A small minority of them do.

PAS was promoted by psychiatrist Richard Gardner in the US in the 1980s. Significantly, Gardner also promoted FMS --False Memory Syndrome. That "diagnosis" was invented by the CIA in the 1990s, to hush up the revelations by children and adults who had been tortured in the MK-Ultra program.

*Richard Gardner, author of a harmful book*

*Psychology Today* supports the PAS, claiming that it involves the "programming" of a child by one parent to denigrate the other, to undermine and interfere with the child's relationship with that parent, and is often "a sign of a parent's inability to separate from the couple conflict."  Granted some parents do that but as it's relatively rare, why make a policy that shares the blame out to everyone -- and with unfair consequences?

Unbelievably, Gardner recommended that **children be cited for contempt of court** if they refuse to visit the alienated parent. He said:

"Once found to be in contempt, the youngster **can be placed in a juvenile detention center for a few days to reconside**r his/her decision…. [Or] the youngster might be offered a visit or tour of the facility in advance while he or she is considering refusal. [Good God!]

"Another consideration, **especially for younger children, would be temporary placement in a foster home** or a shelter for abused children. This is obviously punitive and could help such children rethink their decision not to visit. Such placement could also serve as a transition site for visits with the victimized parent. There is much too much coddling, indulging, and "empowering" PAS children; this would provide sorely needed disempowerment." [Emphasis added]

The Gardner stuff came to Australia via Kenneth Byrne. It is highly favored by Dr Chris Rikard-Bell. On an ABC (Australian Broadcasting Corporation) show, Rikard-Bell said he has diagnosed 2,000 cases of parent alienation. This, he opines, is a form of emotional abuse committed on the child.

You may recall Lena's story in Chapter 1. Like many mothers she had no idea what she was being accused of with such terms as "**parentification, enmeshment, and extremism**." I would not be surprised if the words were made up to see if Lena would be bamboozled by them. (She was.)  Words can be twisted and if it's a cop knocking at your door, even the most twisted words will sound authoritative to you.

As an aside, academic psychiatry in Melbourne was set up by Dr Eric Dax as an outpost of Tavistock, a British group interested in experimenting with complete control of individuals by any method it takes. "Tavi" will be discussed in Chapter 15 below. The Australian expert on this is Diane DeVere.

Now for a word about Ms Rilak of NSW, a Protective parent who has been called a vexatious litigant. The court has not given her an opportunity to see her child for over 2 years, but she is still trying every legal strategy possible. Chapter 13 will present her case. For now, have a look at a US legal firm, called Swiftly Legal, which pitches its admiration for the PAS by showing how the court can defeat a Ms Rilak type.

In relation to the second ground, the Full Court held that the trial judge's **finding** that the mother had not physically assaulted the child prior to the trial **carried little weight**. This is because the trial judge had found that, at the time of the trial, **the child would be at a grave risk of harm** if she were to remain in the mother's care. The risk **related to the mother's unfounded belief that the father had sexually assaulted the child**, and her extraordinary attempts to marshal supporting evidence. [How is that a "risk"?]

For instance, the mother had **embarked on a campaign of interrogating** the child. [I'm guessing: "Darling, were you all right when you were with Daddy?"] The purpose of these interrogations was to elicit information from the child to the effect that the father had abused her.

This led to father's concerns about the **child developing false memories** and sustaining serious psychological harm more generally. [Martin Orne of CIA, eat your heart out.]

**The trial judge had also expressed similar concerns.** This conduct was compounded by the mother's improprieties related to her attempts to gather evidence [including]… **drug tests,** psychological therapy and even a vaginal swab. [Isn't that what a doctor normally does?] The mother engaged in this conduct despite recommendations from various authorities and professionals concerning the deleterious effects they would have on the child.

I assume the above lawyers' ad will mainly attract fathers.

**Another Trick – The Parent Responsibility Contract.** If you are still skeptical that judges are deliberately stealing children, consider the fact that a disabled child is worth more to the system, as agencies can bill for continuing nursing care.

Natasha Cranmore [pseudonym] phoned to tell me about the PRC, and I don't mean the People's Republic of China. She thinks this feature is mainly for the stealing of *disabled* children. She says a disabled baby is "a million dollar baby."

"PRC" stand for Parent Responsibility Contract. A disabled child's mum may voluntarily go to get help or be discovered to be in need of services. For instance, it may be noticed that her daughter needs a speech pathologist.

So far, so good. Any mother of a disabled child exerts twice the effort of an average mother just to get through, so it is proper for society to provide extra help. Mrs Cranmore has so far kept her disabled son but she says "My friends are all losing their kids." This is because when parents request the aforementioned help, they are asked to sign a *contract*. Little do they know with what vigor it might be "enforced."

**Parent Responsibility Contract: Information for Parents** (retrieved February 15, 2019 from Facs.nsw.gov.au)

A Parent Responsibility Contract (PRC) is a **voluntary support agreement** between you and Family and Community Services (FACS). You are being **offered** a PRC because FACS has assessed that there are **concerns for your child's safety and wellbeing**. A PRC aims to support you **to make changes** and improve your parenting skills so your child is safe and continues to remain living with you.

PRCs are to be developed between you and your FACS caseworker in a respectful, collaborative manner. The PRC will include the following information: …

**The actions that will explain what you need to do in order for your child to either remain safely in your care or be safely restored to you.**

Once you have spoken to an independent person to get legal advice, **your caseworker** will organise a case plan meeting with all the relevant parties to discuss, negotiate and develop a PRC that suits your family's needs.  If you have spoken with your caseworker and still disagree with the PRC, **you do not have to sign the contract, as PRCs are a voluntary agreement**....

How long does a PRC last?  for a period up to 12 months.

What does a PRC do?  A PRC is **not a court order**. A PRC is an agreement that is signed by you and FACS, and **registered at the Childrens Court**. [Oh what horrors lie in those five words!]

**What happens while a parent responsibility contract is in place? While a PRC is in place, the caseworker and support services work with you to reduce parenting concerns identified and create change that keeps your child safe.** [Emphasis added]

First let's note the mention of *parenting skills!* "A PRC aims to support you to make changes and improve your parenting skills so your child is safe...." *Child is safe?* That sounds nice. As does this: "PRCs are to be developed between you and caseworker in a respectful, collaborative manner." But wait.

It's a sneaky deal. Remember, it's a contract. Citizens often go to court to sue someone for breach of a contract. In this case it must be done at the Childrens Court. Mum is trapped. She has no due-process rights there. The workings of the Childrens Court are at the heart of child-stealing.

Note: this chapter's discussion of PRCs, regarding disabled kids, deviates from this book's universe, which I specified as being pedo-related cases. The motive for PRCs appears to be money. However, SA's Mullighan Inquiry in 2008 found that institutionalized disabled kids are routinely sexually abused...

# 4. The Lullaby of Law, and George Potkonyak's Insights

*Mary Maxwell interviewing George Potkonyak in Sydney, March 2019*

In 1975, Australia's parliament passed The Family Law Act, which covers all states except Western Australia. The Act deals with divorce, property settlement between spouses, and the custody of children. Prior to 1975 a person wanting a divorce had to sue the spouse in civil court, based on fault such as infidelity or mental cruelty.

The Seventies saw sexual liberation. It was said that discovery of the Pill changed culture. More likely the Pill was brought in *to* change culture, with a goal of weakening the family. (See Chapter 26 for Dr Day's predictions.)

Anyway, easy divorce was welcomed. But it seems to me that the Family Law Act was *worded* to cater to child traffickers.

Let's start with the "paramountcy" of a child's best interests:

> **Family Law Act** sec 60CA, "In deciding whether to make a particular parenting order in relation to a child, a court must regard the **best interests** of the child as the paramount consideration." 60CC  (1) **in determining what is in the child's best interests,** the court must consider the matters set out in subsections (2) and (3).

36

> (2) The primary considerations are   [This is the big item]:
> **(a) the benefit to the child of having a meaningful relationship** with both of the child's parents; and
> **(b) the need to protect the child from physical or psychological harm** from being subjected to, or exposed to, abuse, neglect or family violence.   [Emphasis added]

That A and B were inserted by a 2006 amendment.

The Court looks for voluntary agreement between the parents but **can issue orders** if no agreement has occurred. What if the Court has ordered a child to live with Parent A, can Parent B go and takes the child back? Sec 70NAE says yes, but only few parents have succeeded in invoking it:

> **Family Law Act:  70NAE**  (1)  The circumstances in which a person may be taken to have had, …**a reasonable excuse for contravening an order** [include]:(4)  A person (the respondent) is taken to have had a reasonable excuse for contravening a parenting order to the extent to which it deals **with whom a child** is to live with, in a way that resulted in the child not living with a person in whose favour the order was made if: (a) the respondent believed on reasonable grounds that the actions **constituting the contravention were necessary to protect the health or safety of a person ….**

## Various State Laws

State parliaments enact laws about child safety. That may set up a statutory body, such as a DCP, Department of Child Protection, with a Minister overseeing its work. There have been many names of these agencies: Department of Child Safety (DOCS), Family and Community Services (FACS), etc. The wording of the law may be dreamy in its nice sound.

**Tasmania's** Department of Health and Human Services says: The role of Child Safety Service is to protect children and young people who are at risk of abuse or neglect. In Tasmania, the safety of children and young people is covered by the *Children, Young Persons and Their Families Act* 1997. In that law, risk is defined as follows:

(1) For the purposes of this Act, a child is at risk if (a) **the child has been, is being, or is likely to be, abused or neglected**; or (b) any person with whom the child resides…(i) **has threatened to kill** or abuse or neglect the child and there is a reasonable likelihood of the threat being carried out… [Emphasis added]

**Victoria** says it aims to "promote positive outcomes for children who are vulnerable because of their family circumstances." "*The Children Youth and Families Act* 2005 consolidated and replaced the *Children and Young Persons Act* 1989. The introduction of this Act was accompanied by reforms, given the name 'every child every chance'." [Wow.] That Victorian law commands the Court, to see **parent and child as the fundamental group unit of society** and to ensure that **intervention into that relationship is limited**…. [Holy smoke!]

**Guardianship, foster care, and adoption** are in the state's bailiwick. Application for those matters must go to the Childrens Courts in each state. Typically it is the state's Crown Prosecutor (not DPP) who starts an application that will take a child from its parent and put him/her into guardianship. Many Protective parents are in a panic because *additional* laws have been passed to say that it is bad for a child to remain in guardianship longer than 2 years and so the adoption process should be speeded up (or even forced!).

**George Potkonyak's Insight**. I now quote from a valuable submission that solicitor Potkonyak made to a Senate Inquiry, and then mention how he has been struck off the rolls. The day will come when those who struck him off will regret it.

**To Senate Inquiry (Children in Out of Home Care) 2018:**

The Childrens Court is the first point of call. Each proceeding in the Childrens Court is presided over by a single Childrens Magistrate. ... **The proceeding is closed to the public** with only parties in the case allowed to attend with some exceptions where a relative of the child or a support person of the parent may be allowed to attend with **consent of all parties** and the leave of the Court. There is a provision for **media attendance**, unless the court disallows, but it hardly, if ever, happens....

The District Court is the court to which a party dissatisfied with the final decision of the Childrens Court may "appeal" that decision, as of right. However ...there is a catch: the proceeding in the District Court is a new hearing; **there is no review** of the decision of the Children's Court for an alleged error of law or error of fact... Whatever went ... in the Childrens Court is swept under the carpet and will never see the daylight....

The Act empowers the Family and Community Services **to receive and record "risk of harm reports"** about any child from mandatory reporters or from any member of public. The reporter believes on reasonable grounds that a child is at risk of significant harm. The **identity of the reporter is protected**. Once the report is received, the FACS "is to" carry out investi-gations and make an assessment – if the person responsible considers that the report provides sufficient **reason to believe that the child is at risk of significant harm. If not**, [he or she] does not need to carry out any investigations... If one of the risk-of-harm reports is considered to be serious enough (usually an arbitrary decision by a case worker) the child is removed ... and **placed into temporary foster care**... [Note: it makes no sense to remove from a child from its *Protective* parent here.]

### "Establishment proceeding"
One would expect that this stage of the proceedings, where the court is to establish whether the child is a child in need of care, is where the evidence would be tested according to law. Not so.

[E.g., hearsay is allowed; and the accused can't cross-examine…] It does not matter which kind of "trial" takes place, the magistrate will inevitably find that "the child is a child in need of care and protection", otherwise the magistrate might lose his or her job **for exposing the government to the risk of being liable for damages for unlawful removal of the child from his or her parents**. [Hmm. I never thought of that…] It is too obvious, beyond reasonable doubt, that the cases have been determined even before the parties walk into the court. [Many judges give] "the life sentence" – "Parental responsibility to the Minister until the child attains 18 years of age." [Note this goes on in other countries, too – such as Norway and the US.]

**"Dispositional proceeding"**
This stage of the proceedings is the equivalent to the sentenc-ing stage in a criminal trial. It normally takes place between 9 and **18 months later**. FACS case workers will file hundreds of pages of "evidence" and the poor parent, in spite of allegedly giving consent "without admission" (of any allegations) has to prove now that he or she has "addressed the issues that led to the removal of the child" from his or her care.

Potkonyak's criticism of the system may sound harsh but it could be much harsher. His point is that you can't win. As he says, you would think evidence would be tested according to law, but it isn't. The Family Law Act specifically dispenses itself from The Evidence Act -- and Childrens Courts, which is what George was discussing, seem lawless. A state can snatch a child as it wishes. You *simply have no comeback!*

**Jurisdictional Issues.** Let's note the convoluted nature of the law. Jurisdiction is confusing. You go to Family Court (federal) for child-placing if it's part of divorce. Otherwise you go to Childrens Court. A Family Court judge is required to apply the two criteria of sec 60CC, but the two items are contradictory. (2)(a) is about considering a child's right to parenting. (2)(b) is the part about the kid being in harm's way.

40

The judge is free to ignore B and claim A -- that a kid's need to have a meaningful relationship with two parents trumps all. (Never mind that, in US, a majority of kids have single mums anyway, or that the Army sends women into war with her kids left behind!) None of the 60CC wording matters if the goal is to give the kid to the pedophile parent. The obtuse wording of "A or B" must have been designed for bad reasons. It is a general principle of law that a vague law is void, as people would not know whether they are violating it. In 60CC it is the judiciary that would be hopelessly confused. Prof Elspeth McInnes of the University of SA talks about this on Youtube.

**Getting Struck off the Rolls.** *Potkonyak v Legal Services Commissioner* [2018] Beazley P, Payne JA, Simpson AJA:

The Court of Appeal has dismissed an appeal brought by George Potkonyak against the Legal Services Commissioner finding that Civil and Administrative Tribunal of NSW (the Tribunal) did not err in finding that he had engaged in professional misconduct and ordering that he be removed from the roll of lawyers of the Supreme Court of NSW. Central to the Commissioner's application was the fact that Mr Potkonyak continually propounded an interpretation of the Care Act that was contrary to authority.

The Commissioner's application raised a number of grounds of complaint, including that Mr Potkonyak had: conducted himself inappropriately in court by making various offensive and unsubstantiated [!] statements about a Children's Court magistrate and the opposing parties; breached his duties to the administration of justice and his clients [no he didn't]; misled the court; and consistently engaged in conduct falling short of the standard of competence and diligence expected of a reasonably competent legal practitioner.

Thus we see why most lawyers take the safe route, silence.

## What of the States' *Childrens* Courts?

Why have special childrens courts? Can't good old civil court and criminal court do the job? Ah, not if "the job" is to deliver kids to pedophiles. As I will argue in Chapter 13, childrens courts are not genuine courts (like the Vaccine Injury Court in the US whose purpose is to evade the law of torts). These courts in Australia give a façade of caring for children. As I said, it lulls us to think all is sweet and sound.

These courts are torture chambers for Protective parents. A sad fact is that lawyers go along with it. Typically they dissuade a mum from reporting sexual abuse in the first place "as that may mean you lose custody altogether." If, however,  she is determined to report it, medical records will be conveniently lost by police or social workers, and the Prosecutor (an odd name for the role of the state's solicitor here) will go to any lengths to blame the mum.

The main trick is to say that the child is at risk of future harm in the mum's home -- as *her* persuading the child that abuse has occurred will cause emotional harm (no matter how clear it is to the naked eye that Dad is offending). During the visitations the mum is almost paralyzed, fearing that a remark she might make, like "How are you doing, Dear?" could be construed by the observer as "coaching."

Here is an **order** decreed by Judge Richard Burke in the US:

> "Neither parent will report allegations of physical or sexual abuse to the police, DCP, or the pediatrician. The court will direct such allegations to the Guardian ad litem… A parent who violates that pathway…invites an immediate review of the parenting plan and alteration in access to the children."

Far as I know, "Judge" Burke is still walking the streets today.

# 5. Contempt, Suppression, and Parliamentary Privilege

*St Paul orders pagan manuscripts burned at Ephesus, by Massari*

Evidence that there's something rotten can often be gleaned from the presence of secrecy. This chapter will show the role of secrecy in judicial kidnap. Topics are: gagging of a parent by Section 121 or by citation for contempt, ordering media not to publish, and curtailing talk in Parliament itself.

## Contempt of Court

The judge – who is also known as "the Court" – owns the shop. She and she alone determines how far you can go in language and in behavior inside the shop. And sometimes outside the shop. She can write orders which, if it were a king or president, might be called tyrannical.

The concept of contempt of court has been around since the 12th century. It's beneficial, as we do not want the courtroom to be a rowdy place. Dignity surrounding authority is essential to our feeling of respect for law. Sins for which you can be arrested for *criminal* contempt are:

1. Refusal to testify as a witness 2. Failure, as an attorney to show up in court (unless there is a good excuse) 3. Behavior, as an attorney, that is insulting to the other attorney, or to the judge 4. Behavior as a litigant or a person in the gallery of the

court who disrupts the proceedings 5. Use of vulgar language in documents. Note: The court's power to cite for contempt is *inherent.* A legislature may refine it but cannot erase it. Still, a judge can't "try" a litigant for an infraction of *other* laws.

**What Did Judge Vasta Do Wrong?** I am baffled by the announcement in *Sydney Morning Herald* of February 9, 2019 that the Full Court of the Federal Court sad it was unlawful to punish a dad who refused to show records:

In a scathing judgment, **the Full Court of the Family Court said Judge Vasta had no legal power to** make the orders and it would be an 'affront to justice' to leave them in place. Justices Steven Strickland, Peter Murphy and Michael Kent said they were 'comfortably satisfied' that 'what occurred here ... constituted a gross miscarriage of justice.' There was 'no factual foundation' for the order and the **judge had no legal power to make it**, the judges said. **Even in cases of proven contempt – which was not the case here – imprisonment was 'a sanction of last resort.' the judges said."** [Emphasis added]

Keep that in mind when reading Cuffie's story, Chapter 8. Here is the Family Law Act on what constitutes contempt:

SECT **112AP** Contempt (1) ... this section applies to a contempt of a court that: a) **does not** constitute a contravention of an order under this Act; or b) constitutes a contravention of an order under this Act and **involves a flagrant challenge to the authority of the court.(2) In spite of any other law, a court having jurisdiction** under this [Family Law] Act may **punish a person** for contempt of that court. [Emphasis added]

Contempt may be civil or criminal. If *criminal* you wind up with a prison record. *Civil* may be direct – it happened in the courtroom, e.g., you talked back to the judge. Or it may be indirect, as when you fail to carry out an order.

In 2009, Dr Fredrick Toben of Adelaide, a Holocaust revisionist, was imprisoned for 3 months for contempt. The judge had ordered him to delete material from his website but he did not run home and delete it.  In fact he let it be known that free speech is free speech and he did not intend to take it down, despite Section 18C of the Human Rights Act.

That was a civil contempt of court. If *criminal*, the deed must have been committed beyond reasonable doubt and must involve deliberate intention. The contemnor (love that word!) can appeal and question due process, and often wins.

## Sec 121 To Keep Family Court Proceedings Secret

It is section 121 of Family Law Act that worries Protective parents. They may be in extreme need of telling the world about their situation, yet they fear jail if they talk:

**SEC 121 Restriction on publication of court proceedings** (1) A person who publishes in a newspaper or periodical publication, by radio broadcast or television or by other electronic means, or otherwise disseminates to the public or to a section of the public by any means, any account of any proceedings, or of any part of any proceedings, under this Act **that identifies**: (a) a party to the proceedings; (b)  a person ...in any other way concerned in the matter to which the proceedings relate; or (c) a witness in the proceedings;  commits an offence punishable, upon conviction by imprisonment [up to] one year.

Strictly speaking, the parent is not told to keep silent but is only told by sec 121to keep the parties' *identity* secret. I think 121 is intended to hide court crime; it certainly has that effect.

**Suppression Orders and "D" Notices.** During my attendance at hearings of NSW coronial court, regarding the Lindt Café hostage deaths, I was taken aside and told that I had breached an order – given generally to any attendee and all media – to suppress the name of the police psychiatrist in the *'negotiating"* team. I'd mistakenly thought the name being mentioned was already a code. When it is the government, not a court, that *asks* media to stay hush-hush, it is not – as far as I know – a crime to disobey: A "D Notice" to the press is but a request. (But there *is* black-letter law forbidding media to reveal the name of a child in a court case.)

**KangarooCourtofAustraia.com**

*Shane Dowling, in Canberra*

In 2018 Shane Dowling, webhost of Kangaroo Court of Australia.com, was sentenced 18 months prison for contempt.

"[I had] repeated in court part of an article I had published and for publishing an article about the contempt proceedings in breach of suppression orders. Chief Justice [X] was named as a known paedophile and 17 other judicial officers were named as known paedophiles or suspected paedophiles."

Note: The Australian High Court has recognized a constitutional right to freedom of political speech, in the case of *Lange v ABC,* 1997 -- a suit for defamation of a public figure. In Belgium's Parliament, Laurent Louis called the prime minister a pedophile. He was arrested, although he should have had parliamentary privilege. One aspect of the right to free speech is entwined with the need for all legislators to discuss *anything.*

46

## Parliamentary Privilege

Parliamentary privilege dates to 1689 under William and Mary:

> "The freedom of speech and debates or proceedings in Parliament ought not to be impeached or questioned in any court or place out of Parliament." [British Bill of Rights]

In NSW in 1997 Franca Arena had suggested that the premier and the leader of the opposition conspired with Justice Wood in his role as Royal Commissioner about *police protection of pedophiles.*

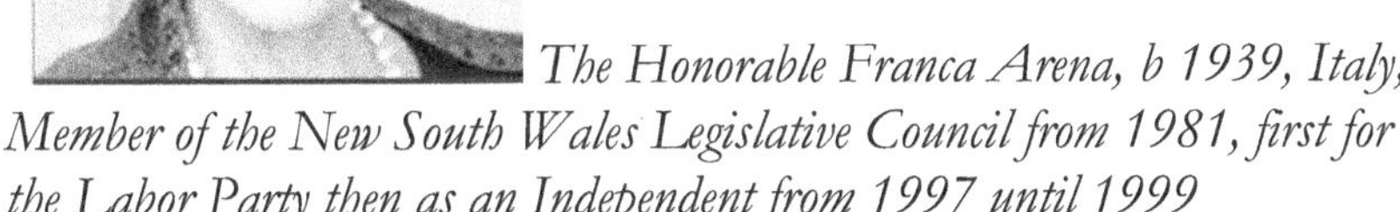

*The Honorable Franca Arena, b 1939, Italy, Member of the New South Wales Legislative Council from 1981, first for the Labor Party then as an Independent from 1997 until 1999*

It is amusing to see how the politicians of the day reacted. They set up a discipline committee! Although members are free to speak, their chamber *can* make an Inquiry about any member.

Section 49 of the Constitution (federal, not state) says:

> The powers, privileges, and immunities of the Senate and of the House of Representatives, …shall be such as are declared by the Parliament, and until declared shall be those of the Commons House of Parliament of the United Kingdom, …at the establishment of the Commonwealth. [i.e., in 1901]

So NSW Parliament passed an Act to hold an inquiry regarding Arena's speech. She went to Equity court and later sought leave to go to the High Court. Leave was denied. The case is *Arena v Nader* 1997. The affair would be laughable today, wouldn't it?

Any of you legislators reading this please note: You most certainly can accuse anyone from the floor. That person can't sue you. How else can the pubic find our certain things? If asked to repeat it outside, just say Pass.  But can the chamber  discipline you or even expel you for "abusing the privilege"? Yes, that is lawful. After all, someone in Parliament could use the privilege for a very personal reason and that would indeed be abuse. But if you are speaking on public matters you are safe.

Ms Arena was smeared, harassed and all the usual tricks, for raising the issue of pedophilia.  A few years ago Arena told a journalist no one has congratulated her for being right. Congratulations, Franca. Goodonya! *See Appendix M for an apology*

## The Ongoing Problem of Secrecy

Note: Documents of Wood Royal Commission remain under seal. There's no legitimate basis for protecting the criminals, and the excuse of privacy for the victims is a joke. Chapter 27 will discuss Lord Cullen's illegal sealing – for a hundred years -- of the records of the 1996 Dunblane massacre in Scotland.

SA's 2008 Mullighan Inquiry papers are also under seal. That inquiry was about sexual abuse of disabled kids. (A change.org petition started by Mia Madsen seeks release of the records.) *The Australian,* on April 1, 2008,  quoted Ted Mullighan's comments:

> "'Nothing prepared me for the foul undercurrent of society revealed in the evidence to the inquiry,' the commissioner wrote, prefacing his 564-page report released yesterday.
>
> "… there were 809 hearings over the inquiry's three years, and their evidence has led to the police investigation of 434 alleged abusers, 14 of which are now before the DPP."

What, we may ask, happened to the other 420?

# 6. Is It the Money?

*(L) US Capitol dome, beyond Supreme Court building (R) insignia adorning Norway's Royal Ministry of Children and Family Affairs*

The human instinct for self-preservation probably suffices to explain why we chase after money. In the modern world that's how you get food. Since there is also a tendency for great amounts of money to accumulate in a few hands, or in organizations, it can become a driving force itself. The logic of money-attainment can lead to absurdities and atrocities.

In this book I claim that a driving force behind bad treatment of protective parents is a plan to harm families. Period. No motive for financial gain need enter in. Yet the workers in the CPS industry do think $ is important. (Recall that they call a disabled child a million dollar baby, referring to the number of care-related jobs it leads to.) Also, "funding" is a way that a national government can exert control over the states.

There is a valuable interview on Youtube conducted by The Herland Report. Dr Einar Salvasen talks about "Atrocities of Norway's Child Protection System." He has been helping Norwegians survive, even *by fleeing to other countries for asylum.* He makes two comments relevant to us. First he says "Once a diagnosis of the mother is made it follows her through all documents even after she has proved it wrong." Why should that be? I claim it is because harassment is an essential goal.

Second, he says, folks were trusting of government in Norway but now that is falling away. I say this, too, is part of the plan. Destabilization is a goal of the powerful. "Drive them nuts."

It often looks like the personnel involved in creating this nightmare – politicians and bureaucrats -- are not in their right mind. This chapter shows members of Congress in 2003 acting like robots at a hearing on child adoption. They all say the same thing and never use their critical faculties!

In 1997, Congress passed the Adoption and Safe Families Act, ASFA. It's supposed to help kids pass out of the foster-care system into adoptive homes. (The legislation refers to "loving homes" but does not list criteria for that lovingness.) The feds pay the state $4,000 for each child adopted out, or $6,000 if the child is categorized as special needs. The House Ways and Means Committee held a review of the law in 2003.  Here is an abridged transcript. Warning: you will be bored to death. Bolding added to help revive you.  I think the speakers are behaving robotically, never deploying natural humanity.

**Opening Statement of The Honorable Benjamin Cardin, a Representative in Congress from Maryland**

The 1997 Act was designed to **ensure the safety of children who come into contact with the child welfare system** [Boy, they'll need it!] and to expedite permanency for children living in foster care. It amended the existing law to require that a child's health and safety be of "paramount" concern in any efforts made to preserve or reunify the child's family [there are none!]. **The legislation also included a provision to ensure that** necessary legal procedures occur expeditiously, so that children who cannot return home may be placed for adoption or another arrangement quickly. Finally, the 1997 legislation also created **Adoption Incentives** program that **rewards States** that increase their numbers of adoptions from foster care...

**Mr. CAMP.** If I might, just for a second, this legislation, which former Member Barbara Kennelly and I worked very hard on -- I agree with much of what the Chairman and Mr. Cardin have said, that it was really brought about **when we saw that the way the Social Security Act was being implemented did not really protect children and families.** So, we came up with this legislation to do that. I am looking forward, Dr. Horn, to the recommendations that you might have to **enhance** the Act….

STATEMENT OF THE HONORABLE WADE F. HORN, DEP'T OF HEALTH AND HUMAN SERVICES. Thank you, Mr. Chairman, for the opportunity… **I'm a clinical child psychologist, and I have devoted my professional career to improving the wellbeing of children. I have a longstanding interest in child welfare policy and practice, and like all of you, I am committed to improving the delivery of child welfare services….** [They all talk like that.]

The passage of ASFA was a landmark in child welfare reform, but the goals of ASFA **remain elusive for far too many** children and families. The ASFA stated that the goals of the child welfare system were **safety**, permanency, and **well-being.**

[Note: the very articulation of those nice words has the effect of dulling the mind of the listener. Yet what is being talked about is really cruel kidnap, at least in many cases.]

ASFA provided numerous tools to States to bring about systemic reforms regarding safety, adoption promotion, and accountability. **The Administration for Children and Families has worked diligently to fully implement** this and **bring State laws and policies into compliance….**We also have continued to work with States to improve information systems and **increase the quantity and quality of data that States collect** [oh-oh]. We made investments in the Statewide Automated Child Welfare -- **31,000 in 1997 to 50,000 in 2001.**

CORNELIA M. ASHBY, GAO DIRECTOR FOR EDUCATION, WORKFORCE, AND INCOME [etc]

Ms. ASHBY. Mr. Chairman and Members of the Subcom-mittee, thank you for inviting me .... My testimony will address four issues: changes in outcomes and characteristics of children in foster care... and practices States use to address barriers to achieving permanency for children in foster care. [End excerpt]

Two interesting tidbits came up at the hearing: 1. "For children who have been in foster care for 15 of the previous 22 months, **the law required States to initiate proceedings to terminate parental rights**, except in specified circumstances..." and 2. "In Texas, the state contracts with **private** agencies to place foster care children with **out-of-state** adoptive families. In Illinois, the state works with a private agency in Mississippi to conduct home studies because **families in Mississippi adopt many Illinois children**." [!]

**Matrix.** Members of Congress share a "matrix," and probably Australian parliamentarians do the same. I am not referring to the woo-woo kind of matrix. *Merriam Webster* defines the noun matrix (plural: matrices) as "something within or from which something else originates, develops, or takes form." The matrix here is **an atmosphere of acceptance** that the government should place your kid in a home that is not your home. What went on at that hearing was pure cheerleading.

**Federalism and States' Rights.** Australia's six states are allowed by the Constitution's Section 51 to "refer" their powers to the Commonwealth i.e., "Canberra" They did so for the Family Law Act, except Western Australia. In the US referring is forbidden by the balance-of-powers principle. Article I, section 8 of the US Constitution lists precisely 18 topics on which Congress is allowed to legislate. For example, Congress can raise an army and can regulate immigration.

In 1787 the idea of federal legislature enacting laws that had to do with the family did not even get a mention; it was so anathema to the theme of the Republic that no one thought to provide *against* it. The "matrix" of the day precluded it. Folks' brains at that time were as unaware of *governmental fiddling with family matters* as they were of motorcars. Since there is no constitutional basis for ASFA, it should be nixed.

**Who Spoke?** At a congressional hearing, persons who are well placed to offer advice get invited as witnesses, or will ask permission to give testimony themselves. But Congress announced that only *invited experts* would speak at the hearing on adoption. Ridiculously, these were the members of the Department of Health and Human Services, the DHHS, the very ones who administer it. (No aggrieved Mums, please!)

The system works by having a lock on its own reality, no matter how greatly this reality may conflict with the social or moral norm. In time it *becomes* the social or moral norm, with everyone using the new language. I'll bet each of the 435 Representatives received some pleas from constituents as to the horrible things that are done by CPS. Why are they silent? One of them should say: "Hey, no 'funding' is needed when a kid lives with his or her Protective parent!"

**Note from the UK.** DailyMail.co.uk: "Foster carers receive on average £20,000 a year per child from the state. Tony Blair personally crusaded a few years back to drive up the number of adoptions by setting councils targets for adoption." (2011)

**In Norway, Is It the Money?** Per the BBC:

"The case of a young couple in Norway whose five children were taken away has fuelled mounting concern. Protesters say social workers are often too quick to separate children from their families, with too little justification. 'Ruth and Marius's life was torn apart without warning one afternoon when two black cars approached the farm where they live in a remote Norwegian valley. ... Ruth was waiting as usual for the school bus that would bring back their two daughters, aged eight and ten. But it never came. Instead, a woman from the local child protection service knocked at the door'."

Pardon me for being jaded but I reckon the BBC's coverage of that story is part of the drive to make people lose faith in government. There was no Mary-Maxwell-type voice on the show urging people to do something about it. Any person in Norway with half a brain can see that it is wrong to steal children. In the enlightening video on the Herland report, Ms Herland mentions that the Norwegian Prime Minister keeps saying it is not a problem, the CPS really tries to help children.

My colleague Dee McLachlan has written to every authority in Australia about the "atrocities," for example: CPS leaders, police commissioners, parliamentarians, vice-regals, judges, lawyers. When they reply it is always with a ping-pong letter, even at the very top. Never do they say "Wow, that is quite a situation you have presented. I'll get onto it this very afternoon."

Norway, Australia, the US. All suffering from the same hand, a hand that organizes it all. In this book I narrow the field of study mainly to judges who are catering to the pedo-rings. Child sex-trafficking is apparently a huge enterprise. (See Fiona Barnett's interpretation in Appendix R, regarding Satanism.)

But, to repeat, I am of the opinion that there is a move afoot to harm society, to break up families. I also suspect that some of the harm-doers simply get carried away by the amazing power they have to control culture and control the fate of individuals.

Congresswoman Tulsi Gbbard recently said "A dark shadow fell over the United States." I think that is more or less accurate.

# 7. Or Is It the Sex?

*Photo source unknown, perhaps the Royal Commission*

The fact that pedophilia is rampant in Australia is now beyond dispute. From 2013 through 2017, under Letters Patent from the Queen, the federal government conducted a massive inquiry known as the Royal Commission into Institutional Responses to Child Sexual Abuse. The commissioner was a NSW judge, Justice Peter McClellan.

The public was invited to make submissions about their experiences and could opt to use a code name such as "BGW." More than 17,000 people came forward. Depending on which institution had been the locus of their abuse, *that* institution was then called in to give an accounting, usually at public hearings. For example: Geelong Grammar School, the Watchtower (Jehovah's Witnesses), the Boy Scouts, the Navy.

A major focus was the Catholic church. In Chapter 1 of this book I floated the notion that the pedophile priests may have been planted, or the whole thing engineered, rather than it being an outbreak of uncontrollable lust. There is evidence that the purpose was to destroy the public's faith in religion. I have covered that in my book *Deliverance: A Royal Commission and Pizzagate Reveal Society's Hidden Rulers*.

The book at hand, *Reunion*, is not interested in sexual abuse of children, other than in the context of Family Court rulings. I got involved when I found out that kids in my state (South Australia) were being seized from good homes. As I theorized earlier, the utterly weird behavior of the courts may mean that they are working for someone whose goal is the general destruction of the family. The sexual aspect may be incidental.

In retrospect I think the Royal Commission may have had a hidden agenda, that of "normalizing" what is going on. Even the formal apology spoken in Parliament on October 22, 2018, seems strange, juxtaposed against the ongoing cruelty of the Family Courts.  Prime Minister Scott Morrison said:

"Silenced voices; muffled cries in the darkness; unacknowledged tears; the tyranny of invisible suffering; the never heard pleas of tortured souls bewildered by an indifference to the unthinkable theft of their innocence -- today Australia confronts a trauma, an abomination, hiding in plain sight for far too long. Why has it taken so long to act? Why were others things more important than this, the care of innocent children? Why didn't we believe?...

"We must be so humble to fall before those who were forsaken and beg to them our apology -- a sorry that dare not ask for forgiveness; a sorry that speaks only of profound grief and loss; a sorry from a nation that seeks to reach out in compassion into the darkness where you have lived for so long.

"Nothing we can do now will right the wrongs inflicted on our nation's children.  So today we gather in this chamber in humility, not just as representatives of the people of this country but as fathers, as mothers, as siblings, friends, workmates and, in some cases, indeed, as victims and survivors. In Ngunawal, 'Canberra' means 'meeting place'. And on this day of apology, we meet together. We honour every survivor in this country. We love you, we hear you and we honour you."

## Could the RC Have Helped Protective Parents?

It is baffling that Australia's expensive and very thorough Royal Commission (RC) could have helped Protective parents but refused to do so. Many mothers went to the RC for help but were rebuffed as their case was not "historical."

Senator Heffernan asked that the RC's terms of reference be extended to cover an investigation of the legal profession and the judiciary, but that was never necessary. The terms of reference in the Letters Patent were wonderfully broad:

> **ELIZABETH THE SECOND, by the Grace of God Queen of Australia** and Her other Realms and Territories …
>
> WHEREAS all children deserve a safe and happy childhood, … Your inquiry will not specifically examine the issue of child sexual abuse but recommendations you make [may] improve the response to all forms of child sexual abuse in **all** contexts.
>
> NOW THEREFORE We do, by these Our Letters Patent … require and authorise you, to inquire into … **what should be done to eliminate or reduce impediments that currently exist for responding appropriately to child sexual abuse.**
>
> … AND We direct you to make any recommendations …that you consider appropriate, including about any policy, legislative, **administrative or structural reforms**….
>
> … recognising nevertheless that you will be informed by individual cases and **may need to make referrals** to appropriate authorities in individual cases; [regarding] the need to establish mechanisms … for the purpose of enabling the **timely investigation and prosecution of offences**…. [Emphasis added]

## Why Does DoJ Concentrate on Viewers of Child Porn?

US President Trump promised that the Department of Justice would crack down on pedophiles. Per US Attorney General "We have arrested more than 2,300 alleged child predators and investigated some **25,200 sexual abuse complaints.**" Justice.gov says "The task forces **identified 195 offenders** who either produced child pornography or committed child sexual abuse." In the early days of people owning PCs, the use of it for viewing porn (mostly adult porn) was said to be very high. I suspect the newer form of porn – child stuff – was put online to encourage pedo crime. Pardon my cynicism but I think this may have been done in order to fill prisons.


## The Jeffrey Epstein Affair – Pedophilia for Blackmail

In August 2019 the newly arrested Jeffrey Epstein died in jail. Trump then found it necessary to sack a Cabinet member, Alexander Acosta, for having given Epstein a ridiculous plea deal in 2008. Epstein had a reputation as a billionaire but it's possible he was a nobody, recruited by Mossad or Tavistock to do the job of "compromising" governmental leaders by inviting them to his island to have sex with jail-bait teens.

His helper, Ghislaine Maxwell, is the daughter of a man who once owned more newspapers that Rupert Murdoch. My guess is that Jeffrey and Ghislaine were both MK-Ultra'd early on, and that their "work" was controlled by higher ups.

Also coming to light recently, such as by Fiona Barnett, is the crazy world of the occult (see "spirit cooking" and Hillary Clinton). I suspect that cults were brought into being to serve the powerful -- it motivates cult members to do evil. My point is that neither money nor sex is enough to account for the corruption of the courts. The pedophile rackets may seem to reflect the human sexual urge but I say it's something else.

# 8. A Ton of Enforcement

*Exodus 2:3 But when she [Moses' sister Miriam] could no longer hide him, she got him a papyrus basket and coated it with tar and pitch. Then she placed the child in the basket and set it among the reeds along the bank of the Nile [hiding the child so he would not be slain].*

In 21st century Australia, hundreds of Protective parents need to "do a Miriam." They need to escape "pharaoh," the abusing ex-spouse whom the Family Court is helping. Alas, the banks of the River Murray do not provide a hiding place for one's baby -- the surveillance systems will track it down. Police or social workers will go after the Protective parent as well as grabbing the youngster!

See the story of Cuffie [a pseudonym] below. At age 75 she was arrested and jailed for not yielding up to police the location of her abused grandchildren. Her daughter, the mum of those kids, is also in jail for the same "crime."

In 2018 the Australian Federal Police, the AFP, went on a kick to show how they were cleaning up "crimes against children." As though trying for Olympic gold in the sport of irony, they arrested Protective grandparents. That is, they laid charges of kidnapping not against any real kidnappers but against kind relatives, and some Good Samaritans, too.

Patrick O'Dea and Russell Pridgeon, MD, are two of the men arrestees by the AFP. They gave refuge to kids who would otherwise defo be with pedo's and whom police had refused to help. The police search was called Operation Noetic. Dr Russell Pridgeon also had his medical license taken away. My late husband was a pediatrician and he was aware that all doctors dread being "struck off the register." Well, OK, you *should* be struck off if you do bad doctoring, or defraud Medicare, or whatever. But not for helping kids in danger. (Believe me, I can say for sure that there are doctors who care greatly about their patients, as George Maxwell was one.)

I'll abridge a letter that Pridgeon sent to doctors, and bold it:

**Dear Colleague**, You have known me as a general practitioner working at Duke St Medical Centre these many years. Amidst the **prurient media coverage** of my arrest you may be aware that I assisted a mother to protect her children from sexual abuse. What I have done is **not a secret** from the authorities; they have known about it for nearly 6 months and have not approached me on this matter until I was arrested.

On 30 May 2018 I wrote to the Minister of Child Safety in Queensland advising her that: "I am one of many people who sheltered and protected them, in the four years that they were free of ongoing abuse. At various times I drove vast distances to transport them between places of safety, and when I was able find safe accommodation for them I sheltered them in a safe house from about Easter 2014 for more than a year.

**"This was one of the greatest privileges of my life to be able to help these children escape** the horrific abuse inflicted upon them by fiends, and enabled by **Rogue Judges, lawyers and Policemen who actively hid the truth, ignored evidence, and facilitated child rape, effectively trafficking these children to paedophiles."**

I became involved in this after the late Prof Freda Briggs, AO, Australia's pre-eminent authority on child sexual abuse, asked me as a doctor, to support the mother, using my experience in trying to save other children. The **children had been taken from the mother and given to the father, despite multiple disclosures of abuse, so their sexual abuse continued for years**. When I heard through the media that she had snatched the children and fled, and when she phoned me for help, there was nothing else to do: I had to help her, I couldn't let her children be returned for abuse.

**I was acutely aware that I was breaking the law**; it was a terrible position to be in. These were not my children, yet **I could not as a moral man, or as a doctor** turn my back on them, and leave them to be abused. **May I bring to your attention that** despite numerous disclosures by the abused children, to the child protection authorities, **the perpetrators of child abuse remain at large, untroubled by the law.** Contrast this to the vast AFP operation to apprehend those who risked everything to protect these children.

The Medical Council of NSW have suspended my medical registration indefinitely. **I believe that my actions were those of a moral man, following the best and the highest traditions of the medical profession.**

Sincerely, Dr Russell Pridgeon, Duke St Medical Centre, Grafton NSW 2460   [Emphasis added]

## Cuffie's Story

Next, please read a harrowing tale by a grandmother, who was arrested around the same time as Pridgeon and O'Dea. I think her imprisonment was intended as a showpiece of cruelty. I have interviewed her and she is as straight as I am. She had no trial. Her daughter is still 'inside' for a total of three years!

**My Story**. I, Cuffie [Pseudonym] am a 75-year-old widow recently imprisoned for six months (with three to serve) for 'contempt of court' by Family Court Judge [name redacted], because I did not advise the Court the whereabouts of my daughter and grandchildren despite a court order to do so.

I did not give them up because my daughter had three years earlier gone into hiding with her two children, then 5 and 6, because of a death threat and ongoing domestic abuse by the children's father. I did not want the children to go back since I had witnessed their trauma when the time came for them to go to the Court-ordered time with their father, and their distressed and unexplained behaviour on their return to my home where they had lived for more than half their lives.

There was no trial as our lawyers agreed we had shown 'contempt of court' although we now understand we could have relied upon Sec 70 NAE(2) and also that **my daughter should not have been given a sentence for longer than twelve months if contempt had been proven.**

I was immediately sent to the Watchhouse where everything I had with me, clothes and jewelry were taken away and I was issued with a tracksuit (no knickers) a towel and a blanket. On that first night, I suffered from extreme cold that exacerbated a severe headache all night, I had none of my medications for blood pressure; I am also under treatment for cancer.

On the following morning after sentencing, the nurse determined that I should be sent to hospital – I was fitted with shackles (I could not believe my eyes when these were being fitted *and* handcuffs) and taken to the hospital in an ambulance.

The symptoms of severe headaches, swollen veins on each side of my face, the best offer of medical assistance I was given was pain relief and chemotherapy!!!!  I was then put into a bed in a general ward with two police officers at my bed-end 24/7.

Late on Monday evening, I was sent to the Women's prison where I was strip-searched and given clothing to be worn at all times – at least there were knickers and a camisole type bra in the kit!  I was also given some bed linen and a doona – so useless as it had no filling in it (just the outer fabric). On the first night, I was in the Secure Area of the prison complex in a room on my own and absolutely froze.

On the third night, my daughter, who had also been sentenced for contempt of court, was allowed to share my cell.  She tried desperately to assist with the headaches (by using sanitary pads to cover over some of the holes through which the air conditioning blew at an extremely low temperature).  She sat by me and held me through the night to try to keep me warm.

A generous fellow prisoner had given me some shampoo, soap, and a hairbrush. The hairbrush – what a luxury! Prison is meant to take away one's freedom, but it also takes away one's self assurance, self esteem and general feelings of wellbeing.  A prisoner's mind and body are controlled by officers whose best saying is "Do the crime, serve the time" no matter why the person has been incarcerated.

After two weeks I lost the sight in my right eye (blind for a time of more than an hour sometimes and then the sight gradually returned).  This went on for weeks.  The medical team checked my blood pressure, suggested I stop the work in the sewing room each day and continued to provide pain relief (when available). Results of blood test had the medical attendant decide to send me to the hospital again. During the time I was there under observation with two officers on hand every minute, I required a visit to the toilet.

The handcuffs were not removed 'as a prisoner had attacked a nurse a few weeks ago.' Imagine the pain of trying to remove my track pants and my knickers and then the effort of getting them back into place with handcuffs still on.

Another huge shock was that every time I was moved from the prison to hospital or when I received a visit from a relative, I had to sustain a full body search — that is, all clothes above waist removed and then replaced, and then all clothes below waist removed. To someone, whose privacy is paramount, it took me weeks to get over it. This was so humiliating to me that I decided I did not want or accept visitors.

My daughter and I ended up in prison for simply loving and accepting our maternal responsibility of taking care of our children and grandchildren!   From the day of the children's discovery, we had both been denied any contact with them That denial continues to this day, nearly 15 months' later.

I am concerned for their health and safety every day and it makes me feel so guilty.  My daughter and I admitted we had gone against the orders of the Court, but believed we both had **reasonable explanations** and medical evidence to support our case.  Also, I was 74 years old at the time, took full care of my 91-year-old aunt and was continuing treatment for bowel and lung cancer.  I got no treatment for my cancer condition while in prison as I could not get access to the natural alternative treatment that I was taking.

Life after prison is unbelievably different and far more difficult than one would expect. The impact of my prison experience has been extreme to the extent that on release, I could not remember how to turn on my computer. Prison turns your brain to mush. Even to go to the shops and face people is daunting and for myself, who was still working as a professional [redacted] before prison, have had some of my credentials taken away.  I had been a member for over 35 years of a highly respected professional international body.

UPDATE: Cuffie has been expelled from her profession as a "not fit and proper person." The mother in jail needs to be out and pronto, for the sake of her kids.  Can you help? -- MM

# 9. A Dearth of Enforcement

*Police Commissioners. Top Row, Left to right: Graham Ashton VIC, Mick Fuller NSW, Grant Stevens SA. Bottom Row: Ian Stewart QLD, Chris Dawson WA, Darren Hine TAS*

What do police do with their time? As Russell Pridgeon mentioned in the last chapter, the abusers that he reported are still at large. Is it fair to cops that they have to hold back on protected persons? They are wearing heavy weaponry. Each carries a baton, pepper spray, a gun, and a Taser. Do they feel silly that they are only allowed to use it on down-and-outers?

What about the fact that they have been trained to say to a Protective parent who brings in an injured child "We can't get involved if your case is before the Family Court."

Don't they feel embarrassed? And do they know it's a lie?

This is not to say that the cops are the blameworthy party. We have **idle prosecutors**, too. We have **Ministers for Police** who won't accept the least responsibility for what's going on.

Turn now to the lack of enforcement of the crimes being committed in Child Protection offices. (CPS is part of police). These have various names, such as the now defunct "Families SA" or the DOCs and FACS (Department of Child Safety, and Family and Community Services). In the United States some of these have been privatized and make a profit.

The office crimes to which I refer are the ones that come under the heading "perversion of the course of justice." Remember that in order for a case to be made against a healthy parent, someone such as a social worker or an ICL (Independent Children's Lawyer) has to lie like a rug.

Lying is not a crime if it is not connected to anything. But in a position that involves court work there is opportunity to perjure and falsify records or conceal evidence. These are crimes and are the stock in trade of the judicial kidnap racket. Oh, and racketeering itself is a crime. Note: I am willing to help any interested American file a *pro se* civil RICO suit.

Recently in the state of Iowa a child-protection social worker was charged with perjury in a case. (See Chapter 16 below.) Iowa's Criminal Law and Procedure Section 720.2 provides:

> A person who, while under oath or affirmation in any proceeding or other matter in which statements under oath or affirmation are required … by law, knowingly makes a false statement of material facts or who falsely denies knowledge of material facts, commits a class "D" felony. [A class D felony gets a maximum of 7 years; much less if no violence.]
>
> Where, while under oath a person has made contradictory statements, the indictment will be sufficient if it states that one or the other of the contradictory statements was false, to the knowledge of such person, and it shall be sufficient proof of perjury that one of the statements must be false."

The arrested social worker was probably ordered by a boss to commit perjury. Note that suborning perjury (recruiting it) is also a crime, of course. In South Australia, the penalty for suborning perjury is the same as for perjuring (7 years):

> *Criminal Law Consolidation Act* 1935 sec 242 (2) a person who counsels, procures, induces, aids or abets another to make a false statement under oath is guilty of subornation of perjury.

In the good old days suborning was much worse than perjury. In his 1769 *Commentaries on the Laws of England,* Blackstone wrote:

"Subornation of perjury is the offense of procuring another to take such a false oath…. The punishment has been various. It was anciently death; afterwards banishment, or **cutting out the tongue**, then forfeiture of goods; and now it is fine and imprisonment…. But the statute 5 Eliz. c. 9. inflicts the penalty of perpetual infamy, and a fine of 40£ on the suborner; and to stand **with both ears nailed to the pillory.**" [Emphasis added]

## 9th Circuit of Federal Appeals: No, You Can't Fabricate

In *Hardwick v Vreeken,* an Orange County California lawyer argued that CPS workers have *the right* to fabricate evidence against a mother. This case reached the US 9th Circuit appeals court in 2017 that court published the following release about the panel (that is, the panel of three appellate judges -- Stephen S. Trott, John B. Owens, and Michelle T. Friedland):

"The panel affirmed the district court's **denial of absolute and qualified immunity to social workers** who plaintiff alleged maliciously used perjured testimony and fabricated evidence to secure plaintiff's removal from her mother, and that this abuse of state power violated her Fourth and Fourteenth Amendment constitutional rights to her familial relationship with her mother. The panel held that plaintiff's complaint targeted conduct well outside of the social workers' legitimate role as quasi-prosecutorial advocates in presenting the case.... The panel further stated that it could not conceive of circumstances in which social workers would not know and understand that they could not use criminal behavior in any court setting to interfere with a person's fundamental constitutional liberty interest."

**Comments to a Youtube Video Uploaded by John919**

The court scene of the above exchange was uploaded by Youtuber John919. Probably he took his name from the Gospel of John, chapter 9 verse 19:

"And they asked them, saying, Is this your son, who ye say was born blind? How then doth he now see?"

There are more than 1800 comments under the video, many indicating that judicial kidnap is common in the US. I grabbed the first bunch of recent comments, did not cherry pick! Here they are -- I've omitted the senders' names and added some bolding. Enjoy some solidarity!

Lady should be locked up for even suggesting it's OK to lie in a courtroom.

CPS is all about the money. **They don't care about anything else**.

How would you like it if a government institution lied in Court to take your children away, put them in foster care and gave them drugs and **let them live with strangers**?

This has been going on for a long time to low-income families. Child trafficking, and low-income families cause of **social engineering**.

WOW A judge with ethics and knowledge of the law….Thaaaaat's something you don't see everyday! My hats off to you YOUR HONOR!! Getting in this system will drain you of your sanity…thanks for bringing this up in the video!

If only **every judge was as good as this guy**, other cases the judge is on the same side as CPS and that's just a mess.

CPS always lie and twist things to steal children off innocent family's! **They get paid to take kids off families** and money is involved so you know it's going to be corrupt to the core. I knew someone years ago who hated CPS so much that he went to their offices at night after a few beers and pissed all over their 'Kidnap Cars,' taking extra care to cover their driver's door handle.

Yes… CPS does falsify documents…it's called **"Security Protocol."** This representative is lying through her teeth…

Man, our founding fathers are rollin' in their graves!! I don't even recognize this U.S. of A.

Never let DCF in your home unless warranted. By letting them in you give them an opportunity to say that your home is a mess, untidy, they saw alcohol, and medications visible and within reach of child, **no child locks on cabinets, open windows** where a child could fall out….

Go after that president for human trafficking and CPS kidnaping human trafficking.

That judge gave a **little boost for humanity**.

If your home is neat and tidy and you are an excellent Mom, many DCF investigators and **social workers will simply fabricate evidence** to use against you in court.

If you are live in **low-income** housing, **DCF will prey on you** upon the first complaint they receive. Once DCF has custody of your child, it is highly possible that your child will suffer irreparable emotional and **psychological harm of which no amount of intensive trauma therapy can fix.**

DCF obtains custody, **they will attempt to alienate you from your child**, and say nasty things about you to your child. My investigation of DCF employees in Worcester, Mass. office indicates that some of these workers had suffered traumatic childhoods including rape and incest...

In the words of Jesus, it would be better if that person would hang a millstone around their own neck and be tossed into the ocean than for that person to hurt a child. Please pray for the conversion of all D.C.F. workers. **They lie all the time**.

They are not just going after low-income people anymore because they've gotten most of their kid it seems, but after living in a large city for the past 20 years **I now know that a teacher with no criminal record not even a speeding ticket can have her kids taken away for nothing.**

**That old white judge is my spirit animal**.

It's happening in Tennessee, too. It's heartbreaking. D.A.'s and attorneys and sheriffs' detective who are all involved in their own criminal actions, and them who covered for them, of doing their own crimes of the fake family court.

To repeat: that is only a handful of the 1800 praises for the ruling against the perjurer, plus "Me Too" statements. In Appendices E and K you will find more of such rejoicing over proper happenings -- in the UK. Goes to show that people (including me) are getting educated by exposés. It will be good to see some rejoicing in Australia, in the near future.

70

# 10. Truth Commissions (Plural) Are Needed Now

*(L) PM John Howard at Port Arthur, (R) thesovereignsway.com*

All the chapters of Part One have reported some dishonesty. We are a dishonest species; it is all part of self-preservation, and getting ahead. But it has to be slowed down. Unfortunately, humans can live with amazing dissonance. We can say the best interest of the child is paramount, and proceed to act as if it were the least important factor.

Here is a perfect example of the absurdity that ensues. In Missouri, a Protective parent had her little boy taken away as she was accused of Munchausen by Proxy syndrome (meaning she imagined the child to be ill, and over-doctored him). In fact he had a rare disease. She sued for the way the Child Protection Service had treated her and was awarded $3 million. Yet they **do not give her son back to her**. She is allowed "supervised visits." Madness!

## Truth Commissions

I suppose a truth commission is the way to go. If you are willing to start up a small one, please do. The usual thrust is that people who were victims come forward to pin blame and those who did the victimizing hopefully come forward for forgiveness or to make a deal to avoid punishment. Willingness to negotiate is valuable on both sides.

No two TC's -- truth commissions -- are alike. An example of a truth commission is the one held in El Salvador in 1990s. Its official document (quoted at the website usip.org) says:

> "Between 1980 and 1991, the Republic of El Salvador in Central America was engulfed in a war which plunged Salvadorian society into violence, left it with thousands and thousands of people dead and exposed it to appalling crimes, until the day, 16 January 1992, when the parties, reconciled, signed the Peace Agreement and brought back the light and the chance to re-emerge from madness to hope. Violence was a fire which swept over the fields of El Salvador; it struck at justice and filled the public administration with victims; and it singled out as an enemy anyone who was not on the list of friends. Violence turned everything to death and destruction, for such is the senselessness of that breach of the calm plenitude which accompanies the rule of law...."

*Anglican Archbishop Tutu of Cape Town*

TC's should *not* be run by officials. Each time the govern-ment sets up an Inspector General, an Integrity Commission, or suchlike the situation actually gets worse. More cover-ups become needed. South Africa was lucky to have a respected, non-government person associated with its TC, a bishop.

That Truth *and Reconciliation* Commission had the job of reconciling two bitter-enemy races. The atrocities done by the authorities to the Blacks could not be left unmentioned. For our agenda, I recommend that there be many leaders not just one. With many leaders it can have many styles. And if the group working in one city does a bad job, let them see how other cities are making a better success of it. Note: victims shouldn't be the TC leaders; impartiality must be observable.

**You Do Have the Authority**
The ultimate authority in society is society. It is society that gives a government legitimacy (at its pleasure) and can revoke it. While it is true that some governmental inquiries have been brought into life by statute, *anyone* can conduct an inquiry.

Dee McLachlan did just that. (Her Family Court survey is in Appendix H.) By hosting a survey she had to depend on people's willingness to answer questions. In a "real" truth commission, there would be the power to subpoena, and maybe the resources to give rewards. But truth has its own dynamic; it wants to get out there, no matter what, and it will.

Note: a private truth commission, if conducted in good faith, would avoid the problem of the "aura of awe" that often accompanies an official inquiry. We all have a general instinct to worship authority. Nowadays this can work against us.

**A Grand Jury Is Somewhat Like a Truth Commission**
Grand juries are part of common law. They seem to have disappeared in Australia – but if they were never statutorily repealed they have merely fallen into desuetude. In the US they are guaranteed by the Bill of Rights Fifth Amendment:

> "No person shall be held to answer for a capital, or otherwise infamous crime, unless on a presentment or indictment of a Grand Jury, except in …the militia… in time of War….

As formal police departments came into existence only in 1820, what did we do about crime before then? It was up to citizens to bring information to their Grand Jury. That grand jury would look into it, protecting the privacy of the accused until such point at which they may decide he was indictable. They would then direct the state to try him. Over time, the public got lulled into thinking that the grand jury has a boss, the state prosecutor. No, sorry, it's the other way around. Moreover, Australia has an outrageous set-up for prosecutions, an unaccountable DPP (Director of Public Prosecutions). See Chapter 23 about that.

## Moot Court at Law Schools Or in Your Backyard

Here's an idea. In law schools, they put on moot court trials, either for real persons of the past or made-up cases. I have twice run a moot court trial for someone whose actual trial was improper. The first of these moots, concerning the convicted Martin Bryant, took place on stage at the 2016 Adelaide Fringe Festival. The second, concerning Jahar Tsarnaev, took place in 2018 at the Watertown Public Library.

I did not get thrown into jail, or sued, in either case. I say you can do this, too. The Protective parents may wish you would run a proper, fair trial for them (as I did for Bryant and Tsarnaev) or they may be pleased if you would put on the trial the state *did* provide in their case, warts and all. Section 121 of the Family Law Act requires you to disguise identities. Feel free to dramatize this book's stories of Lena, Cuffie, or Carol Woods. Heck, make an opera out of Russell Pridgeon's arrest.

The bottom line is, we need a Truth Commission, or something like it, to circumvent the brick wall that has been set up by the authorities, as regards judicial kidnap. Note: you can be sure that the authorities will send infiltrators. Don't get your knickers in a knot about it – chalk it up to experience.

How to let your immediate neighbors know you are running a truth commission? Put up a lawn sign. Or hang a big notice in your front window. Too afraid visitors will rob you? Look, the Big Boys have been training us for decades to distrust one another. You can find ways to determine if a person is OK. Main rule: don't give up in advance. Keep tryin'.

## The Shyness-Humbleness Problem

If you lived in a small society you would not have any worries about offering to help when help was needed. But in our huge societies everyone automatically feels small. What's worse, we've assigned all the helping functions to designated "positions" – in government offices or even in charities.

Listen to me. I'm a tellin' ya: your assistance and initiative are needed. Whatever role you are talented to play, you can play. The idea of a Truth Commission is very appropriate as a solution to the loggerheads we are at regarding judicial kidnap. But it won't just appear in the firmament.

I notice that several Protective parents are begging for a new Royal Commission re Family Court. That is *not* smart.

Please create a *local* Truth Commission. The first meetings could consist of your friends writing up a mini-constitution for the group. I'd suggest you even write up a loyalty oath. Per state constitution of NSW, its legislators can't take a seat until they have come clean as to whom they are working for:

Section 12 (4). The oath of allegiance is to be in the following form: I swear that I will be faithful and bear true allegiance to Her Majesty Queen Elizabeth II, Her heirs and successors according to law. So help me God.

No doubt you'll come up with something more appropriate. And if you do, you can show it to newcomers. That will make them want to join your circle of associates. Note: if the name "Truth Commission" sounds too formidable, why not make up a different title.

Soon after forming your group, please create a small victory, as nothing succeeds like success.

# PART TWO:

# ANALYSIS OF THE ISSUE

CHILDREN AND YOUNG PERSONS (CARE AND PROTECTION) ACT 1998 -- New South Wales

SECT 10A Permanent placement principles

(2) (a) Wherever a child or young person is able to form his or her own views on a matter concerning his or her safety, welfare and well-being, **he or she must be given an opportunity to express those views freely and those views are to be given due weight** in accordance with the developmental capacity of the child or young person and the circumstances.   [Emphasis added]

# 11. Freda Briggs Summarizes All in Her RC Submission

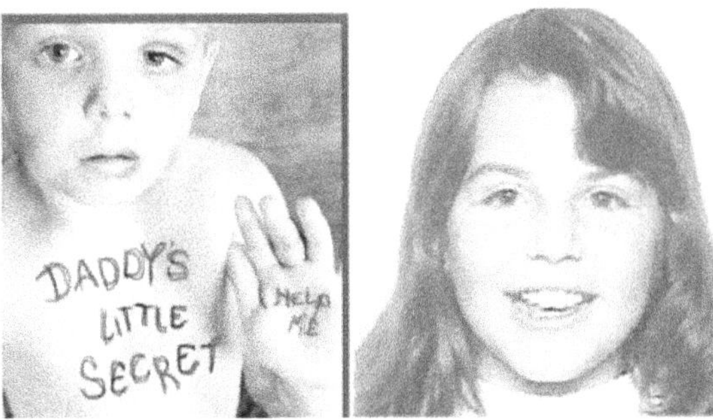

*(L) statmanyexchange.org.  (R) Louise Bell, 1973-1983, RIP*

The material below came from the late Freda Briggs, Emeritus Professor of Social Work at University of South Australia, UniSA.  She devoted forty years to attempting to improve Australia's child protection system, and wrote many books.

I never met Freda but I'll pretend to be interviewing her. I'll insert my remarks to break up parts of her 2014 submission to the Royal Commission. The numbers shown were in the original. All quotes are verbatim. I added some bolding.

**Mary**: Professor, thank you for such a comprehensive report. I ask you first to tell us about your faculty-based effort to get the University of South Australia to include **training in the signs of child abuse** as part of the curriculum for students majoring in Social Work, given that social workers are, like teachers and doctors, mandated to report any child abuse they observe. How does academia fit into the overall issue?

**Freda**: 1.2. For years, UniSA **fought against** providing mandatory reporting training for student teachers and it was only **when lawyers advised the university that it could be sued by students** that this changed.  1.3.  Over the years, government ministers and FamiliesSA CEOs met successive Deans of Social Work at UniSA (and, I believe, at Flinders

University) and failed to influence change in undergraduate courses.

**Mary**: I see that you have commented on the difficulty of navigating the legal aspects where a parent accuses the other parent, in Family Court, of child abuse.

**Freda**: 2.2. It has long been widely believed among staff, CEOs and state parliamentarians that state services/police are *not allowed* to intervene if there is a Family Court Order in place or there is a case in Family Court involving the child; and that the Family Court will conduct the investigation when, in reality, it is not resourced to do so.

The failure of FamiliesSA to investigate allegations of incest has resulted in children being ordered to live with their accused abusers (sometimes *convicted* child sex offenders), enduring further abuse. When additional evidence of abuse is reported, FamiliesSA's response to parents (and me) has been "The file is closed".

**Mary**: This is exactly what parents have been telling me.

**Freda**: 2.3 The criminal justice system does not cater for incest/child sex abuse victims who lack the maturity and sophisticated communication **skills needed to withstand cross examination by barristers** in the criminal court.

**Mary**: Aha! Plus we have Prosecutors obstructing us.

**Freda**: 2.4. If the perpetrator is not convicted, and the department **does not have the incest victim assessed** and/or the abuse is not "substantiated", the protective parent faces a dilemma. If s/he does nothing, the child can be removed into the care of the [state] minister.

The perpetrator is likely to seek residence of the victim through the Family Court **because of the ease with which it can be claimed that the protective parent (usually the mother) either (a) trained the child to make false allegations of abuse or (b) is delusional.**

**Mary**: Oh dear, that is unconscionable. Clearly a game is being played here in order that child abuse will flourish!

**Freda**: 2.5. The **notion** that children and mothers lie about incest is alive and well, contrary to international and Australian research. A mythical mental illness that only affects mothers in incest cases was accepted into Australian family law in 2003. Called Parent Alienation Syndrome (PAS), this was **the creation of a paedophilia-supporting American named Richard Gardner in 1985. This would have been laughable** had it not had such serious consequences. Although neither Gardner nor his idea had scientific credibility, the "Syndrome" gained acceptance.

**Mary**: Sadly, the same guy, Gardner, was involved in the CIA masterstroke, "False Memory Syndrome" that shut down the efforts of **victims of MK-Ultra torture** to speak out.

**Freda**: 2.6. Through FOI it was found that, in successive years, the Family Court **made around 40 requests for intervention by FamiliesSA and the requests were refused.** There is a long history of resentment relating to federal (Family Court) versus state funding.

FamiliesSA workers **have a history of concocting reports to justify their actions or inaction.** Some have been caught **blatantly fabricating reports for the Youth Court** as well as Ministers.

**Mary**: I bet such things have been hard for you to bear.

**Freda**: 3.1. In the Family Court case of *Grange v Langmeil*, FamiliesSA persistently said that the children had been assessed on three occasions since 2008 after reporting **anal rape by their father and yet when asked for the dates of the assessments, CEO Tony Harrison admitted that no assessment had ever taken place. Damning documents [were] removed from FamiliesSA files.** 4.1 Social workers gave examples of how they were **bullied by senior staff**. Case workers, **teachers** and police **gave evidence that they were deterred by line managers from reporting abuse**.

**Mary**: What do you see as a way around that?

**Freda**: 6.2. A report was sent to Attorneys General in 1995 recommending that there should be an inquisitorial court for child sexual abuse cases involving child witnesses. This would be staffed by a panel of rostered child abuse experts with authority **and means to investigate all of the evidence**. However, the SA Attorney General commented that the legal profession would resist change because the current **system makes it easy for lawyers to "get their clients off" when children are the only witnesses**.

**Mary**: I am deeply ashamed of the lawyers.

**Freda**: 6.4. In 1999, *Four Corners* showed a documentary, *Double Jeopardy*. This showed how the court system **inflicted** psychological abuse. Some of Australia's senior judges, prosecutors, defence lawyers and victims agreed that this was intolerable. **Justice Helen O'Sullivan and Justice Robinson courageously said** that if their children were sexually abused they would never allow them to suffer the ordeal of a trial…. A report was published : "*Alternative Models for Prosecuting Child Sex Offences in Australia*" **It has been ignored**. [That report is on the website of Dr Annie Cossins at University of NSW Law School.]

**It Has Come to This: Holding Your Baby Is a Crime**

Case 6: Four indigenous children living with their parents on a property out of town. [Case submitted to NCPA.org]:

On the Friday night of the June long weekend, when the father was home alone with the 4 children as the mother had not yet returned from town, five police officers and a couple of DOCS workers arrived without warning to forcibly remove the children. The reason was not that the parents were a risk to the children but *another* man, living in his own house on the same property, 'was considered to be a risk', and the department falsely claimed that the family had left one of their children alone unsupervised with this man.

In fear and shock, the father picked up his two youngest babies and held onto them trying to argue that this allegation was false. The police forcibly removed the children from his arms and then arrested him for resisting police in front of his children who were all screaming. Thus, this father now has a criminal record just for trying to hold onto his babies.

The children were separated and placed with strangers in foster care. *The 2 oldest went through 4 placements* and the 2 youngest had 3 placements until they were all placed together in a residential facility that is only approved for children aged 12 to 17, but these children were aged 1 to 8, and had to contend with the instability of a rotating roster of staff.

Meanwhile, the department were promising restoration, but *at the same time* made an application for a two-year order and *the day before the first court hearing*, legal aid informed the parents that they were withdrawing their grant because they decided there was no merit in their case – in other words Legal Aid had prejudged the case and decided the parents could not win, so they would not fund their defence. This is happening more and more. So, the parents appeared in court by themselves with no idea what to do *and the department got an interim custody order.*     [Emphasis added]

# 12. Dee McLachlan's 2018 Family Court Survey

*(L) Susan Kiefel, Chief Justice of Australia*
*(R) William Alstergren, Chief Justice of the Family Court*

When Protective parents started to hear about our articles at GumshoeNews.com, they phoned the Editor Dee McLachlan to tell about their luck with Family Court. She felt she was listening to almost identical stories.  Dee then decided to conduct an online survey in hopes of obtaining a statistical view of what was happening. The first screen said:

This is a survey is about the FAILURES of the Family Court in AUSTRALIA to protect children. It is for Protective Parents regarding their experiences…. It is broken up into these categories:

a)  Disclosure [to whom did the kid reveal the abuse?]
b)  Believing the child [who believed and who didn't believe]
c)  Family Court and  Finances
d)  Disregarding and DESTROYING Evidence
e)  Coaching, Record Falsification and Punishment
f)  General questions, and Threats
g)  Damage, and Outcomes

McLachlan hired a professional survey company to administer it; the responses were made to that company, anonymously. It was open from October 8 to December 14, 2018.

Seventy-nine persons responded. It must be emphasized that the results are not of scientific standing. The ideal method of taking a survey involves aiming the questionnaire at people who are not already known to think alike. Dee acknowledges that her survey was aimed at aggrieved parents, and, as you see above, it stated that it is about FAILURES of the Court.

Still, the survey said "Please be scrupulously accurate." We have no way of knowing the responders' honesty, but there's a wide range of answers, some surprising. To me, that gives it credibility. Here are four of the questions:

**2. How old was your child when you realised that SEXUAL ABUSE (or a serious injury) occurred? Number of responses:** [79 responded to this question]

- Less than 2 years: 11x chosen (13.92%)
- 2 – 4 years: 33x chosen (41.77%)
- 5 – 8 years: 27x chosen (34.18%)
- 9 – 12 years: 7x chosen (8.86%)
- Older than 12 years: 1x chosen (1.27%)

**4. Who did you contact once you realised there had been abuse? Number of responses:** 77, These were multiple choice questions, and the responder was invited to tick *more* than one box, e.g., MC [multiple choice]

- Family (40)
- The police (41)
- My doctor, the hospital (34)
- Child Protection Services (48)

**32. Who do you believe CHANGED, or FALSIFIED REPORTS, or COMMITTED PERJURY?** [53 replied]

Members of my family (7)   Doctor, medical personnel (5)

The police (17)     Your psychologist / psychiatrist(9)
Social workers, supervised visit personnel (12)
Child Protective Services (26)
ICL, Independent child lawyer (28)
Court reporters, pre-court services (25)
Court appointed psychiatrist (16)
Court appointed experts (15)
The judge (the court) (21)        Other (19)

## 5. When you confronted the perpetrator about the abuse, did they do any of the following? [77, MC]

- Deny the allegations (60)
- Threaten with violence (24)
- Advance proceedings into Family Court (34)
- Call me delusional, resulting in me having to undergo mental health assessments (37)

Re "advance proceedings into Family Court" the 34% figure is very significant. I believe the "other party" – i.e., the abuser, has already been instructed (if I am correct about his/her being a cog in the wheel of child sex trafficking) to *approach* the Court. Isn't that intriguing? Instead of fearing the judicial system because he is a wrongdoer, he feels his 'advancing' will be greeted nicely.

And that is so. In the twinkling of an eye, the court – having been advised by Department of Child Protection -- will turn the spotlight on the mother. All interest in his abuse will dissipate and she will start to be accused of abuse, even if only to the extent of abusing by coaching or abusing by parental alienation.  The deck is stacked!  Amen.

**Survey Answers Criticize Court Reporters and ICL's**
From mid to late 2018, Dee McLachlan and I published articles knowing only about Family (federal) Court.  We only found out

in 2019 that the state Childrens Courts are just as harmful, especially as they can award guardianship. We had not yet become aware of the power of two little-known groups of "professionals" – the **ICL**'s and **court reporters**.

The latter write up what is said in court -- reminiscent of the FBI's policy of not taking signed statements. FBI agents conduct an interview and write a report on Form 302. If there is corruption in government, this is a perfect method for hiding it. In fact I think the practice of having "reporters," when modern technology can do better, is itself very telling.

The ICL – the Independent Children's Lawyer is like the US's "Guardian ad litem." They are supposed to represent the child. But it most cases they don't meet the child. Their lack of interest in the child came out clearly in the survey.

Question 7 asked "Who DID believe your child? Did someone (even one person) from the categories below believe your child?" 71 persons answered; they were allowed to tick as many boxes as were relevant in their case.

Note: I will now put the answers in descending order for your convenience. These people  DID believe the child:
Members of my family (58)
Your psychologist/psychiatrist (41)
A doctor, nurse, medical personnel (29)
Anyone in the police, detective etc (21)
Child Protective Service Officers (15)
Social workers, supervised visit personnel (12)

Court appointed experts (6)
Court appointed psychiatrist (3)
Court reporters, supervision services (3)
ICL, independent child lawyer (2)
The judge (the court) (2).

Imagine that! The child's own lawyer chooses not to believe her, despite Australia's media telling about the findings of the Royal Commission that most children's disclosures are true.

Now please look at Question 32, shown above. The ICL ranked worst of all responders.  The question was:  "Who do you believe CHANGED, or FALSIFIED REPORTS -- or COMMITTED PERJURY?" 53 people answered.  More than half -- 28 persons -- ticked "ICL" The only other professions who made it into the twenties were:

Child Protective Services (26)
Court reporters, pre-court services (25), and
The judge (the court) (21).

That's perjury we're talking about. And by judges! Disgusting.

I mustn't let the court-appointed doctors off the hook. Did you notice how 43 ticked the box "Your psychologist, psychi-atrist believed" but only 3 *court-appointed* psychiatrists did.

**Article by now-retired barrister Maurice Kriss: "Mothers being forced to agree to shared parenting or lose the child"**

Please circulate this 2016 article. Kriss was an attorney in criminal law, no doubt a key to his understanding Family Law. A mother asked for his help and soon he found himself doing *pro bono* work in many other cases of the judicial kidnap type, in all six states. Boy, did the scales fall from his eyes.

I am the President of the National Child Protection Alliance of Australia. I joined the NCPA where I was asked to assist a number of mothers who had their children taken from them by the Family Court after reporting that their children had been sexually abused …. **I noticed a distinct pattern: the mothers were treated with abuse and disrespect. They were called liars and accused them of coaching their children to lie. The**

**fact that very young children at the time were bleeding from the anus or vagina did not move police**. The conduct of the court in most of the cases in which I had appeared, were abominable. The 'Magellan List' was an orchestrated corrupt system that was designed to discredit mothers. It took me some time to realise that the mothers had lost their children from the moment they filled in a Form 4 reporting sexual abuse.

I endeavoured to report this to friends but was met with disbelief and their belief that mothers lie to stop their husband from seeing their children. I was accused of being …crazy. The Myth of lying mothers was deeply entrenched in the community.

Why is not written in the newspapers or magazines or on the TV? The reason is that the Family Court has a complete gag order, which can punish anyone who breaches this order of silence with 12 months' jail. It is s121 of the Family Law Act. S121 is for the protection of Judges, employed selected psychologists, and the so-called Independent Child Lawyers in their immoral and illegal conduct in removing mothers from their children. [The gag makes it] difficult to raise these issues.

The NCPA charges the Family Court, with knowingly and consistently **committing mental torture**. It is a worldwide problem, at least in the UK and the USA, Denmark and Ireland, where children are removed from their mothers for doing what they are mandated to do, care and protect their child. Unfortunately, many mothers are too scared to put pen to paper lest they reap the wrath of the Family Court. The Court can and does refuse the mother to see her children until the child is 18 …

If the child is not old enough to be cross-examined, very little if anything, is done. *On the few occasions when a report substantiates the child has been abused*, the Family Court has been known to dismiss the report "for the mother is a liar and the child has been taught to lie." Young children have no concept of adult sexual activity, and no matter how you try to put such concepts into a child's mind it would not work. Even older children cannot maintain a sexual lie under investigation. You may ask if there's no proof that the mother is lying, on what basis can a Court order the child to live with the abusive father? If the mother can be shown to suffer from a mental illness.

**[The Three-Fingered Judge]** An ICL said to me "The judge will give your client three chances to agree with his orders. He will raise his hand and show three fingers, after each time he will ask you the same question three times, if your client does not agree she will lose her child, do you understand me?"  The father was accused of anal penetration of his 3-year-old child, had one computer with 82,000 pornographic images on his computer. His Honour dismissed the pornographic material and other evidence. Raised his three fingers ….

Some mothers are **forced to admit that they were delusional when they reported the sexual assault.** Having now admitted, the mother is given a gag order preventing her reporting further sexual abuse to the police or any other authority. Ordered: that the **mother cannot take the child to a doctor, hospital, or psychologist** without the **father's approval**. [Emphasis added]

Chapter 4 showed that George Potkonyak lost his license to practice law in NSW as he had "spoken up." He was alone, just as the mothers were alone, until Facebook, Youtube, and other methods of communicating taught them that what happens on their case is standard. Such parents are accused of abusing the kid emotionally "because they have delusions and they alienate!" I know two more lawyers who were warned to shut up, or else.

This can now come to an end. The judges, the discipline board officers, and others who foisted this game on us must face the music. The ICL's job needs to end, and most court-appointed psychiatrists' license should be revoked. Not that these four categories of persons should suffer only the loss of employment. They should be indicted for their multitudinous crimes.

# 13. Rilak Case: Recusal, Mandamus, Abuse of Process

*A famous mother-child bond: Diana and the princes*

The case of *Rilak v Tsocas* has run for years in Family Court, Sydney. You can find all of it on the website austlii.edu.au, hosted by the Australian Legal Information Institute. First I will quote the part where the mother, Ms Rilak, asked for a recusal of the judge – Justice Ann Ainslie-Wallace, from her case. The transcript begins by dismissing that application.

## REASONS FOR JUDGMENT about Recusal

On 23 March 2018, on the Court's own motion, two appeals instituted by Ms Rilak ("the appellant") were listed before the Full Court to determine whether they should be dismissed. On the day before the hearing of that motion, the appellant, by Application in an Appeal sought that I [Ainslie-Wallace] recuse myself from hearing the matter. In the affidavit in support of the application, the appellant contended that I had been involved in six appeals instituted by her and that I had "rejected all of her applications" (Affidavit filed 22 March 2018. Par 12.)

In oral submissions, the appellant said that she does not have faith in me and that **she feels I am impermissibly prejudiced against her and will not afford her justice in the hearing ….** In July 2015 the appellant sought expedition of an appeal instituted by her against interim parenting orders made on 5 June 2015 during the final parenting proceedings ("the interim parenting orders appeal"). The appellant had earlier sought and been granted expedition of the recusal appeal. …

[Ms Rilak hasn't been able to see her girl, born 2010, in over 3 years, or even to receive phone calls, for absolutely no reason.]

On 12 July 2017 I dismissed the appellant's application for extension of time in which to bring appeals from an order of Justice Stevenson made on 7 July 2016, and an order of Justice I made on 22 July 2016. In both cases the time for filing an appeal had long passed by nearly 12 months ….

Finally on 13 October 2017, on the application of the respondent, **I ordered the appellant to provide security for costs in relation to an appeal** instituted by her against a costs order made by Rees J resulting from **the appellant's unsuc-cessful application that the respondent [Dad] be dealt with for contravention of the parenting orders**.

[The father is in utter breach of orders to allow visits!]

The law in relation to disqualification on account of apprehended bias is well settled. [That's the problem!] In *Johnson v Johnson* (2000) the plurality of the High Court (Gleeson CJ, Gaudron, McHugh, Gummow and Hayne JJ) held:

> "... It has been established by a series of decisions of this Court that the test to be applied in Australia in determining whether a judge is disqualified by reason of the appearance of bias (which, in the present case, was said to take the form of prejudgment) **is whether a fair-minded lay observer might reasonably apprehend** that the judge might not bring an impartial and unprejudiced mind to the resolution of the question…[Our way] is based upon the need for public confidence in the administration of justice."

I observe that in one of the matters which the appellant said had given rise to her concern, **I was but one member of a bench of three** who came to a unanimous decision on the application.

90

I am comfortably satisfied that the fair minded reasonable observer understanding the context of the applications decided by me and the Full Court would not apprehend that I would fail to bring an impartial mind to the issue to be determined in the present appeal. **Thus I refused the application that I disqualify myself from further hearing the appeal.**

## Nemo Judex

There is a list of maxims (overarching principle of law) later in this book. One of the maxims says "No man can be judge in his own case." It is expressed in Latin, the language used in British courts for centuries, as: *Nemo judex in causa sua debet esse.*

Are you ready for more of Ms Rilak's case? She tried several approaches that are the only hope a citizen can have. She tried to get: 1. declaratory relief, i.e., to have a judge say she acted lawfully or that the other side acted unlawfully, 2. an injunction to restrain the judge, 3. mandamus, via Section 75(v) of Australia's Constitution, to coerce a court person to fulfill a job.

Predictably, Rilak was blocked on each road, and was told that **she was committing abuse of process.** It's described in the following snippet from one of her other many trips to court:

**Rilak v Tsocas.** As to the main proceedings, the plaintiff seeks (i) declarations that she was denied procedural fairness, declarations that reports were not prepared according to law and oral evidence was not received according to law, and a declaration that the trial judge should have recused himself from the main proceedings and (ii) a writ of prohibition or **injunction against the second defendant, the Chief Justice of the Family Court,** restraining him from relying upon various evidence and findings in the main proceedings and, a writ of **mandamus** compelling him to "do his duty according to law" in relation to written complaints made by the plaintiff on 30 July 2015 and 7 September 2015. To the extent that the application relates to the main proceedings, it is an abuse of process.

As Nettle J noted in *Construction Forestry Mining* (2016)

"The high constitutional purpose of s 75(v) of the Constitution is to make it constitutionally **certain that there is a jurisdiction capable of restraining officers of the Common-wealth from exceeding Commonwealth power.** It is not to provide an alternative means of remedying judgments of superior courts from which there are adequate rights of appeal."

In the same way a litigant must generally exhaust statutory rights of appeal before this Court will contemplate an application for a constitutional writ …. An attempt to leapfrog that process via the original jurisdiction of this Court is, for the reasons just given, also an **abuse of process** in this case. [Emphasis added]

## The National Benchbook – Regarding Abuse of Process

I believe it is the *perpetrators* that abuse court procedure on a regular basis. Here is a fascinating document, from a National Benchbook on Domestic Violence that alerts the judge to this very behavior. Note that this benchbook seems to be an instruction for the judge to pin down, and discipline, the *real* abusers-of-process. (Or is it a guide to helping them?)

It was retrieved from dfvbenchbook.aija.org.au April, 2019. *Source:* The Australian Institute of Judicial Administration, in partnership with the University of Queensland Law School:

**National Domestic and Family Violence Benchbook**

[Be alert to] various forms of … abuse of processes that **may be used by perpetrators** … to reassert their power and control over the victim. A party to proceedings in domestic and family violence related cases **may use a range of litigation tactics to gain an advantage over or to harass, intimidate, discredit the other party.** These tactics may be referred to in legislation …as malicious, frivolous, vexatious… Perpetrators … who seek to control the victim before, during or after separation may make multiple applications and complaints in multiple systems … with the **intention of interrupting**, deferring, prolonging or dismissing judicial processes, which may result in **depleting the victim's financial** resources and emotional wellbeing, and adversely impacting the victim's capacity to maintain employment or to care for children.… This tactic is known as 'burning off', and is prevalent where a victim lacks the financial resources to engage legal representation, and the perpetrator is either financially well-resourced or wiling to incur debt… and fund multiple actions over extended periods.

Where the perpetrator is aware that the victim may be in a financial position to engage solicitors, the perpetrator may use a different tactic known as **'conflicting out'**, which involves seeking preliminary advice from multiple lawyers [especially in small towns] so as to deny the victim access to legal representation, on the basis of conflict of interest.

Although there is a widespread belief in the community that mothers … fabricate allegations to influence family law proceedings, …**it is more likely that they will be reluctant** to raise allegations for fear of having their motives questioned.

Cross applications for family violence protection orders may be used by some perpetrators to intimidate the victim into withdrawing their application. Perpetrators in these circumstances may seek a cross order to neutralise the effect of the victim's order. Some cross applications may be genuine, but those that constitute intimidation **may have the effect of trivialising or silencing the victim's claims** for protection.

Some commonly reported examples include the perpetrator: failing to appear in court; repeatedly seeking adjournments; **appealing decisions on tenuous grounds**; obtaining a protection order against the victim and misleading the victim into breaching the order; …. A victim may feel intimidated, isolated or neglected by, for example: having to sit in proximity to the perpetrator and their family and friends in the courtroom; experiencing condescending language from defence lawyers or judicial officers; in some courts, being cross-examined directly by the perpetrator (who may have chosen to self-represent so as to secure this opportunity)….

Judicial officers may need to weigh up and assess requirements for procedural fairness [against] the perpetrator's exploitation of the justice system. Processes, when used by a party with improper intent, could amount to malicious prosecution, abuse of process or a criminal offence. [See appeal in *Baron v Walsh*.]

In 2014, the WA Supreme Court of Appeals ruled in *Baron v Walsh*, that it does not (necessarily) abuse process to use legally available actions, such as making multiple interlocutories…, but the intention is what matters. Some litigants misuse the law illegally to thwart the function of the law. In Chapter 17, I will show how you can make use of two torts of abuse of process and malicious prosecution, to try to right this wrong.

**Court As a Show Institution?** The Protocols of the Elders of Zion is a 1905 work of contested authorship. I quote:

"In all ages [people] have **accepted words for deeds**. They rarely pause to note, in the public arena, whether promises are followed by performance. **Therefore we shall establish show institutions.** …Our directorate will have knowledge of all the secrets of the social structure…with the whole **underside of human nature**, with all its sensitive chords on which they will have to play. **Persons [who disobey] our instructions, must face criminal charges** or disappear." [Emphasis added]

It is hard to avoid seeing Family Court as a show institution. School systems should move quickly to teach students about habits such as our proclivity to accept words for deeds….

# 14. The Perfect Crime: "Family-Court-Ordered Rape"

*Banner from a supporter at Dr Pridgeon's hearing*

So far, this book has described factors of "legal kidnap." Now Dr Russell Pridgeon, one of the persons arrested in the AFP's "Operation Noetic," has taken the matter to a new height by calling it "the perfect crime" and by labeling it "Family-Court-ordered child sexual abuse."

Recall that in Chapter 2, British social worker Carol Woods learned that when she refused to falsify records, she got smeared, harassed, and threatened. Other whistle blowers, see Chapter 28, end up in the morgue. So the treatment of this physician so far has not been as bad as it could be. It's a pity, though, that more medical colleagues are not protesting.

## Dr Pridgeon's Speech, April 5, 2019, in Brisbane

"This case [my arrest] is not about child stealing, it is about child protection. It's about the desperate efforts of good people, good law-abiding Australians, desperately trying to protect children from the worst sort of sexual abuse. We are not criminals.

There is no law in Australia against protecting children from rape. We have a right to protect our children even against court ordered child sexual abuse, Family Court ordered child sexual abuse. We have a duty to protect our children. If we didn't protect these children we would be breaking the law. The criminal code …

[SEC 286 of the Criminal Code Act 1899, Queensland] **demands that we protect children**, keep them safe, and we've done that, yet we are being charged with crimes.

"The people who have abused these children are not being charged, they are being protected, they are being protected by the AFP. The AFP are denying this abuse, even though they know that these children have been abused. This denial is absolutely blatant, and absolutely brazen. It's quite wrong.

"Raping children is a crime. It is an abomination. Ordinary decent Australians regard it with horror and disgust, but the AFP apparently do not. And the public servants who were supposed to protect these children did not.  Apparently they don't regard child sexual abuse as a problem here. The child protectors, we the child protectors, are being prosecuted by the very people who failed to protect these children in the first place. This is a crime to hide a crime.

"The AFP knows the full effect of these children's abuse. They have access to the police databases. **They have taken our computers, they've taken all our documentation, and that documentation that was leaked with the description and evidence of the children's abuse. Yet they do nothing, yet they continue to lie about the children's abuse.  They say the abuse did not occur, it occurred!** [Emphasis added]

"The descriptions that we have of the children's disclosures are graphic; they are horrendous. They know this, and yet they lie. The AFP know what we know. They know that these children have been sexually abused. We protected these children from abuse. Whatever we've done, we can say that we have given these children four years of freedom from rape. These children made 40 plus disclosures to 13 different adults when they were between the ages of 4 and 5, over a period of about 18 months.  Only one of those adults was ever **interviewed** by the police. This wasn't an investigation; it wasn't a bona-fide investigation.

It was a cover-up.  Professor Freda Briggs did a report on these children. She was so disgusted with what she found, she made a complaint to the **Crime and Misconduct Commission**. [They found] the officers did a poor quality investigation. Nonetheless, there was no remedial action, it wasn't re-investigated. So the false narrative that these children were never abused, continues.

"Incestuous child sexual abuse is a crime of secrecy. It occurs in the privacy of the family home. It occurs behind closed doors. There are no witnesses. **If we choose to disbelieve the children, then we create the perfect crime.** Our Prime Minister, **Scott Morrison, promised the children of Australia that they would be believed**, and would be protected, and that's what we did. We believed these children. We believed them and we protected them. This is a very dark moment in the history of the Australian Federal Police. Their behaviour is appalling. They have shamed Australia."

In my opinion, this was a thrilling moment for the Protective parents of the world. The AFP surely misjudged their quarry if they though Pridgeon was going to submit to such accusations.

Mainstream media is not telling the world. Channel 7 was there in Brissie filming the event but has not broadcast it. **See? Media is the problem.** Other news outlets have in fact blasted the doctor, in line with the official false accusations making him sound like a real baddy. A heavy attack can be found at The Sunshine Coast News, online. Reporting Pridgeon's original arrest back on November 8, 2018 -- along with Patrick O'Dea and other elderly persons -- the DailyMail.co.uk, wrote:

"AFP Assistant Commissioner Debbie Platz said the 'syndicate' demonstrated a complete disregard for the rule of law and decisions of the courts. '**The actions of this group [Russell, O'Dea, et al] do not protect children.** What it does is potentially endanger the safety and wellbeing of them,' she said. 'Parental child abduction can have harmful physical and emotional effects on the children abducted. They can suffer the loss of contact with their family and friends, miss their educational stability and are often hidden away from people around them. They are removed from almost everything familiar to them including their toys, daily routine, and sometimes even their name'." [Emphasis added]

It is so typical of the media to mislead us. Of course the fault lies with Assistant Commissioner of Federal Police Debbie Platz for using that deceitful language. But journalists could have dug into this a bit. *The Brisbane Times* ran an article emphasizing the ankle trackers that Pridgeon and O'Dea have to wear. Their article included a significant typo as follows:

"Flanked by two women in suits, Pridgeon accused police of deliberately ignoring evidence of child sex abuse that his group had collected from the children. 'They say that abuse did not occur. It's absurd,' he said."
No, Russell did not say "It's absurd." He said "**It occurred.**"

**Suggestions for Russell Pridgeon's Defense at Trial**

Under common law it is legal to take aggressive action to defend oneself *and also to defend others*. You may be arrested, but self-defense is a defense in court so you should win an acquittal. The Australian High Court precedent for this is very clear. In a 1987 ruling in *Zecevic v Director of Public Prosecutions*, the justices said:

"The question to be asked in the end is quite simple. It is whether the accused believed upon reasonable grounds that it was necessary in self-defence to do what he did. If he had that belief and there were reasonable grounds for it, or if the jury is left in reasonable doubt about the matter, then he is entitled to an acquittal. Stated in this form, the question is one of general application not limited to cases of homicide."

Russell might also take the lead provided by NSW barrister Terry Shulze. In a Gumshoe article, "Review of Australian Law and Its Decline," dated June 19, 2018, Shulze explained:

In English law, extrinsic aids to interpretation of a law relied primarily on the concept of searching for the "mischief which the statute was designed to remedy." (See Heydon's Case, 1584) That ancient language is the 'rational basis' or 'rationale for the legislation' or the *'raison d'etre'*. In American law there is a term "substantive due process". It was developed from the concept that a person cannot be seen to be receiving due process, when the law itself lacks the substance of law.

No matter how proper the procedures may be, a person does not receive the benefits of due process when the law itself is corrupt. My submission [is] *if there was no reason for the legislation*, the legislation was a denial of substantive due process.

Pridgeon could also invoke *Minister for Immigration v Teoh*, a 1995 High Court case. Teoh, an alien, was the sole supporter of citizen children. Convicted of drug crime he was slated for deportation. Australia had ratified the UN's Convention on the Rights of the Child in 1990. Teoh's lawyer, Stephen Churches, argued on the basis of Convention's Article 3:

"In all actions concerning children, whether undertaken by public or private social welfare institutions, courts of law, administrative authorities or legislative bodies, the best interests of the child shall be a primary consideration."

It *gave Australians an expectation* that the best interest of the child would be paramount. High Court: Mr Teoh can stay.

**What about Section 70NAE?**  The fact that Operation Noetic is a public relations stunt, to scare us all, can be seen in the fact that Family Law Act sec 70NAE specifically says it is proper to remove a child from a dangerous place *against court orders:*

**Family Law Act: 70NAE  Meaning of reasonable excuse for contravening an order.**

(1)  The circumstances in which a person may be taken to have had, for the purposes of this Division, **a reasonable excuse for contravening an order** [include]:

(4)  A person (the respondent) is taken to have had a reasonable excuse for contravening a parenting order to the extent to which it deals **with whom a child** is to live with, in a way that resulted in the child not living with a person in whose favour the order was made if:

(a) the respondent believed on reasonable grounds that the actions **constituting the contravention were necessary to protect the health or safety of a person ....**

## The Crimes of the AFP

Dr Pridgeon claims that **he had been informing the police, for months,** of his actions, trying to get their help. Many parents say they ring the police about desperate cases and get rebuffed. I lived in Adelaide for most of 40 years in blissful unawareness of these crimes. But even if I had learned of it, I'd still have assumed that police are on the side of the public, not on the side of the criminals.

Dr Pridgeon has turned the thing on its head – how could he not? The kidnappers, the judges, virtually *order child sexual abuse.* I wish Russell would go on the offensive instead of the defensive.  AFP Assistant Commissioner Platz had the gall to say that "the 'syndicate' (the O'Dea elderlies) demonstrated a complete disregard for the rule of law." But it is she who does not know *rule of law* from a bar of soap. I allege she has committed the crime of *perversion of justice.* Syndicate indeed.

I recommend that the Assistant Commissioner be citizen-arrested. It is legal to citizen-arrest a person who is caught committing a felony. You'd have to read Platz her rights, specify the charges and call for back-up. Do not use excessive force. If your quarry does not cooperate, you can add the charge of *resisting arrest*. All cops present are likely complicit in her crime.

Might she sue you for attempting to arrest her? Yes, if you failed to meet the requirements just listed (that a felony was being committed and that you informed her she is under arrest.)

**The Medical License**

I also think Russell should sue the Medical Association, which is a private organization. The Health Practitioner Regulation Law says *unprofessional conduct* is "that of a lesser standard than might reasonably be expected of the [doctor] by the public or professional peers," including "(c) conviction of the practitioner for an offence, the nature of which may affect the practitioner's suitability to continue to practise the profession." Pridgeon has not been convicted of anything.

Isn't it normal for doctors to support colleagues? The Medical Board of Queensland heard the awful case of a doctor who hog-tied a boy in his office (that is, tied the child's hands and feet together behind his back). The Mum took a photo of it.

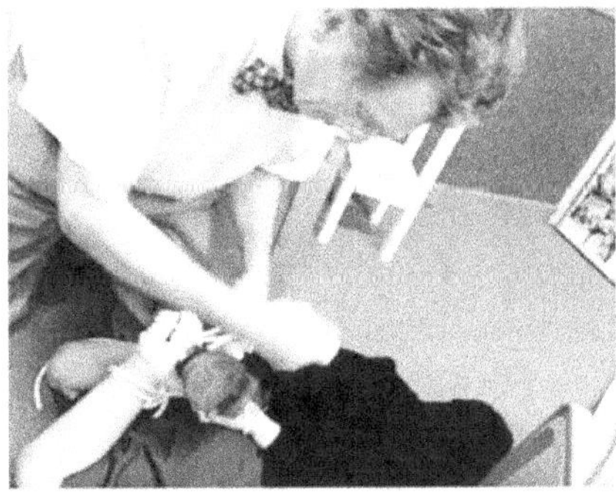

*Doctor tying the autistic child*

Dr Neville Davis, was convicted in 2015 of assault by sitting on that boy's back. According to the *Courier Mail*, Magistrate Paul Johnstone released Neville on a 12-month, $1000 good-behaviour bond with no conviction recorded. The Medical Board gave him only a reprimand.

Hello?

# 15. Police State, CIA, Tavistock, Childrens Courts

*NSW Police carried M4 rifles on New Year's Eve.  Theguardian.com*

Our situation is getting worse every year. To name a few items: the police are becoming militarized, schoolteachers are handed a strange curriculum to use, customers have to pay whatever the monopoly firms want to charge, TV entertainment has much violence, respect for religion has plummeted, judges make arbitrary decisions....

Local leadership seems to have disappeared. This is because everything local is now overwhelmed by the apparently marvelous Big Stuff.  Technology is vey complicated. Nations join in global formations such as the mysterious "NATO" (whose name omits any revealing of its purpose -- North Atlantic Treaty Organization, what a joke). Celebrities, some as young as twenty, command attention on every magazine cover. The average person no longer feels empowered.

I am old enough to remember when we all felt empowered — heck, we're each as powerful as the next guy. And I don't see any reason why that could not be revived. In this book, the reviving consists of getting to the bottom of the judicial kidnap fandangle. Specifically it consists of seeing how courts do what they do in "child protection" cases. Now for the  intriguing question:  WHO IS BEHIND THIS?

**The CIA.** In the 20th century it's certain that one group, the so-called Central Intelligence Agency of the US, got deep into the study of how to control people. The CIA used such means as LSD, shock treatments, sensory deprivation, and sexual humiliation on adults. They filled children's brains with wrong information and reactions. (Data on that is now declassified; no need to be called woo-woo if you discuss it.)

Probably the ability of "coverts" to carry out such illegal work depended on nobody finding out. If folks did find out, they could be killed or simply discredited. There was also the protection of authority. If the crimes got reported, police would "lose" the information, and courts would acquit.

The current epidemic of pedophilia is not random. I think the behavior got deliberately installed. As for the urge to treat people with brutality, that's in our species' repertoire. It earns praise when used on an enemy. Most American citizens don't take an interest in their country's use of torture. Also they're unbothered by the fact that mainstream media can publish counter-information, to audiences of millions. As regards cults, CIA-type entities set some of them up as experiments in mind-control. Cult members become imprisoned, mentally.

**Tavistock.** Tavistock is a registered educational charity in the UK. I use the name 'Tavi" for any groups – some go back to ancient times – that carry our secret mind-control activity. Where parents want help, they find blockage in every institution, as we have seen: the parliament, the police, the media, child-help groups such as CPS, or ombudsmen.

I speculate that Tavistock is the major coordinator of child abuse and that its purpose is most likely mind control. The Tavistock leader Dr John Rawlings Rees (1890-1969) was able to get access to "broken" soldiers of World War I and experiment further on them. Mothers losing their kids in

Australia is not only for child sex trafficking but is a fun game for Tavi-types, to see how far they can tease Mum's mind.  **A** famous psychology book, *Attachment and Loss,* shows how a child gets depressed when taken from mother. The book's author, John Bowlby, did his study under Tavistock auspices.

**Attenion!  Childrens Courts Are Not Actually Courts**
The Childrens Courts seem to be as much a barrier as the Family Court for keeping family members separated. Every state has one. South Australia calls it Youth Court. I shall now argue that it is not really a court. It is an administrative body that answers to the police. Yet the public does not know that.

Say a parent has reported injury of his kid, yet the abuse gets covered up by the *social worker* or the *police,* and never reaches the court. Of those two entities, who should be blamed? Is it the *police's* duty to pursue the matter of child abuse, to the point of pressing charges?  Yes, despite the fact that the law is worded to lay the responsibility on many others, too.

And here is a how'dya'do: the DCP social workers are actually *part of the police.*  The public does not know that, but there you are! As Dee McLachlan and I bumbled around sleuthing, we thought it was naughty that the DCP and police are in bed together, but it turns out they are supposed to be in bed together. It is officially DCP's job to assist the police.

**The Six Minsters for Police.** More complications. What is the role for the parliamentary *Minister* for Police?  Let's say a 10-year-old boy discloses sexual abuse to a teacher. She is a mandatory reporter. She passes the word to police (which is done by phone, not in writing). Is it the police's duty to do something about it?  I assume so. Why else have a law about mandatory reporting? (Tut, tut, no sarcastic replies, please). But if you write to the Minister for Police, he'll ping-pong you to the Department of Child Protection. It's  joke.

It would be good to hear each of the six Ministers for Police delineate their turf. Perhaps they will be honest and say "My job is to look the other way" – and -- "I always block emails from irritants like Dr Russell Pridgeon."

**Children's Court and Guardianship**

Guardianship is a possible basis for taking a child. Please sample this tidbit from the Queensland government website:

The law gives [Department of] Child Safety the mandate to protect children from significant harm or risk of significant harm and whose parents are unable …to protect them.  This Act also provides the **legal framework for decision making** by Child Safety staff, such as decisions to: place a child in care with the parent's consent [or] apply to the Childrens Court **for an assessment order** and have custody of a child…**Childrens Court process** is a complex one, involving a range of legal processes and rules. [Emphasis added]

See how an innocuous sounding organization can steal kids under the appearance of benevolence! As already noted, the DOCS virtually own the Childrens *Court*. Tell me if that's not a Star Chamber. Now get this, from qld.gov.au:

"**The Office of Child and Family Official Solicitor** (OCFOS) is a team of legal officers based in Child Safety who provide legal advice and **support to Child Safety staff.**  They apply for urgent orders such as assessment orders and temporary custody orders, and prepare referrals and briefs of evidence for the Director of Child Protection Litigation."

The word "urgent assessment orders" means the Protective parent will be sent along to a psychiatrist to determine her ability to care for her child.  (I'm wondering if my mother would have made the grade. In the days when the Church forbade the eating of meat on Friday, Mom made macaroni. I mean there was not the slightest variation in our diet. Friday = macaroni. Friday = macaroni. Maybe I needed a guardian.)

**Due Process.** Let's try rephrasing the question about chain of command. I'm getting the impression that most portfolios are in fact empty of content. The guy or gal holding "the portfolio" is meant to DO NOTHING. They need only obey the chain of command that says "Stay quiet."

So: **To what entity should the parent turn to procure some due process in the matter?** Say he has received a Notice that the state reckons the child is in danger. The Childrens Court is not a court where two litigants strut their stuff hoping to "win the case." It is a place where the might of the government will come crashing down on the loner —but that's the very thing for which due process was invented!

It's "illegal" for you to have to duke it out with the mighty state. Over centuries, the citizen has become entitled to all sorts of shields, like a right to counsel, a right to subpoena evidence and cross-examine witnesses, you know the routine.

From what mothers have told me, the Childrens Courts do not go in for due process. Mum will not be able to "make her case." The person representing CPS is a "Crown Prosecutor." Mothers have also told me that they get yelled at by the judge! It is a bullying situation, and could lead to suicide.

Bottom line: if there is no due process *this is not a court.* One will have to overcome the temptation to believe that a thing is something according to its name. And as Confucius said: It is the beginning of wisdom to call a thing by its right name. I take it that a Childrens Court is an administrative arm of the police. (And they don't spell 'Children's' with an apostrophe!)

## "Fixated Person's Investigations Unit"

The latest Tavi imposition on us is NSW's "Fixated Person's Investigation Unit." Police Commissioner Mark Fuller has the unmitigated cheek to say he has authority to hold a fixated person for 14 days – *no he doesn't*. There's no Fixated Persons Act. The FPIU is a flagrant tactic to scare whistle blowers. I don't mind admitting that it scares me. The rumor is that some people get "injected" upon arrest. Injected with what?

Would I meet their definition of "fixated"? It means a person who files lawsuits or writes to multiple ministers or who – wait for it – criticizes government. It's like the "querulous litigant" diagnosis by Dr Paul Mullen of Monash, or the person who suffers ODD: "Oppositional Defiant Disorder." I am very interested in opposing, defiantly if necessary, the outrages being committed today.   Aren't you? Think what will happen to you in a police state.

Note: On June 9, 2019 I attended a Red Pill Expo in Hartford where I was handed a leaflet about a guy, Ross Schaefer, held in a secret ("black-site") US prison. I assumed it was wrong. No, it's unfortunately correct. Schaefer's "crime" has a vague connection to money laundering. Yet he's incommunicado. Same with 'bomber' Jahar Tsarnaev – *not allowed to talk at all!*

**More on the So-called Childrens Court**

As argued above, Childrens Court is not a court **and what goes on there is not adjudication**. Childrens Courts are adjuncts of the police. The "judge" herself writes an order as instructed. (Trust me, **she is not a judge** if the phrase "due process" doesn't ring a bell with her.) Childrens Courts should be abolished. If the police need to take a child from a harmful parent, it can be done by charging the parent with a crime.

**Now for a surprise**. The very top of CRIMES ACT 1914 - SECT 3CA Nature of functions of magistrate says:

(1)  A function of making an order conferred on a magistrate by section 3ZI, 3ZJ, 3ZK, 3ZN or 3ZQZB **is conferred on the magistrate in a personal capacity and not as a court** or a member of a court.

(2)  Without limiting the generality of subsection (1), an order made by a magistrate under [those sections] **has effect only by virtue of this Act** and is not to be taken by implication to be made by a court. [This is an amazing admission.]

(3)  A magistrate performing a function of, or connected with, making an order under [those sections] has the same protection and immunity as if he or she were performing that function as, or as a member of, a court. [So you can't sue her for making a wrong call, but she can be prosecuted for crime.]

(4)  **The Governor-General may make arrangements with the Governor of a State**, … for the performance, by all or any of the persons who from time to time hold office as magistrates in that State or Territory, of the function of making orders under [those] sections.  [Emphasis added.]

It seems the judiciary has a regal connection. Indeed, per the state constitution of NSW, its *legislators* can't take a seat until they have come clean as to whom they are working for:

Section 12 (4).   The oath of allegiance is to be in the following form: I swear that I will be faithful and bear true allegiance to Her Majesty Queen Elizabeth II, Her heirs and successors according to law. So help me God.

In NSW courthouses, the banner above the judge's head says *Honi soit qui mal y pense*, the motto of the Order of the Garter.

# PART THREE

# OPERATION CRACKDOWN

**Fabricating, altering or concealing evidence.** Sec 243— A person who— (a) fabricates evidence or alters, conceals or destroys anything that may be required in evidence at judicial proceedings; or (b) uses any evidence knowing it to have been … altered, with the intention of …(d) influencing the outcome of judicial proceedings… is guilty of an offence. [Max. Imprisonment for 7 years.]

-- Criminal Law Consolidation Act 1935, South Australia

# 16. Purge the Bench, Make Room for Great Judges

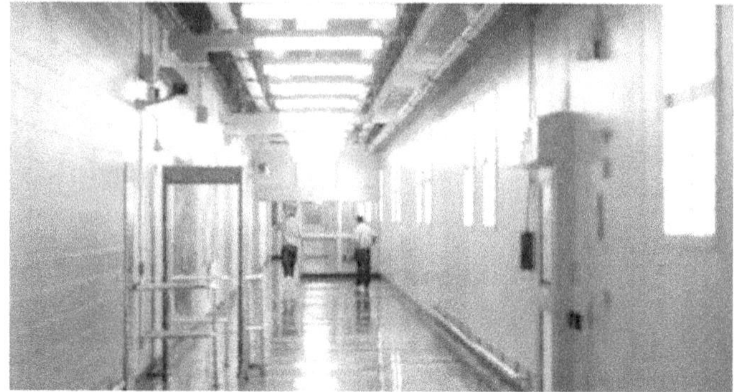

*An unusually clean-looking prison   Photo: Brookings.edu*

So what is the issue this book deals with? It is the practice of taking children from a good parent or parents and involving them in some kind of sexual activity (and sometimes torture, though I have avoided that topic). The foregoing 15 chapters presented arguments, respectively, on these 15 points:

1. There is a deliberate plan to hurt both kids and parent.
2. Australia's Family Law Act is part of social engineering.
3. A Royal Commission apologized to 17,000 abused kids.
4. Dr Pridgeon had asked in vain for authorities to help kids.
5. Victims of judicial kidnap tell the same story worldwide.
6. Gardner provided a key tool: parental alienation syndrome.
7. Contempt of court is used to stymie protest and truth.
8. In Congress, committeemen's minds seem entrained.
9. A whistle blowers' fate is always death, jail, or discrediting.
10. For disabled, beware the Parent Responsibility Contract.
11. Academic Briggs exposed all the tricks to the RC in 2014.
12. From her survey, McLachlan discovered what ICLs do.
13. Rilak asks a judge to recuse, gets called a process abuser.
14. After his arrest, Dr Pridgeon lays the AFP out in lavender.
15. Childrens Courts are police-run Star Chambers.

# What Does Australia's Constitution Say about Judges?

> Constitution Sec 72. "The Justices of the High Court and of the other courts created by the Parliament: 1. shall be appointed by the Governor-General in Council;   2. shall not be removed except by the Governor-General in Council, on an address from both Houses of the Parliament in the same session, praying for such removal on the ground of proved misbehaviour or incapacity...."

The phrase "other courts created by Parliament" means by Commonwealth parliament; this is not about *state* judges. It does apply, however, to Family Court judges.

Note that the "address from both Houses of Parliament" mentioned in the Constitution only "prays" to the Governor-General; it doesn't tell the G-G he must act. I believe the Crown is at the head of Australia's judiciary.

In the US, a majority of members of the House of Representatives can *impeach* a federal judge, and send it to the Senate for conviction. If a majority of senators vote to convict, the person is removed from office instantly.

## In Colonial Times

Until Australia's Constitution came into effect in 1901, there were six colonies, each with Crown-appointed judges. To tip them out, for bad behavior, the colony could appeal to Britain to "amove" the bad judge.   Ten judges – from various colonies – were so "amoved."

High Court Justice Michael Kirby listed some in his 1983 Boyer lecture.  For example, Tasmanian judge Algernon Montagu (1802-1880) was amoved by the Lieutenant Governor over "questionable financial transactions."

John Walpole Willis of Melbourne had previously been removed as a judge in Canada. His sins in 1842 were "cantankerousness and foibles." Note that what these judges had done was of a personal nature. This is almost always the case in US. The most recent judge impeached by Congress was tipped out for not paying child support.

Happily a judge in US was *transferred* by an Ethics Panel in response to parents' complaints. This could happen here too:

**Judge Younge Transferred re Violating Parent's Rights,** Brian Hickey, *Philly Voice*, July 2, 2018, Pennsylvania

"Lyris Younge, a judge for the Philadelphia County Court is transferred [after Judicial Conduct Board investigated] after several parents and lawyers issued complaints against her involving due process violations and 'creating **judicial parental alienation.'** [That's a new one!]

"Critics say Judge Younge ruled by intimidation, not the law. Parents claimed their children were wrongly taken, and rights violated, when Judge Younge **refused to allow them to address the court or present evidence.** [Typical in Oz, too]

"A **petition was also created** by concerned parents to remove Judge Younge **from the bench.** The petition reads, "Hundreds of families have been affected due to Younge's **unsupported decisions.** Younge is supposed to preserve the family unit, and ONLY place children who are in danger. Lyris Younge has made it her goal to terminate parental rights, and **adopt children out.**" [Emphasis added]

**Judicial Immunity**

Ah, aren't judges immune in regard to any rulings they make from the bench? Well, yes, of course they have to be protected from civil actions for their judgments – or they might make lenient rulings in fear of being sued. But they never have immunity from criminal charges. There is only one person in Australia who is immune from criminal liability. "The king can do no wrong." If judges commit a crime they get punished like anyone else. And that crime could be something they do on the bench. Of course. That is where they can inflict a lot more harm than beating their wife.

**Something Less Than the Full Sacking**

Both in the US and Australia there are "boards" you can go to with a complaint about a judge. These boards are made up of judges. Will they actually discipline their colleague? They might. In the US some of the 50 state legislatures have a Judiciary Committee, these can tip a judge overboard.

The American Bar Association has concocted a model Code of Ethics for Judicial Conduct. For example:

CANON_1 A judge shall uphold and promote the independence, integrity, and impartiality of the judiciary, and shall avoid impropriety and the appearance of impropriety.

CANON_2 A judge shall perform the duties of judicial office impartially, competently, and diligently.

Surely you'd think anyone who is a judge does not need to be told those mundane rules. But it may help a complaining citizen to be able to point to a specific breach. In Australia, **NSW and SA** each have an ongoing Judicial Commission for receiving complaints. If that board finds the matter serious enough it may get moved to Parliament.

There is material in the *Crimes Act*, Commonwealth 1914. Its Part III is about crimes in the administration of justice. Section 32 says that a judicial officer who

> (b)    **corruptly gives, confers, or procures, or promises or offers to give, convert, procure, or attempt to procure to, upon, or for, any such judge, magistrate, or Commonwealth officer, any property or benefit of any kind, on account of any such act or** omission on the part of the judge, magistrate, or officer; shall be guilty of an indictable offence. Penalty:  …**10 years**.   [Emphasis added]

## On Beyond "Corruption"

It is disappointing that attention is always focused on the judge's selfish interest, such as swinging a case a certain way in exchange for *money* – as if this were the only type of corruption going on. We need a provision for judges who do the wrong thing because someone is leaning on them, maybe has even threatened his/her life?  It would be good to make that an indictable offense similar to taking a bribe. Once a provision is on the books, at least people can talk about it. What about the fact that many judges are *appointed* to carry out the agenda of a sinister secret society?  I think we need a specific law to keep secret-society people from the bench.

## Prosecution of Lionel Murphy

In Australia the only High Court judge *prosecuted* was Lionel Murphy.  (But it was a state court that prosecuted, re his previous behaviour as a state judge).  He continued to sit on the High Court as he went through appeals of his conviction. Murphy's case is complicated; it is unresolved as he died at age 64 of cancer.   The material in Murphy's case was sealed for 30 years back in 1986, so it emerged into daylight in 2016. One item caught my eye.   In his desire to see a certain mafia company get a construction contract, Murphy asked someone to find out if particular AFP cops were "approachable." The answer came back: "No, those two are straight."   Two handy vocabulary words for us -- "straight" and *"approachable."*

114

## Judge Sees the Light in Iowa City, Iowa

This just in! We can switch from criticizing mode to celebratory mode.  All hail a good judge, Adam Sauer. In February of 2018, he got a bench in Iowa, when he was only ten years out of law school. In June he overruled the decision of another judge in a case who had where four children had been unfairly removed from their parents.

Because there had been discrepancies in the **testimony of the social worker**, Judge Sauer ruled, that the case could be thrown out:  "Providing false testimony of any kind is an **unfathomable violation** of the trust that the people in the State of Iowa place in their public servants and cast a dark and permanent shadow upon all of us."  [Emphasis added]

The social worker, Chelsea Grey, age 30, was arrested. Scott Reger signed the affidavit outlining alleged perjury:

1. She testified that she had spoken with their teachers about academic and social concerns the kids were exhibiting at school. Later she admitted she had not spoken to teachers.

 2. She testified that she went to the foster home to check on the children once a month, as required by law, but later admitted she did not visit them.

3. She testified that she would recommend a foster care placement keeping all four children in the same home, but it was found that she had in mind to separate one of the children from the other three.

Recall: WA Supreme Court of Appeals ruling in *Baron v Walsh* says it is **not an abuse of process to make a police report of a perjurer whilst one has an ongoing case**.  Great!

Everyone has the right to bring a dispute to court. The law maxim relevant here is *Ubi jus, ibi remedium* — Where there is a right, there is a remedy. The place to sue is not Family Court; it is civil court or possibly the Court of Equity. Note: I am not referring to the *appeal* of a case.

The parent's goal is to get the kid back. The lawsuits I am about to mention are *not* aimed at that. Still, they could lead indirectly to that in two ways.  First, the act of suing causes your opponent (your oppressor) to get the label "defendant" — that will make you feel you are no longer on the defensive. It puts you in the driver's seat. Second, the improprieties of the Family Court show up more vividly when compared to *normal* civil court procedure.

## What Remedies Are Available in Common Law?

People go to civil court for three things:  1. To claim damages; 2. To ask the court (via injunction) to constrain someone's behavior; 3. To seek a declaratory judgment. That last one is relatively rare, perhaps because it yields no lucre.

**Damages.** It is a normal duty of a court to award money as a way of making justice happen. This is called private law. If someone breaches a contract, the other party may request that the judge force the breacher to perform. If that's impractical a judge can order a cash payout instead.

**Torts.** People also sue under the law of tort. The WEX Legal Dictionary gives this definition of *tort*: "A tort is an act or omission that *gives rise to injury or harm* to another and amounts to a *civil wrong* for which courts *impose liability*.

How is it that you get to be civilly liable for harming a person? No state legislation is needed; the common law does it. (A parliament can modify common law by statute, though.) And who created common law? It was built up over time by cases. Today's lawyers look for the relevant precedent.

Then it's all stuck in the past? Nope. A High Court today can make a ruling in a new case that will change the pool of pre-cedents. The UK Supreme Court as recently as 2015 breathed new life into freedom of speech while ruling on the tort of IED – infliction of emotional distress, in *Rhodes v OPO*.

The defendant, James Rhodes, wrote his autobiography, *Instrumental* (it's marvelous), describing the sexual abuse he endured as a child. His wife sued for an injunction to prevent its publication, as it would cause IED to their son. The lower court granted it but the UK Supreme Court overturned it:

> "Freedom to report the truth is a basic right to which the law gives a high level of protection …. [Furthermore] a right to convey information to the public carries with it a right to choose the language in which it is expressed in order to convey the information most effectively."

Torts include: *assault* (I threaten you), *battery* (I hit you), *conversion* (I steal from you), *false imprisonment* (I lock you in my car), *trespass* (I invade your property), *defamation* (I harm your reputation), *malicious prosecution* (I used prosecution process for

the purpose of harming you) and *infliction of emotional distress.*
Torts also include *depriving someone of a right*, such as to privacy.

One must prove that the defendant intended the harm, or was
negligent. The category of neglect of duty occurs where these
is a duty of care. Hence if you get sick from eating bad food
you can sue the restaurant as it had a duty of care to feed you
safe food.

**Child As Plaintiff.** Let us ask what a child could sue for. First,
identify an injury. Perhaps the defendant raped her or assaulted
her by threats. He destroyed her privacy by putting her in porn
films. (I am not referring to criminality.) But note that a
parent's wish to sue on behalf of child is thwarted if the child
is "in care" as she is not the guardian.

**A Mother As Plaintiff.** The mum needs remedies from the
law, first as against her ex-partner, the perpetrator, and also
against many people who caused her to be injured by invading
her legal rights, or caused her harm, such as loss to her health
or wealth. *Injury* and *loss* are part of tort claims. In the US,
parents can claim for *loss of parental rights* as such.

**Can Governmental Entities Be Sued?**

It's generally hard to sue government employees as they will try
to invoke sovereign immunity and the judge may grant that.
But you can sue them "in their individual capacity." So even if
they have some immunity at work, if the thing they have done
is "not in their job description" – e.g., it is not in a cop's job to
conceal evidence, why should they be immune?  To grant them
immunity would suggest that anything any badge-wearer does
is OK.  Possible civil-servant defendants:

-- Police who refused to listen to urgent reports of crime or
imminent danger to a child, or who discarded evidence.

118

-- Social workers who wrote a false notification that the protective mother has mental health issues. Recall *Hardwick v Meeken* in Chapter 9 above.

-- Mandatory reporters of child abuse, such as teachers or nurses who did not report it even when they knew of it. By the way, it is a legal fact that the school acts *in loco parentis* during the school day, and has the same duties to protect a kid as does a mum or dad. I think school principals often wish to help but are scared of breaking orders. Just tell them they can help Protective parents *in order* to avoid being sued!

**Abuse of Process and Malicious Prosecution**. It came as a surprise to me to learn that you can sue for abuse of process (I though that was a phrase that only a judge could throw around.) It is a tort. A hotel keeper told a lady he would have her arrested for disorderly conduct for not paying her bill. She sued him for the tort of *malicious prosecution* and won. He had her charged with a crime she did not commit as a way of getting her to pay. She could as well have used the tort of *abuse of process* -- that's when you cause the law to go through its motions for a purpose other than its intended purpose.

**Injunction**. In the hands of a civil-court judge, an injunction is a powerful tool. He can "enjoin" someone to *do* something or to *refrain* from doing something. Why not petition for an injunction to get your parental rights back? Or petition for the court to enjoin the perpetrator to return the kid? Injunctions can be handled on an emergency basis, like restraining orders. Indeed they can be issued *ex parte,* with the other side not being given a chance to oppose it until a few days later.

Trust the law. At least trust it to have thought of your needs years ago! I have put on the last page of this book a template for a chit. The plan is to get some community action going but once your chit is ready, try using it to get an injunction.

## Can a Writ of Habeas Corpus Get the Child to Safety?

Writs of *habeas corpus* do not really belong in this civil-suit chapter. They're usually sought to help prisoners. However, a *habeas* writ can also be used for an adult who is confined against his will in hospital or a child illegally held by someone. AustinTexaslegal.com offers this at its website:

"Let's say your spouse is refusing to drop off your child as scheduled. You communicate with him or her and it turns out that your spouse isn't planning to return your child [yet]. You could also want to have more time with your child than what is decided by the court. However, a parent just cannot do what he or she wants when a court order regulates your time.

"Habeas Corpus is an option available to you if the other parent refuses to return your child back to you…. Since the orders are signed by you and your co-parent, this signifies that you have read and acknowledged such guidelines. Violating the terms of these orders means a legal violation.

"You have to make sure that you have a valid order that states that you have the right to have possession of the child when you say you do. In order to initiate habeas corpus in a child custody case, you will have to file a petition for it in the same court where the court order regarding your possession of your child was signed and released.

"The judge will check if everything matches legally. If it does, the judge will order the other parent to return the child. It's not something the other parent can argue with. He or she will have to comply with the judge's order whether he or she likes it or not. The judge will enforce the order as fast and as efficiently as possible."

[I haven't heard of *habeas* used successfully in Australia.]

# 18. Think Maximally -- High Principles Did Not Die

*Picture of a law school lecture, manuscript in St John's College*

A mum called to ask me if she can refuse to give back the child to the pedo father at the end of her current 2-week visit. I'm not a practicing attorney, but I'm not an idiot. I know that 2 and 2 make four, that the sun rises in the east, and that the capital of Florida is Tallahassee. And naturally I know that a parent does not have to hand a child over to a person who is almost certain to harm that child.

Is there anyone, anywhere, who does *not* know that?

Of course this mother wants to hear more than my common-sense prattle. She wants to hear law. I think Section 70NAE of the Family Law Act can be useful to her, but the first thing that popped into my head to tell her was the **law maxim** *Necessitas non habet legem* – "Necessity has no law." In extreme situations, do what you must.

I've gathered together some maxims that are on point for the mother in question. She may ask *"Do they supersede what the Court has to say?"* I believe they do. Maxims are high legal principles. A judge should honor them.

Given that she is living in a state of fear, I expect her next emailed question will be "Can you please show me the proof that they supersede it?" Yes I can, Mrs X, but first let me power you up with 12 maxims that say, basically, "**A parent's gotta do what a parent's gotta do.**"

Here are the maxims *du jour*: I won't clutter it with the Latin.

1. No one is bound to do what is impossible.
2. To a judge who exceeds his office or jurisdiction no obedience is due. [Holy smoke!]
3. No one is bound to arm his adversary.
4. When laws imposed by the state fail, we must act by the law of nature.
5. The law regards the order of nature.
6. Necessity makes that lawful which otherwise is unlawful.
7. Let justice be done, though the heavens fall.
8. Nothing is more just that what is necessary.
9. Nothing against reason is lawful. [Ahem]
10. What is prohibited in the nature of things, cannot be confirmed by law.
11. What necessity forces, it justifies. [Tailor made for Mum]
12. We must have recourse to what is extraordinary, when what is ordinary fails. [Chits, for example]

I think it may help to give the Latin just for Number 2 above, so Mrs X can be extra-assertive vis-à-vis the Court. It's: *Judici officium suum excedenti non paretur.* So there!

And maybe number 11: *Quod necessitas cogit, defendit.*

**In regard to a Protective parent's typical circumstances,** the following 12 maxims may come in handy:

13. An act of a judge that does not relate to his office is of no force. [That's a biggie for Childrens Court]
14. It is a fraud to conceal a fraud.
15. The law does not require that to be proved, which is apparent to the court.
16. Mayhem [violence, destruction] is incipient homicide. *Mahemium est homicidium inchoatum.*
17. Paternal power should consist in affection, not in atrocity.
18. Offences against nature are the heaviest. *Peccata contra naturum sunt gravissima.*
19. What is proved by the record, ought not to be denied. [Ask parents how their report is discarded.]
20. The safety of the people is the supreme law.
21. It is safer to err on the side of mercy.
22. Where there is a right, there is a remedy.
23. Force is inimical to the laws.
24. What has been admitted against the spirit of the law, ought not to be heard.

Number 24 recalls Terry Shulze's theory in Chapter 15. Shulze says Look for the mischief that the law intended to correct. The law criminalizing kidnap is about people grabbed against their will. Dr Pridgeon's kids were grabbed by him in conformity with their will.

**You can send the following dozen maxims directly to the attention of the judge:**

25. Twisting of language is unworthy of a judge. *Augupia verforum sunt judice indigna.*
26. Violence may also put on the mask of law.
27. One out of the pale of the law (an outlaw) is civilly dead.
28. The laws themselves require that they should be governed by right. [Well, son of a gun!]

29. A multitude of ignorant practitioners destroys a court. [Refer to Family Court survey in Appendix H!]
30. The law always intends what is agreeable to reason.
31. A greater inheritance comes to every one of us from right and the laws. [Bewdy]
32. An evil custom is to be abolished. *Malus usus est abolendus.*
33. What is done contrary to the custom of our ancestors neither pleases nor appears right.
34. Power should follow justice, not precede it.
35. Truth fears nothing but concealment. [Hot dog!]
36. Where there is culpability, there punishment ought to be. *Ubi culpa est ibi paena subesse debet.*

**Waiting it out** may seem to the Protective parent to be the best option. But the law does not favor that and actually sees holding back as **condoning** the status quo:

37. Time runs against the slothful and those who neglect their rights.
38. An error not resisted is approved.
39. The law always abhors delay. *Lex dilationes semper exhorret.*
40. The laws serve the vigilant, not those who sleep upon their rights.
41. He who does not prevent what he can, seems to commit the thing.
42. He who spares the guilty, punishes the innocent.
43. **One absurdity being allowed, an infinity follow**.
44. He who consents cannot receive an injury.
45. Consent removes or obviates a mistake.
46. Evil deeds ought not to remain unpunished, for impunity affords continual excitement to the delinquent. *Impunitas semper deteriora invitat.*

*Note: All these numberings are arbitrary, added by me.*

# 19. Prosecute Any Accomplice or Accessory to Crime

*Even the cleaner at a visitation (contact center) could be an accessory; perhaps a guard at the Childrens Court?*

Let's scan the horizon to see what kinds of persons could be indicted. Let's consider the *principal* crime to be the act of removing a child from a parent against that parent's wishes (excepting where it is clearly warranted). I claim it is the judge who makes the kidnap happen and so I consider him/her to be the principal offender. It does not matter that the judge was not physically present at the crime scene. A person who *orders* a crime, *commits* it.

## The Lesser Criminals: Accomplices and Accessories

So the question is: **How many other persons** have participated criminally in state kidnap? Who qualifies as an accomplice or an accessory, or as an aider and abettor?

When a man robs a bank, the person driving the getaway car may be named as an accessory. But if that driver also helped plan the robbery, he may be charged as an *accomplice.*

In the New South Wales Criminal Trial Courts Bench Book, at Judcom.nsw.gov.au we see directions for the judge to use at trial. I have abridged it and added bolding:

A person is guilty of being an **accessory before the fact** where at some time before the crime is actually carried out, he or she intentionally **encourages or assists the principal offender** to commit that crime. Therefore, there must be some act committed by the accessory that was intended to bring about the crime… it can be **assisting in the preparations** for the commission of the crime.…

Before a person can be convicted of being an accessory before the fact, the Crown must prove beyond reasonable doubt that, at the time of the … assistance, the accused **knew all the essential facts or circumstances which would make what was later done a crime**. This includes the state of mind of the principal offender when those acts are carried out. **The accused need not actually know that what he or she encourages and/or assists the principal offender to do is in law a crime**. The accused does not need to have the legal knowledge that the conduct to be committed by the principal offender actually amounts to a criminal offence. …

It is my claim that in, say, Adelaide, the infamously murderous pedophile ring is connected to (though not perhaps majorly dependent on) the way in which kids can be captured by means of a court order that takes the kid from its Protective parent and hands it over to an abuser.

**Which Occupations Are Involved?**
I hypothesize that there are many helpers. Examples could be: cops, lawyers, ICL's, psychologists, and social workers.

They may think the judge is doing good by, say, taking a child from a mum who alienated that child against the father. Or they may think it is a good thing to save a child from living with a mother who has psychiatric issues such as anxiety or delusion. But note that the NSW Bench Book, above, said that an accessory is one who "intentionally **encourages or assists the**

126

**principal offender** to commit that crime." And that "The accused **does not need to have the legal knowledge** that the conduct to be committed by the principal offender actually **amounts to** a criminal offence."

In a typical case, of a Protective parent losing his/her kid, the various occupational groups come into the story:

-- **cops** may go to the home of the parent and actually take the child by force
-- **lawyers** may advise their clients to be hush-hush in court regarding "sexual abuse of the child"
-- **psychologists** may write up a report of interview with the pedophile that makes him (or her) sound nice, and may, in reporting the mental problems of the Protective parent, tell lies or exaggerate the facts
-- **social workers** may interfere in the procedure by which a Protective parent comes to the Department of Child Protection for a weekly "supervised visit" with the child, or may make a false report downplaying signs of abuse.

Use you imagination to fill in the appropriate words in the square brackets. The benchbook looks like this

The Crown alleges, and must prove beyond reasonable doubt, that [*the accused*] [*specify the act relied upon by the Crown*] intending that [*the principal offender*] would commit the crime of [*specified offence*] later. The Crown must prove that by these acts [*the accused*] intentionally [*encouraged and/or assisted*] [*the principal offender*] to commit the crime of [*specified offence*].

So far we have talked about accessories *before* the fact but now let's look at **accessories after the fact. I offer a journalist named Meg** as the person who is being tried. Instead of "he/she" I'll say **she** for Meg and **he** for principal.

Why did I select the occupation of journalist? Because the media are known for committing cover-up.

The benchbook, says "The offence of being an accessory after the fact can be committed by rendering assistance either to the principal offender or to a person who aids and abets the principal. …" Let's stick with the simple bit, Meg aids the judge kidnapper, Judge Smyth. Here's what one should say:

The Crown does not allege that <u>the journalist, Meg</u> was involved in the commission of the crime carried out by <u>Judge Smyth.</u> The charge brought against <u>the journalist, Meg,</u> is that she assisted [*the principal, Smyth*] after he committed the crime of kidnap, and **gave that assistance with knowledge that [*Smyth*] had committed that crime. …**

A charge that a person is an accessory after the fact to a crime committed by another is an allegation that the person giving that assistance has … committed a crime. It is a separate and distinct offence from that committed by the principal ….

Here, the Crown must prove beyond reasonable doubt both the commission of the crime of "kidnap by <u>Judge Smyth</u>" and that <u>the journalist, Meg</u> assisted Smyth knowing that the crime had been committed. A person is an accessory after the fact …[by, for example] disposing of the proceeds of the crime, or by doing an act intending to hinder the arrest, trial or punishment of the principal offender.

… The Crown says this was done with the purpose of [*specify the alleged reason for the assistance rendered by the accused (please insert "cover-up")*]. To be guilty of being an accessory after the fact, the Crown must also prove beyond reasonable doubt that <u>the journalist, Meg</u> knew that <u>Smyth</u> acted in a way…. and with a particular state of mind that gives rise to a criminal offence. <u>The journalist, Meg,</u> **does not need to have the legal**

**knowledge that those facts amount to a crime**…. It will often be the case in a charge of accessory after the fact that the accused is said to have known of the commission of a crime simply on the basis of what he or she is told by the principal offender or some other person ….

**The accused** -- <u>the journalist, Meg</u> -- **may come to know that a crime has been committed by the principal offender <u>Smyth</u> from inferences that the accused has drawn from facts which he or she believes have occurred.**   [Emphasis added]

An aside:  In the case of the Boston Marathon bombing, in which I nominate the FBI as principal offender (that is, I say the FBI did the bombing), journalists who are accessories after the fact, such the editors of the *Boston Globe*, would have been able to "make inferences that they drew from facts." We can see this when they *avoid* interviewing key witnesses.

**An Exercise for a Protective Parents (a Dad)**

Without further ado, you should be able to give jury instructions, using the NSW Crime Benchbook. Choose any person whom you have identified as an accessory to crime regarding your child. Insert that person's name as the accused, and name a principal offender. Then **read it aloud** as follows:

The Crown alleges, and must prove beyond reasonable doubt, that [*the accused*] [*specify the act relied upon by the Crown*] intending that [*the principal offender*] would commit the crime of [*specified offence*] later. The Crown must prove that by these acts [*the accused*] intentionally [*encouraged and/or assisted*] [*the principal offender*] to commit the crime of [*specified offence*].

Wow. You did great!  You're bench material!  Go for it.

# 20. Declaratory Judgments, Equity, and Coram Nobis

*If there's a kangaroo and an emu on the badge, it must be federal court*

A review of Part Three's chapters thus far shows that there are many ways to try to stop, or to avenge, what has been going on in regard to judicial kidnap: **Purge** the bench by "amoval" or impeachment of a judge. **Sue** in torts for money damages to a child or parent, use the **maxims** to reassert high principle. **Prosecute** accessories and accomplices no matter how minor. The next chapters will add: **draft** corrective legislation – including legislation on due process, demand **inquests** into suspicious deaths, catch out the **structural** problem of the Office of DPP, **defrock**, that is, deregister doctors and lawyers, and something similar for journalists and cops, and bring into being some **Truth** Commissions.

## What Is a Court?

A court is a place where disagreements are settled. It is a place where the might of the law is able to coerce any individual or organization. It is a place where society's thinking about fairness over the centuries ends up in a magnificent body of jurisprudence. It may be very helpful to a person to get a court to say whether such-and-such is a breach of the law, even if no damages are sought and no criminal complaint is made. When someone knows a wrong has occurred, he or she wants at least to tell friends and have friends say "Yes you are right, that was a terrible injury."

The recent formal apology by the Prime Minister to abused children was a great reliever of stress to many victims. In my own life someone wronged me in a business deal. Many years later I ran into the businessman and the first thing he said was "I apologize." I was flabbergasted. It also surprised me that a big burden was lifted off me just by those words. It was almost dizzying.

Anyway, the courts are able to give *declaratory judgments*. Lawyers seldom pursue this but I suggest it may help a Protective parent to seek declaratory relief. I note that Shane Dowling has recently boasted that he has "instituted criminal proceedings" against an official. Technically all he has done is filed in court for a declaratory judgment. But that's fine. It could lead indirectly to indictment. He is right to try *anything*.

**A Writ of Mandamus**

There are several writs in ancient English law of which the writ of *habeas corpus* is the best known. The writ of mandamus asks a court to order a government official to carry out his job. When interviewed by Dee McLachlan, Justice Michael Kirby hinted that using mandamus, which is specified in sec 75(v) of Australia's Constitution could be a way to get the Tassie govern-ment to deal with the wrongful incarceration of Martin Bryant.

**What about the Writ of Error Coram Nobis?**

In good old English fashion there is another remedy, to help a court correct what it did, if it had been fed the wrong facts. "Error coram nobis" means "errors before us" – *us* being the royal we. I have tried to use it in a US state court to help Troy Davis avoid being executed in 2011, but was not listened to.

Since then it has been successfully used by others, even for parking violations cases! When I tried it in Tasmania in 2015 I got the reply that it is not recognized by Tasmanian law. I believe that is incorrect. You may try adapting the following:

**Petition for a Writ of Error Coram Nobis** [a "template"]

To the Family Court (or a state's Childrens Court)
From [name of Protective parent]    Date _________

I hereby petition for a Writ of Error Coram Nobis

Error Coram Nobis is one of the ancient writs. It protects the Court. The petition is sent to the judge that originally made a ruling if he had been defrauded by any member of the Court.

The writ of error coram nobis was described in 1894 by Henry John Stephen's *Treatise on the Principles of Pleadings in Civil Actions:*

"A writ of error, like an original writ, is sued out of Chancery, directed to the judges of the court in which judgment was given, and commanding them, in some cases, themselves to examine the record, … in order that some alleged errors in the proceedings may be corrected. The first form of writ, called a writ of error *coram nobis* is where the alleged error consists of matters of *fact;* the second, called a writ of error generally, where it consists of matters of *law."*

The judge in [my case] could not have made the right ruling if he had been defrauded. I can show below that he was deceived as to facts, and that fraud-upon-the-court was thus involved.

This ancient writ arrived in Australia with the Common Law on the First Fleet and has never been statutorily repealed in Australia. In the US there is much jurisprudence to keep it alive, the most recent US Supreme Court decision involving the fraud-upon-the-court was Korematsu the case. (1984)

In an earlier case, *Hazel-Atlas Glass Co. v Atwood* (1944), Justice Robert Jackson wrote for the majority of US Supreme Court:

**"No fraud is more odious than an attempt to subvert the administration of justice.** The court is unanimous in condemning the transaction disclosed by this record.… The resources of the law are ample to undo the wrong … Remedies are available to purge recreant officers from the tribunals on whom the fraud was practiced. Finally… **to nullify the judgment if the fraud procured it**.… Such a proceeding is required by settled federal law."   [Emphasis added]

In [my] Family Court case the judge was defrauded by police, CPS social workers, and a so-called Independent Children's lawyer. They all hid from the court the evidence that my daughter was being sexually abused by the father. They suppressed photos of her injuries, recordings of my conversation with her at "weekly visitation," notes from her schoolteacher to me, and doctor's records. I attach these now.

The writ of error coram nobis is a way of upholding justice and of supporting the sacredness of the court. It does not entail any court fees and need not involve the steps of appeal. The petition (as this one) is sent to the original court, not a higher court, asking that the original court correct the errors made. I cite two of the maxims: *Lex non requirit verificari quod apparet curiae.* -- The law does not require that to be proved, which is apparent to the court. And: *Peccata contra naturumsunt gravissima.* -- Offences against nature are the heaviest.

I ask that you set aside the ruling [___] and do so in haste as my child is suffering needlessly.

Yours respectfully, _________     Date _________

Signature witnessed by _________ Address _______________

**The Court of Equity.** Here is a helpful maxim: "When a common remedy ceases to be of service, recourse must be had to an extraordinary one." *Ubi cessat remedium ordinarium ibi decurritur ad extraordinarium.*

You can go to the *court of equity* to get a creative solution to your problem. Under English law the court of equity was separate from the court of chancery. In 1873 they were combined in the UK via The Judicature Act. Even after that, however, a person could still use the coordinated court to ask that the judgment be made per the *principles* of equity.

In Australia, it took the state of New South Wales a century to get around to combining the courts, via its Law Reform Act (Justice and Equity) in 1972. Other states had already done so. Australia's High Court recognizes the principles of equity as still extant.

Can a child ask for Equity? Yes. Equity specifically says "Equity assists minors." Equity allows a judge to go outside the strict law and make a "constructive remedy." It is especially used when the law as such would result in an obviously unjust outcome.

Since the twelfth century in England, the Court of Equity has included a provision for the "disgorgement of ill-gotten gains." As everyone knows, child trafficking is a lucrative business. Surely everyone knows that the lucre involved is ill-gotten. Let the disgorgement begin!

Maybe Equity could be approached on behalf of the desired Reunion. A creative judge could put together a package, re-uniting child with parent *and* ordering compo. That sort of thing is known in the equity trade as "constructing a remedy," possibly with a "constructive trust." Why not?

# 21. Legislate To Upgrade Law, and Run for Office

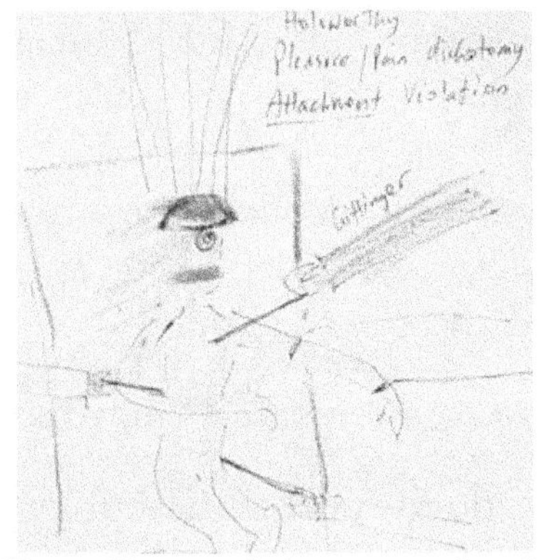

*(L) Fiona Barnett being tortured at Holsworthy Army Base, age 5*
*(R) Senator Bill Heffernan defended her, has now retired to the bush*

At this point we are halfway through Part Three's "Opera-tion Crackdown." I am inventorying any proper means that people can use to achieve the goal of Reunion of child with Protective parent. One such means is new legislation. Let us think for a moment of laws that could be enacted to counteract the scandalous state of affairs in the Family Court, the Childrens Courts, and child protection agencies.

## Amend Bad Laws -- Federal

Federal Parliament right now, without further ado, could repeal or amend any part of the Family Law Act that is bad. One possible bad part is: the Family Law Act's waiving the Evidence Act. Parliament could re-impose many of the standards of evidence developed over centuries in common law and statutory law. While it can be a *good* thing for Family Court judges to have more flexibility than in criminal court, it is crazy to give them absolute discretion to dispense with due process. Really it offends the sacredness of law.

The infamous section 60CC could also be changed. It quite ridiculously tells the judge to do two things that are outside his ability to do. Subsection (a) tells him to assure a meaningful relationship of the child with both parents – this is not a job for government or law; it is nature. Subsection (b) tells the judge to watch out for the child's safety, yet there is no mechanism for him to investigate an unsafe situation.

Also, Sec 112AP of the Family Law Act could be amended to clarify the particular contraventions of orders that constitute contempt. Parents are confused and scared about this.

**Legislate for Child Protection Agencies and Guardians**

The word *appalling* does not do justice in describing the capriciousness of the CPS in determining **that a mum has coached, that she has thereby emotionally harmed the child, or that she is lying about the sexual abuse**. It is as though there are no standards. Even contradictory items in file are not considered to be a problem to solve!

There should be action on this by *Parliament*, not by the courts. The basic relationship of legislature to judiciary is: parliament *makes* the laws and courts *apply* those laws. If I understand it correctly today (and believe me it is obtuse), the typical mum confronted with false accusations by CPS and destruction of records, thinks it's for the judge to sort.

A judge is a manager of any case before him. Thus it *would* be possible for him to question the fairness of any procedure or the competence of evidence collection. But the CPS should not have done a bad job in the first place. Let me name a few legislative ideas that could relieve some mums:

1. Get rid of the deceptive wording in Parent Responsibility Contracts. Why should a mum *not* be told that keeping her kid out of school for a family trip will lead to guardianship?

2. *Criminalize* any extortion-type threats by CPS workers – and also by judges – such as "If you don't sign this agreement to share custody, you won't see your child again."

3. Remove all aspects of financial incentives for governments that put kids into state care or adoption. We know that in any area of life a financial incentive can pervert the values that are supposedly at hand (e.g., he "needs a stable home.")

4. Simply do not allow forced adoptions. (There is a helpful UK website forced-adoption.com). A mother has the right to her child. So does a father. See *Johnasen v Norway* case in Appendix J.  And don't forget, Congress is in a "matrix."

5. It may be wise to legislate CPS out of existence.  We can see that any agency with a license to grab children is very likely to become part of the trafficking network. This sort of temptation is known in the insurance industry as "moral hazard." Legislation often seeks to counter moral hazard.

**Legislate for the Childrens Court (a.k.a. Youth Court)**

Someone in each state parliament decided that the normal courts weren't suitable for family matters. So a special court was set up to try juveniles for crimes and to be the handmaiden of the CPS, which is the handmaiden of police. Ha!

As Potkonyak pointed out, the court runs "dispositional proceedings" and "establishment proceedings." That looks like obfuscation to me, and it's worse in the US, which has "adversary hearing, status hearing, initial permanency planning," and other, pardon my French, garbage. The result is that families spend all their time, money, and nerves on it. To repeat, it is for parliament to control this; it's their baby.

**Can Parliament Control Police?**

I have the impression that police do not answer to politics. *The Police Act* 1988 SA legislates such things as how police should take a urine sample. But can it get police to stop kowtowing to pedo-rings? That is the job of the DPP. And thereby hangs another tale; see Chapter 23 please.

## How We Can Help Fiona Barnett Survive to Old Age?

On July 18, 2018, Fiona Barnett, a survivor of MK-Ultra, read an hour's worth of stunning testimony to the International Tribunal for Natural Justice. (See Youtube.) In my opinion, human history changed the minute she spoke. Fiona has more than just allegations; she has insider knowledge. By luck, one parliamentarian helped her: Senator Bill Heffernan

On the following page I've drafted a piece of (amateurish) legislation to show how easy it is to do. Many laws are written by corporations or other interested parties, and handed in to the legislature to be enacted. You can do this, too. I'm calling mine the Heffernan bill -- it will seek to investigate what Fiona says goes on in Holsworthy Army Base basement.

Fiona says child protective services are riddled with child-traffickers. And she came down hard on universities, identifying many scholars who she thinks are members of a Luciferian cult. At Holsworthy, she says, you may find children being "bred" for various uses. See Appendix R.

See how easy it is to legislate?  Politicians, paralyzed for a long time, may seem reluctant to act. But maybe they'd gladly jump on the bandwagon if you start it going. Try giving "the Heffernan bill" to your MP.

Once there is a bill in parliament, interested members can call for a division – thus the ayes and the nays get identified. (They stand on opposite sides of the room – it's rarely done, but it's legally provided for.) Every MP would find himself asking "Am I for or against child-stealing?"

Note: under present state law, indictments are the prerogative of a "Director of Public Prosecutions," a DPP. No worries. Someone in each state Parliament and in Canberra could draft a bill called "The Abolition of the Office of Public Prosecutions Act." Easy. Piece o' cake.

**Draft of a "Heffernan Bill" for Parliament to Consider!**

*An Act for an Investigation of Holsworthy Army Base*

-- Recognizing that there is a powerful criminal contingent in Australia today,

-- Acknowledging that bringing suspects to justice has been hampered by secrecy and fear,

-- Realizing that the citizenry was shocked by the findings of the Royal Commission into Child Sexual Abuse,

we enact this statute to investigate Holsworthy Army Base in regard to crimes against children and to facilitate the bringing of powerful persons to justice. It begins with a questionnaire.

Within 30 days of receiving The Questionnaire, designated professionals must answer it under oath, divulging the extent to which they were aware of sexual abuse of children or any unauthorized experimentation on children at any time.

*Children* here means: persons under the age of 18.
  [other definitions. Etc]

Refusal to register or to answer the questionnaire is an offense. The penalty is a fine of $500,000 and 2 years prison. No one who *voluntarily admits* that they failed to report crime will be charged with having failed to report crime.

Parliament will establish a panel (hereinafter "The Panel") that will be accountable to the Attorney General. Panel members will be vetted to eliminate conflicts of interest. Attorneys-General will liaise with Commonwealth Minister of Defence concerning the military. The state Attorneys-General will liaise with the Commonwealth Minister of Home Affairs about any involvement of ASIO. The Prime Minister will brief any foreign government if needed.

This law comes into effect 14 days after receiving royal assent.

## Society Is the Boss

Citizens today need to have it drummed into them that *society* is in charge of society. Citizens need to hear that all persons are accountable. Were you shocked when I said Holsworthy will be investigated? I was shocked myself! Let's go around shocking everybody with the news that top brass in the armed forces (and police forces, and ASIO) are not above the law. And remind everyone that **cover-up of crime is a felony.**

What else would you like to make legislation for? Until 1991 there were laws in Australia to prevent anyone owning too many news outlets. Then the big owners got Parliament to repeal that law. Just get Parliament to repeal the repeal. Easy.

You could make laws to do anything that does not violate the Constitution. But you can't criminalize a deed retroactively. How about court fees that make a mockery of Magna Charta's promise that law will not be bought or sold? You can repeal the Childrens Court's $4.95-per-page photocopy fee!

## Stand for Parliament

Why not just become a legislator? Start your campaign by getting your name around, in connection with any beneficial activity. Or start by running for a small office that nobody wants, to get a foot in the door! Perhaps you should join one of the small parties; they need candidates to put forward. To run as an Independent you need to collect signatures well in advance. It's a lot of work but it's definitely doable.

Even if there is little chance of winning a seat in Parliament your candidacy can educate people about the issues. I have tried it myself twice (in the US). The public was very welcoming. They want new ideas. They are dying for honesty.

They want you.

# 22. Demand an Inquest into Prof Freda Briggs' Death

*(L) Emeritus Professor Freda Briggs, photo by Tricia Watkinson*
*(R) Vickie Chapman, Attorney General of South Australia*

Dear General Vickie,

We need a coronial inquest into the death of University of South Australia's Professor Emeritus of Social Work, Freda Briggs. She devoted her life to increasing the protection of vulnerable children.

Freda's 2014 submission to the Royal Commission is loaded with accusations about policies of government that result in no protection for children. She was 85 years old when she died in Royal Adelaide Hospital in April 2016. I do not know what her death certificate says. In SA a member of the public cannot obtain the death certificate of a non-relative.

For all I know, God may have taken Freda in the usual way, by natural causes. Eighty-five is good innings. But the other day a woman in Adelaide told me that Freda had invited her to visit her home a few months before she died. This woman did not rush to take up the invitation as she was busy and didn't think time was running out. Freda seemed "as fit as a horse -- fighting fit." Maybe the old professor had another decade in her. An inquest may help the public peace of mind.

In fact, that is the purpose of a coronial inquest. Under the current law we must look at any suspicious death, or disappearance, or death in custody. If a doctor claims that a death at home was expected due to an illness, there is usually no inquest.   If a person died in hospital, there is usually no inquest.  Freda died in hospital.  That does not satisfy me as a reason not to inquire. Did someone "bump Freda off"?

My many years of research into the CIA tells me that in the US there is an employee in every hospital and nursing home whose unofficial job is to kill patients and another whose job is to change records, as needed.  A head nurse may suit. A top administrator is even better. He or she need not be a ruthless individual; such persons are under mind control.  I personally know an MK-Ultra victim who killed many people, yet she is as nice as pie.  I've encouraged her to turn herself in and make a case for diminished responsibility, but she's afraid of being tortured in prison. (See my *Prosecution for Treason* 2011.)

Let us not forget what Peter Lewis (1940-2015), Speaker of the House in the South Australian Parliament, said:

"I [was] bringing some of the people who had made the alleg-ations to the point where they might pluck up enough courage and confidence and swear the truth of those allega-tions, enabling them to be more carefully investigated. But they were being 'bumped off'– that is, murdered and viciously assaulted – quicker than I could get them to write [it] down.

The most outrageous thing [is] organised activities of those pedophiles in high public office – that is, the judiciary, senior ranks of human services portfolios, some police and MPs."

A Coronial inquest has long been a public right. At times it is a helpful inquiry into a disaster such as a fire or the capsizing of a ferry.  It is not like a civil court case but more like an open inquiry in which there are not parties, as usual. The Evidence Act of 1929 doesm't need to be observed at Inquest and it is at the judge's discretion to call this or that witness.

On the very same day as the Port Arthur massacre, the coroner for southern Tasmania, Mr Ian Matterson, began an inquest. He was later required by law to desist when a criminal suspect pleaded guilty. The same arrangement holds under South Australia's Coroner's Act, 2003.

I note that in New South Wales, the Coroner's Act says that the state's supreme court can quash a coronial finding, or order a new one if there is: "fraud, the rejection of evidence, an irregularity of proceedings, an insufficiency of inquiry, or the discovery of new evidence or facts." I intend to ask the NSW Supreme Court to quash the findings of the Lindt Café Inquest. I sent to Coroner Justice Michael Barnes, before he concluded the Inquest, a compilation of "Ninety-nine Things That Do Not Add Up." (He did not reply.)

In Boston, I have asked the state Medical Examiner, Dr Mindy Hull, to conduct an inquest into the deaths of Tamerlan Tsarneav, apparently murdered by the FBI, and a John Doe who appears to me to have stood in the place of Tamerlan to undergo a fatal shootout. (She has not replied.)

If a racket is big enough to damage untold numbers of kids' lives, it is big enough to have someone available to knock off a strong witness such as Freda Briggs. Recall from Chapter 14 that it was at the request of Professor Briggs, that Dr Pridgeon helped spirit two kids to safety, in light of the cruelty they were undergoing. I don't mean Briggs was fond of law-breaking. Not at all. But she knew her priorities.

I do not claim to *know* that she was killed. But anyone who brought evidence against government, especially if she's a person who had standing and credibility, is entitled to cry out from the grave "Please investigate my death." Oh, how we tend to neglect all such crying's.

**Queensland Suspicious Deaths**

Chapter 28 will discuss Matthew Condon's book *All Fall Down*, about Queensland's Fitzgerald Inquiry. The sheer number of suspicious deaths is telling. Usually the death is not a punishment for having "ratted" on the powerful but rather is a precaution against their telling any more. What a touching testament to law! Here's an example:

"In April, the former Police Chief of the Cairns region, Kevin Dorries, was dying of cancer. …Dorries, by way of confession [to get his $275K superannuation payout released] wanted to share some documents with [the Fitzgerald Inquiry]. He possessed some information so powerful it could almost instantly bring down the government.
"[According to a family member, Deputy Premier Bill Gunn] went and spoke to Dorries in a motel room. He, Dorries, wanted to give up [intelligence he had] on a paedophile ring. Bill promised he would go after this. But Dorries died of cancer before Bill got around to this."

Postscript to SA Attorney General Vickie Chapman: How about Peter Lewis? Did he die of natural causes at age 75? It would seem that he deserves the honor of an Inquest.

You might also call for a massive inquest into the deaths of 600 orphan children that are reportedly part of the sealed-up Mullighan Report. In fact while I have your attention, General, please unseal all that stuff. There can't possibly be a privacy issue regarding the deceased. Even if there were, there is always a way to override one value with another, here the value of us getting to the bottom of child-stealing. Thank you.

# 23. Catch the Structural Problem: The Office of DPP

*Photo of prosecutors from website odpp.nsw.gov.au*

Two Australian women, Fiona Barnett and Rachel Vaughan, have provided their testimony to a private group, the International Tribunal for Natural Justice, the ITNJ. Both told of their direct experience of extreme abuse as children, and their witnessing of murders of children.

Their main complaint is that no matter how many times they reported these things to the police, they were rebuffed. It was shocking to them, and it will be to you also if you hadn't realized it, that the government prosecutors will not prosecute, or even charge, any of the numerous criminals in government. "No way, José."

They are happy to prosecute your local drug dealer and your local car thief. They will even charge a pedophile as long as it is an isolated one, not in the protected group. Such behavior by prosecutors it itself plainly criminal.

This chapter quotes a complaint by a good judge, Justice Peter McClellan of New South Wales Supreme Court, who was head of the Royal Commission into Institutional Response to Child Sexual Abuse, which lasted from 2013 to 2017. He took the ODPP to task over prosecutorial discretion, a nice name for "protecting the baddies."

Australia does not have a DoJ type prosecutor. It has the ODPP, Office of the Director of Public Prosecutions. This was copied from the UK. Its excuse for existence is the "independence" of those who will enforce the law.  See *Fisher v Oldham* (1930).  How nice – he or she "will be non-political and fearless." But this is crazy on the face of it.

The DPP does not answer to Parliament. He/she does not answer to anyone. Just ask: what person can stand up alone to the mafia? It is a recipe for rule by the mafia, isn't it?

I have written a book, co-authored by Dee McLachlan, called *Port Arthur: Enough Is Enough*. It shows how the alleged killer, Martin Bryant, was definitely not the man who massacred 35 people in 1996. His case was handled with outrageous injustice by Tasmania's DPP, Damien Bugg, who subse-quently became the Commonwealth DPP.

Here is a lengthy excerpt from McClellan's speech. It's very somber and restrained. I've added some bolding.

**"Seeking justice for victims," by Justice Peter McClellan, April 13, 2017**

The establishment of independent prosecuting offices has been described as 'one of the more significant improvements to the criminal justice system in this country in the 20thcentury.'[20] In *Price v Ferris*, then President Kirby described the object of having a Director of Public Prosecutions as 'to ensure a high degree of independence in the vital task of making prosecution decisions…"

The position of Director of Public Prosecutions was first established in Australia, in Victoria in 1982. The move in Victoria followed the establishment of a Crown Advocate under the Tasmanian Crown Advocate Act 1973, in Tasmania.

The Tasmanian Act, however, **did not provide guidance on the relationship between the Crown Advocate, the Attorney-General and the Solicitor-General**. This was seen as a significant flaw.

In [Victoria] the second reading speech to the relevant bill stated: "A major aim of the Bill is to remove any suggestion that prosecutions in this State or, indeed **the failure to launch prosecutions** can be the subject of political pressure. [Right. It's now the subject of criminal pressure.]

The Australian Law Reform Commission [had] described the process of prosecution in Australia … as 'probably the most secretive, least understood and poorly documented aspect of the administration of criminal justice.' [But] the degree of transparency, and the capacity for scrutiny, of the prosecution process has increased. [e.g., by] the promulgation and publication of Director's Guidelines.

Director's guidelines are, probably, the primary mechanism in this country for the control of prosecutorial discretion. However, they are only part of the picture. A report by the Australian Institute of Criminology almost a quarter of a century after the creation of independent prosecuting agencies, stated the following:

"... The considerable discretionary powers vested in prosecutors employed by the state and territory Offices of the Director of Public Prosecutions are exercised in accordance with prosecution policies and guidelines, but the decision making process is rarely subject to external scrutiny." This lack of external scrutiny or oversight has emerged as an issue for the Royal Commission [of which I, McLellan, am the head].

…the Commission has been required to examine the issue of DPP complaints and oversight mechanisms.

For those of you who may not be aware in Case Study 15 the Commissioners found inadequacies in the processes of the ODPP of New South Wales. The Commissioners further found that the **Queensland DPP failed to comply with its own guidelines, including in relation to consulting with complainants.**

Concerns in relation to DPP processes emerged again in Case Study 17 in relation to the Northern Territory…. The Commissioners again found noncompliance with the Northern Territory DPP guidelines **in relation to a decision to discontinue a prosecution.**

These case studies confirm that the mere existence of the Director's guidelines is not sufficient to ensure the level of accountability and transparency the community might reasonably expect. This is not surprising. [Too right, mate]

The [RC] Commissioners are conscious that there is a tension between ensuring DPP accountability and DPP independence. Given that independence was essentially the *raison d'etre* of ODPPs, concern in relation to how greater accountability might be achieved is understandable. However as former Victorian DPP, and later Justice, John Coldrey observed:

"Whilst it is argued that prosecutorial independence is an essential element in the proper administration of criminal justice it must be equally recognised that **inherent** in an independence without accountability is **the potential for making arbitrary, capricious and unjust decisions.**

[Hooray for Justice Coldrey!]

Currently **there is no formal mechanism through which a complainant can challenge, or seek review of, the exercise of prosecutorial discretion** including in circumstances where the decision making process has not been in accordance with the relevant Director's guidelines.

Further, **the general community has no body or mechanism it can rely on to be satisfied that the DPPs and staff are adhering** to their guidelines. [Would it matter? *Would they be saints* where all others are sinners?]

In the Report of Case Study 15 the Commissioners stated:

"Any body that is given statutory independence and that cannot be subject to any external reviews is at risk of failure in its decision-making processes. **When the decisions being made are critical to the lives of the individuals involved,** ...it is relevant to ask whether the current structure, where there is **absolute immunity from review of any decision** is appropriate. ..."

Requirements in the guidelines to consult **before decisions are made to discontinue** [i.e., let the guy off the hook] recognise the importance of these decisions to complainants. Insufficient consultation before deciding to discontinue a prosecution or accept a negotiated plea is likely **to cause victims to experience distress.** [like a sunshiny day is likely to cause happiness] The ACT Victims of Crime Commissioner told [us] that "it is **the procedural justice issue** for many victims of crime that **stays with them** as much as the crime itself."

[Note: As far as I am aware, Justice McClellan has not been in a car accident since giving that speech.]

'The point at which the prosecutorial discretion to commence a prosecution is exercised is one of the key points of attrition in the criminal justice system.[30] As the ALRC has stated 'prosecutors play a key role as gatekeepers determining which victims of crime have access to justice'.[31]

[My] Commissioners consider that all Australian DPPs should be able to implement a number of minimum requirements. Those requirements are: 1. The adoption of **comprehensive written policies for decision-making and consultation with victims and police**. 2. Ensuring that all policies are publicly available and published online. 3. Provision of a right for complainants to seek written **reasons** for key decisions. [Rachel Vaughan will be pleased to find out why the murderers she reported did not get prosecuted.]

In relation to a complaints mechanism the Commissioners recognise that the CPS [not *the* CPS] is significantly larger than the offices of all Australian DPPs combined.

We also recognise that ... decision-making in Australian ODPPs already occurs at a more senior level than in the CPS. Accordingly there is a capacity for some degree of informal review [OMG] before a decision is made.

...there is merit in the provision of a formal internal complaints mechanism which would allow **victims to seek merits review** of key decisions…that result in a prosecution not being brought or being discontinued. There is a further option – an **audit** of compliance with DPPs guidelines and policies. If the results of any audit were **published** this would advance the transparency and accountability of DPPs and their offices, and might negate the need for an external audit process. [Emphasis added]

*Merci beaucoup* to the author, Justice McClellan.

Note: I think the existence of a DPP takes the spotlight off of the Attorney General, on whom the spotlight should be.

# 24. Defrock 'em: Doctors, Lawyers, Journalists, Cops

What is your real complaint about the Family Court or the CPS system? If it is not something that can be remedied by the crackdown methods discussed above – e.g., suing, impeaching, prosecuting, or enjoining -- maybe it could be tackled by causing a bad professional to lose her livelihood.

## Doctors

It's well known that a doctor may be sued for malpractice. Perhaps she wrote a faulty prescription or let the scalpel slip. However those are not the types of complaint most likely to appear in connection with child-stealing. For this book's topic, the "malpractice" is likely to consist of a GP's failure to report abuse, or a psychiatrist's playing along too readily with the party line – e.g., advising a judge that the Protective parent is a delusional mental case.

This may be criminal. Mere *failure* to report abuse carries a fine, $15,000. Falsely testifying about a "mental case" under oath is perjury, a felony. (Felons get jail time). If not given under oath, bad reporting is just slander (but you can sue for damages). The remedy we are looking at in this chapter is society's control over the livelihoods of professionals.

For a doctor, that consists of an *ethics board*. It may appear to be a board with only doctors on it, but permission for an occupational group to police itself is granted by *legislation*.

Doctors are accorded great trust, in return for which they must be accountable to the community. It is up to parliament to decide what amount of self-policing is okay. Almost certainly in your state there is a way for you to put a bad doctor's job in jeopardy. And the doctors know this.

**Lawyers**
Same with lawyers (and judges, but they were discussed in Chapter 16). We constantly hear from Protective parents that their lawyer advised them not to mention child abuse. Is that acceptable on the basis of "strategy'? That is, can the lawyer justify it by saying "I know it will harm my client's case if she accuses her ex of pedophilia"? No. Emphatically no.

It's not acceptable, as it would amount to lawyers abetting the bad behavior of judges. In fact it's a crime to support a crime. And it is an additional crime to fail to protect the child.

For lesser sins there are ethics boards. (In SA the Law Society had the task, but it has now moved to an Ethics Complaint Commissioner.) The complaint most frequently dealt with is over-charging. Two others are conflict-of-interest and bias.

Law schools should inform students that a lawyer should be mindful of the maxims. These intellectual standards can help any lawyer or judge see what justice demands. Once again:

It is a fraud to conceal a fraud.
An error not resisted is approved.
The law always abhors delay.
He who does not prevent what he can, seems to commit it.
He who spares the guilty, punishes the innocent.
One absurdity being allowed, an infinity follow.
Let justice be, though the heavens fall. *Fiat justitia ruat caelum!*

Why have such marvelous wisdom and be afraid to use it?

**Journalists**

Standards for the journo profession are really bad. In fact maybe journalism should be called an occupation, not a profession, as the word profession implies high standards and a taking on of social responsibility by the practitioner. Mind you, a few decades ago employees of newspapers did accept a set of ethics that the community liked – and they were proud of it. Some of the famous boundaries were:

1. Don't print a story without corroborating it from at least one other source.
2. Don't accept pay from the party who wants coverage.
3. Respect people's privacy – don't gang up at their home.
4. If writing your opinion do it in an editorial not in the news.
5. If blaming someone, give him a chance to rebut.

As you can see, those rules are all honored in the breach. In Australia where study for a bachelors degree in journalism takes six semesters, I've heard that the first five semesters are devoted to teaching the old ethics. Then in sixth semester the lecturer says "Ha ha, just kidding."

This chapter is named "Defrocking" as there is a way to get a profession to remove from its noncompliant members from practice. However, journalists are not licenced by the state in the first place, so can't be defrocked. It is simply up to the public to demand ethical behavior. Not to do so is a disaster. The government-owned Australian Broadcasting Corpor-ation has a charter and a complaint board. It has no teeth. This lack could be corrected by legislation, at any time.

**Cops**

Is there a way to get a bad cop fired? Of course. Think what it would be like if there weren't! (This subject also relates to CPS, which is a part of the police, although its staff are social workers not cops.) If cops mistreat a citizen their behavior can usually be found to be criminal.  Yet people are reluctant to make the proper complaint as the first line of complaint is to the police itself and "we all understand" it will go nowhere. I say it goes nowhere *because* we "all understand that."

The public should be sure to remove the practice of police policing the police. It is ridiculous. In the US, Congress made sure that people could sue. This should act as an inhibitor to a brutal cop – he'd hate to be impoverished by a lawsuit. (However in many cases the Police Benevolent Association pays the bill.) Also, it is prosecutable:

18 USC 242 "Whoever, under color of any law, statute, ordinance, regulation, or custom, willfully subjects any person in
any State … to the deprivation of any rights, privileges, or immunities secured or protected by the Constitution or laws of the United States, … shall be fined under this title or imprisoned not more than one year, or both;
… and if death results from the acts committed in violation of this section or if such acts include kidnaping or an attempt to kidnap, aggravated sexual abuse, or an attempt to commit aggravated sexual abuse, or an attempt to kill, shall be fined under this title, or imprisoned for any term of years or for life, or both, or may be sentenced to death."

**Doctors, Again.**  Recall the discrepancy, in McLachlans's survey, in regard to the number of people who did or did not believe the child's allegations of abuse, according to whether it was the child's own psychiatrist or a court-appointed one. Why is the ration 41 to 3?  This needs disciplinary handling.

In Chapter 29, I will reviewed a superb book by Keith Snow, *The Worst Interests of the Child.* It seems that in some states of the US the baddy is the doctor. Snow covers a case in which the doctor is also officially part of the court's decision-making as a "cutody consultant." And boy do they lie.

# 25. Try Citizen's Arrest, Outlawry, and Legal Self-Defense

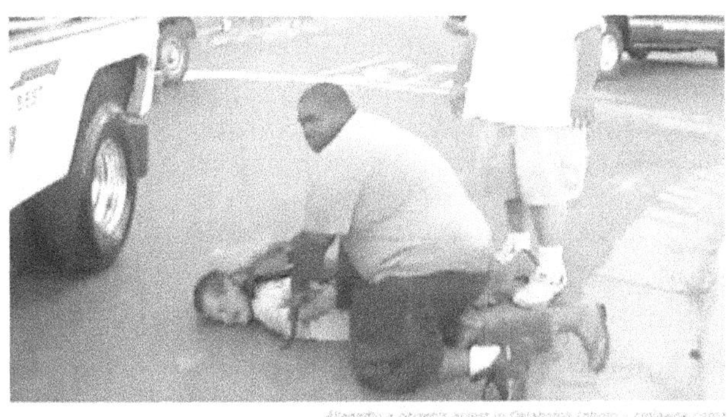

Allegedly a citizen's arrest in Oklahoma (photo – cnhawd.com)

First, the violent arrest shown in the picture is not the kind we'll be discussing here.   Second, note that in the term "citizen's arrest," the apostrophe goes before the S. It is the proper spelling – you could say "official" spelling.  So what is the meaning of *official* anyway? The Olympics, which is a private organization, has "official" insignias. The queen's "official" birthday is other than her real one. Don't worry about the officialness of citizen's arrest, please. Worry about its purpose. The purpose is to help society.

What is society? It is a group of people, originally an ethnic tribe, a big clan that combines roles of each fellow so they can work together. "Work together" means there has to be order. Folks automatically come up with rules. Later, rules seem to have a life of their own.

When I flew into Brisbane on March 7, 2019 I was afraid I was going to be arrested – having to do with my nosing into the matters discussed in this book. If they had said "You are under arrest" I was going to say "So are you."

I believed they would not be doing it to me lawfully and so they would be using "color of law" to assault me. What other means does a citizen have but to arrest an assaulter? That may have resulted in tragedy, I don't know. But now let's go over the "official" way to do citizen's arrest. Very few Americans know that if an FBI agent says to you "I'm arresting you," he is doing it as a *citizen's arrest*. He is only a citizen. The Federal Bureau of Investigation is not police and has no legal basis for doing "law enforcement" -- and they know this very well.

Trust me. Every state of the US allows citizen's arrest if for no other reason that they let FBI guys do it. Long story short: you can do it, but within certain limits. Here they are: Only do it if there's no other way for the person to get stopped from doing crime. Only do it if you tell him you are doing it – otherwise he can kill you on the spot in self-defense. Then call 911 (in Australia, 000) fast, and hand him over.

I know you want me to tell you the official *words* to use. Don't be silly. Forget officialness. Think purpose. The purpose is: SOCIETY enforces the discipline, the rules. It is society's job and at that moment *you are* society. Even if a lady's stealing your bike and you stop her you are doing it for society although it may look selfishly motivated.

*Law Professor Cherif Bassiouni*

In his famous monograph, Professor Bassiouni taught us that it is not OK to use citizen's arrest for misdemeanors, only felonies. (Kidnap is a felony.) Also, Bassiouni said, only use it if you know for sure that the person did commit the crime.

Rev Kevin Annett in Canada has set up a common-law court that prints arrest warrants. Fine. And How about bringing your stack of bedbug letters to show that arrest is a last resort.

**The Law of Outlawry**

In the olden days before policing was institutionalized, some people – bandits – couldn't easily be caught. They were outlaws, officially! It fell to everyone to catch them. You could say to them (Thank God some official words here): *Caput gerat lupinem*. "Yours is the head of a wolf." It means "You are outside society. You are civilly dead."

It was your duty to kill him. True. If instead you fed him or harbored him, that was a crime for which you could be arrested. Why? Because society wants rid of him. See?

As far as I know, *the law of* outlawry came to Australia with the First Fleet and has only ended if a state repealed it by statute. Tasmania did repeal it in 1924.  Look for your state's code on Google and you will see if there were any repeals. If not, it's machete time. No, I AM KIDDING. I just mean we should all understand why the law is where it's at.

**Self Defense Law Has Not Been Repealed**

Chapter 14 provided a High Court case as precedent for a person who kills or injures another in self-defense. The law of self-defense includes defending your loved one -- or anyone in your vicinity who's about to be injured.  That High Court case was *Zecevic versus the DPP*.

By the way, on a 2015 Youtube video I declared that I think all DPPs in Australia are outlaws as they are not ever going to prosecute themselves. Are they? (I mean *if* they commit a crime.) No one can reach them. Technically the Attorney General can. But he/ she would say "That's too political."

See what we're up against? It's necessary today to penetrate the fog of wrong ideas and overcome our fear of all persons who wear a badge. *You* wear a *natural* badge. Please deploy it.

# PART FOUR

# THE BIGGER PICTURE

Former cabinet member Stewart Udall, *Myths of August* (1994):

> I've known people who've acquired [security clearances] and I have a pretty good sense of what the effects of receiving [it] are. First you will feel like a fool for having studied, written and talked about these subjects... for years without having known of the existence of all of this inside information …
>
> Then… you will forget there ever was a time you didn't have it, and you'll be aware only of the fact that you have it now and the others don't … **and that all other people are fools.**
>
> Over a longer period of time, it will become very hard for you to learn from anybody who doesn't have these clearances… You'll become incapable of learning from most people in the world, no matter how much experience and knowledge they may have.   [Emphasis added]

# 26. Dr Day Has a Meltdown at the Adelaide Fringe

*Palm House in Adelaide's Botanic Gardens: Photo by pepitus*

Part Four, "The Bigger Picture" will now attempt to put the subject of legal kidnap into a context. I see it as part of a social engineering. This will be described in five chapters:

Chapter 26 presents the insider predictions that Dr Richard Day made to a medical audience in 1969. Chapter 27 zooms in on the 1996 massacre of children at Dunblane, Scotland. It is clear that a ring of pedophiles – elite members of society – were behind it. Chapter 28 uses Matthew Condon's research into the Fitzgerald Inquiry into police corruption. Talk about familiar! Chapter 29 celebrates law. Chapter 30 is about the anticipated Reunion of kids with Protective parents.

**Now to Dr Day**

The following was written with the intention of having it performed at my 2019 Adelaide Fringe play entitled "Crikey! Adelaide Conspiracy Theories." It got axed just before the show (not related to censorship). You'll see me ask Dr Richard Day, about predictions he made in 1969. The world did not know about them until 1988 when Dr Lawrence Dunegan revealed them on Randy Engels' radio show.

**Mary:** Doctor, it's good of you to be interviewed for Gumshoe News. I want to go over some of your famous work from 1969. You see at this moment in Australia, exactly fifty years later, we are having quite the *family* problem. You had predicted a break-up of the family as being a *good thing* for society.

**Dr Day:** [very stiff] I said it would restrain population growth.

**Mary:** But now it has come to an extreme. It's almost as though the people who were told to make it happen, which I understand were Rockefeller's people, went way too far. There is now a scheme of child-stealing, not by your basic weirdo's or criminals but by *judges*.

**Dr Day:** I think I know what you are going to say. These people turn the tables and accuse the *mother* instead. The next thing you know the kid is sent to a foster home.

**Mary:** Right. So the planning must have been *prior to* 1969.

**Dr Day:** Yes, we did arrange it.

**Mary:** I noticed that Dr Lawrence Dunegan, the guy who publicized your speech after mulling it over for 19 years, was already your critic before he even left the medical dinner that night. He disapproved of your prediction that men would be sent to jobs far away, and this would lead to an increase in divorce. Dunegan used the word *diabolical* for that.

**Dr Day:** It wasn't diabolical. It was being business-like.

**Mary:** That's why I am here. How far can "*business*like" go when it comes to the entire set of human relations. My beef is about the judges. You said a child would be sent to foster care. It's the *judge* that signs the order for that. But, once you have so corrupted a judge to get him to do *that*, you have no prospect of the judiciary being decent in *any* matter. Justice is going down the gurgler.

**Dr Day**: Is it too high a price to pay for *population* control?

**Mary**: I'm thinking Bible. What does it profit a man if he gain everything he sets out to gain – in your case "planned parenthood," so-called – but loseth his soul. I mean the soul of society in general, what we used to call *humanity*. No decent judge, no justice. No justice, law of the jungle. Who can survive in that setting?

**Dr Day**: Hopefully the *strong* can survive.

**Mary**: How could you be so foolish? The strong cannot survive. No one could endure the law of the jungle today. In a big city, food arrives in supermarkets from far away. There will be no food *at all*. And we're all dependent on public works, such as the water supply. It is necessary that we have a government, one that enforces justice.

**Dr Day**: I willingly entertain the idea that we "overdid" it.

**Mary**: Thank you. It's a relief to hear you say that. In fact many people like the bit in your 1969 speech where you said "People don't ask the right questions…."

**Dr Day**: If I recall correctly – but it was 50 years ago – the thing I was referring to was people's willingness to accept wrong information even when it's *illogical* on the *face* of it.

**Mary**: A funny thing, those medical students in your audience prove that point. *They* took what you said as acceptable – just because *you* said it. Even when you said the cure for cancer was under lock and key at the Rockefeller Institute, nobody threw a shoe at you. Did anyone even clear their throat?

**Dr Day**: We had put a little something in their wine. [pause] Still, it was an experiment, and we took a chance.

**Mary**: But in the long run, your speech *did* reach us. People are using it to overcome "Rockefeller-ism." You see, Dr Day, the race is not always to the swift.

**Dr Day**: Nor the battle to the strong, neither yet bread to the wise, nor yet *riches* to men of understanding, nor yet favour to men of skill -- *but time* and *chance* happeneth to them all.

**Mary**: Dr Lawrence Dunegan was taken aback by your remark that night, that not only was the Church going to *collapse* but the clergy would *help* make this happen. I imagine you did not specifically foresee that large numbers of Catholic priests would get outed for molesting children.

**Dr Day**: I *did* know about that.

**Mary**: [suddenly angry, bangs on desk]: *How dare you!* How dare you, fifty years ago, on some kind of putrid mission for your employer, decide that it was OK to wreck the life of a child before he or she had a chance to grow up?

**Dr Day**: [closes his eyes and sighs] I suppose I was brainwashed.

**Mary**: Well, then, you'd better *un*-brainwash yourself. [yelling] You'd better figure out which of your mission-accomplished colleagues are as un-happy as you are and *do something* to turn this around.

**Dr Day**: [shyly] What do you recommend?
**Mary**: [yelling] What do *I* recommend. What do *you* recommend.

**Dr Day**: My son and grandson are not too thrilled with me.  I will ask them what *they* recommend.

**Mary**: [calms down] Just asking could heal a rift in the family.

**Dr Day**: Rift in the family isn't the *word* for it. I'm an *ass*. They know it.  I couldn't see it. How many people have I hurt. [looks distressed] Seven or eight at least. Maybe more.

**Mary**: Try a *million*, maybe a hundred million?

**Dr Day**:  This is horrible.  I feel sick. I am going to throw up. I should never have done it.

What craziness this *all is*. How could it have happened? How could anyone get it so *wrong*. [whispering] What ever happened to my conscience.

[He gets up and starts to pace around]  My stupid conscience. [Pause]  If I could live my life *over* again. [Pause] It's unbel*iev*able what we did.

How can we make up for destroying the ocean. Was it even possible to destroy an ocean? Yes we did it *deliberately*. [screaming]  We did all kinds of stuff secretly.  You know why? Because we could get away with it.

We thought it was funny. [Pause, starting to cry]

It's our fault. It's my fault. Mea culpa. Mea [expletive] culpa. Mea [expletive *expletive*] culpa.

# 27. We Can Learn a Lot from Dunblane

*Lord Cullen*          *Lord Robertson, later head of NATO*

It's uncomfortable to talk about something terrible that is happening in one's own country but usually easy to discuss overseas events. In 1996, we awoke to the news that 16 first-graders had been killed in Scotland. (That was 6 weeks before the Port Arthur massacre in Tassie.)

After reading Sandra Uttley's book *Dunblane Unburied*, I felt sure she was correct -- that the authorities knew more about it than they admitted and that information about the killer, Thomas Hamilton, were being hidden.

For purposes of this book on Australia's child stealing I will come straight to my conjecture. I say the lords "did" Dunblane. And while I am being frank, I speculate that the toffs of Australia are the main protectors of the pedo-rings.

I am determined to evade any woo-woo topics (such as satanic rituals, cannibalism, or spirit cooking) in this book as the focus should be on the newly-recognized judicial kidnap. Lord Burton, a Mason, said that the Masons are responsible for the Dunblane massacre. Masons are a powerful force in the legal profession and the judicial system in the US.

164

Except for Lord Burton's accusation against his own mates (divulged by him to the newspaper *The Scotsman*), I have no way to pin it on the Masons but I can pin it on the toffs – a British slang word for the upper class.

The etymology of *toff* has something to do with eating toffee that sticks to the teeth and makes a person talk funny. The Aussie vocabulary has a fairly close equivalent – plummy (you talk like you have a plum in your mouth).

In brief, the official story is that Thomas Hamilton was an unpleasant loner who had run camps for boys. No explanation was provided for his sudden criminality much less his suicide. In early years after 1996, complaints surfaced that the police had complaints in file that should have led to his not being allowed to re-register a gun and not be given the use of public grounds for his camps.

Sandra Uttley found other issues. Highway surveillance showed Hamilton that morning going off a ramp that did not lead to the school. And an off-duty cop who was in the gym where the shooting took place was not called as a witness. Parents complained that bullet holes in the gym wall didn't match the story -- so the gym got razed.

For my money, another significant point is that the folks of the town were told it should not be discussed for a whole year due to trauma – plainly this is suppression. A bigger clue is Lord Cullen's *sealing the records for 100 years!*

## Tim Minogue's Research

There is an article by Tim Minogue entitled "Savile isn't the only obnoxious paedophile being covered up by the system." (Referring, of course, to Jimmy Savile, born 1926, died 2011). Find it at dunblaneexposed.info.

Minogue learned a lot from Glenn Harrison who had been housemaster from 1989 to 1991 at The Queen Victoria School, the QVS, also in Dunblane. Harrison saw bullying and suspected sexual abuse, especially as the boys were sometimes taken away for weekends. Eventually he tried every which way to use the proper system – police, parliament, judiciary, royalty – to get help for the kids, but he kept hitting a brick wall. *What does that tell you?*

In Australia, Denis 'Dinny' Ryan, a police detective from Mildura, told the 2014-2018 Royal Commission that he couldn't get his fellow cops to deal with the matter of sexual abuse of kids by a priest. So cops must have been in on it. Glenn Harrison (I will call him Glenn) contacted many officials of Queen Victoria School, *and higher ups*, and – in my opinion – proved that "they are *all* in it." Toffs, that is.

Supposedly the lone gunman, Hamilton, had "turned the gun on himself," and laid his corpse down there on the gymnasium floor for all to see. When Hamilton, was identified on TV, Glenn recognized him immediately.

Not only had Hamilton come wandering around the dormitories at QVS, he had been reported on, by this Housemaster, in an effort to get him kicked out. This was around 1990. You would think a housemaster making such a complaint would be listened to, right? But all his letters went unanswered or were handled dismissively.

In June, 1991, Glenn decided to resign. His contract required that he give one term's notice, so he would depart in January. On December 11, he wrote to the parents of his 57 boys to warn them of the danger of bullying and abuse at the school. This responsible behavior on the part of the Housemaster led to someone throwing a stone at his window. Frightened, he went to the police. Well, that was a mistake. While he was not home, another batch of police broke down his door at QVS with a sledgehammer and stole some of his papers.

I feel as though I shouldn't say "stole." After all, the police have a duty to enter a premises and check on something don't they? Maybe we should say they "seized the goods for inspection," or something like that.

Nah, let's call a spade a spade. The point of using a sledgehammer was surely to scare him, and the point of taking his papers, which they never gave back, was to deprive him of the evidence that was in those papers – such as copies of letters to Ministers.

Once he was situated in a new job, at Baltasound, Glenn wrote more letters, this time to the Secretary of State of Scotland and to the Duke of Edinburgh in his role of patron of the Queen Victoria School. Nothing came of it. (I got all of the Glenn story from stickybeak Tim Minogue.)

A key complaint was the fact that people using the name "Friends of the QVS" would take the boys away for weekends. Glenn and his wife lived near the front gate so they could see flashy cars driving up on Friday night to get the boys. He says the boys would return looking stressed but with a lot of money.

**Australian *Déjà vu*.** Many of the "friends" were recognizable to Glenn as they were famous people – a veritable Who's Who of Society. By the way, Fiona Barnett said that when she witnessed a baby-murder of that kind in the Great Hall of the University of Sydney, the audience consisted of Sydney's "high society."

In Mildura, VIC, Detective Ryan had discovered that one of his colleague-cops worked for ASIO (Australia's intelligence agency). I ask: do ASIO members realize whom they actually work for? I think the Dunblane story, especially the cover-up, shows that many police and covert agents are **working directly for the toffs**. And they are toff-protectors.

For whom did the CIA perform the unbelievable sins of MK-Ultra? CIA director Allen Dulles, had previously been in the OSS. The letters O-S-S are supposed to stand for Office of Strategic Services, but its nickname was "Oh So Social". In other words, members of America's upper class were all supporting OSS (headed by Bill Donovan).

British journalist Tim Minogue had, *prior* to the Dunblane mass murder, attempted to get legislation requiring members of the Freemasons to declare their membership if they were a parliamentarian or a judge. This seems to me a good idea. I recommended similar in my 2011 book, *Prosecution for Treason*.

When President George W Bush was asked about his fraternity, Skull and Bones, he said he was not allowed to discuss it. Thanks to First Amendment rights, a Bonesman, like any other US citizen, can be as silent as he wishes. But if he won't discuss his conflicting loyalties, a law should prevent him being elected. No talkie, no White Housie.

I want to make a point here about the way in which Minogue was treated, for his efforts. He is a journalist who went about his inquiries politely and "by the book." But he found that the police had started an investigation on *him*.

When he asked why this was happening he was told that it was because Lord Robertson (one of the persons he wrote to) was a public figure and therefore deserving of police protection. Makes me think it was like a pioneer of the "fixated persons investigations unit."

Minogue says: "[I wrote] to those legally responsible for the safety and wellbeing of the pupils in a private boarding school, the board of governors, which in this case of Queen Victoria School were Her Majesty's Commissioners. The head commissioner is an ex-officio post held by the Secretary of State for Scotland.

"I wrote to my MP, the late Rachel Squire and asked her to ask the then Secretary of State, Mrs Helen Liddell (Baroness Liddell of Coatdyke), if she was aware of any group such as the 'Friends of QVS.' … My MP would not take on my concerns and suggested I contact the Secretary of State directly. I replied to my MP stressing the seriousness of the allegations and copied the letter to the then Secretary of State, Mrs Helen Liddell. By a return e-mail I was told by Mrs Liddell that … the matters I had raised "are devolved to the Scottish Parliament" and my letter had been forwarded to my MSP Scott Barrie!

"I responded to the Secretary of State's 'palming-off' of my enquiry to my Member of Scottish Parliament by pointing out that she could not shirk her responsibilities as a Chief of Her Majesty's Commissioners, which were invested in her by Royal Warrant…"

Minogue was then told that "he should write to the Chief Executive/Headmaster of QVS." What nonsense.

Minogue did not get any satisfaction, and found those officials to be unaware that Hansard (i.e., official record of Parliament's business) had contained information about the Housemaster's complaints. So Minogue widened his search, this time writing to the headmaster of the school for the years 1989-1991 and all the then commissioners. He also wrote to Lord Cullen (ahem) and Lord Robertson (ahem, ahem) who had been **visitors to the school.**

Minogue then used the Internet to search the Dunblane Inquiry and found that three persons had said under oath that they knew of a Hamilton connection to the school:

Grace Jones Ogilvie, a neighbour of Hamilton, said she knew of him taking his boys' clubs camping at Loch Lomond and at the QVS. Ian Steven Boal said that his friend Hamilton had got him a job at a QVS summer camp. Robert Mark Ure who lived across the street from Hamilton said his estranged wife had been at the firing range at QVS with her friend Hamilton.

Did Minogue get anywhere with the Ombudsman? No because the police are one of the exclusions from the list of offices that ombudsmen can investigate. Minogue did find in 1993 Hansard that the Chief Inspector of Schools had carried out an inspection, and that it was discussed in Scottish newspapers in 1992 – only the matter of bullying, not abuse, and nothing about the letter Glenn had sent to parents.

**Lord Burton**. Most interestingly, Minogue was contacted by Burton: "Lord Burton knew of my contact with The Housemaster and we had an exchange of views. I found him to be a pleasant, and I believe a decent man, but he was over-keen to protect his organisation (Masons) and **blamed the Speculative Society clique in the judiciary**, and the police for a cover up 'at the highest level' of the Dunblane tragedy. He told me that a Scots Tory Law Lord and member of the Speculative Society had pounded his fist on his desk in the House of Lords to emphasise that he [Burton] should let the matter [of the Dunblane massacre] drop." [Emphasis added]

Getting the downlow about the QVS from Minogue's article has been quite a shock. My late adored husband George grew up near Dunblane. All the folks I've met through him are morally solid. I thought Scots had cornered the market on decency – and that, like Bobbie Burns, they scoffed at toffs.

Tim Minogue has now published a list of the Speculative Society's members. Whew! Many judges. What do they think they are doing? All guilty of *obstruction of justice* regarding this serious 1996 crime. William Scott, a concerned citizen of Dunblane, found that that there was **no statute authorizing Lord Cullen's 100 sealing of records**.

Wait a minute. *Why* did Lord Cullen and his mates cover up the massacre? In order to keep pedophilia hush hush? Well yes, but it's much worse than that. I speculate that the massacre was group-planned. Some people somehow thought it good to send sixteen darling children to their graves.

*Teacher and Kids*

Note: Cullen "made his name" by running the Lockerbie case. He also ran a 5-year investigation of the North Sea oil spill known as Piper Alpha. I'll bet both were frauds. I see that Lord Robertson has sued *The Sunday Herald* over the fact that a commenter indicated Robertson was responsible for the Dunblane massacre. The newspaper [insider?] paid an out of court settlement of 25K pounds to Robertson.

*The Guardian* wrote: "The case in 2004 forced internet publishers to re-double their efforts to ensure internet users posting on their message boards do not libel people."

Nonsense. Citizens must look around for murderers and they need to debate it. By the way, Robertson was a Labor MP. In 1999, having been UK Defense Secretary for 2 years, he was made a peer. The he became NATO secretary general from 1999 to 2001. Now he works for a defense contractor.

To repeat, all this was turned up because one native, Sandra Uttley, could be bothered, and her friend, Ms Hagger, helped.

**Toffs Did It**. I believe that Thomas Hamilton was not the killer. He had no reason to cause his own death like that. Someone else did everything and threw Hamilton's body onto the gym floor. You can see the trickiness of the case at various websites, and in Uttley's *Dunblane Unburied*.

I say the persons who do the cover-up are the guilty parties. As stated in a law maxim: *contra spoliatorem, omnia praesumuntur*. "Against the one who destroys evidence, all things can be presumed." In fact, denying the very existence of such a group as "friends of the QVS" is a clear sign of guilt that the friends do bad things. If they are doing good, wouldn't they want to boast about it? Or at least take a modest bow?

**It's Clinic Time**. Can we please stop saying that various patsy-terrorists are nuts and use basic diagnostic skills to see who is really sick? How sick is the mass murder of children?

I don't have much hope of getting upper-class child-killers into Broadmoor (or in America, Bellevue, or in Adelaide, Glenside). But they *can* be forcibly sent to a clinic. This is called "sectioning," after a section of the law that allows the freedom of the mentally ill to be curtailed, legally.

I propose a new clinic. Toffs' Clinic. This is not a joke. The toffs should be in prison as murderers. If they "didn't know better" they should be in hospital. Take your pick, Toffs.

172

# 28. Fitzgerald Inquiry on Queensland Police Corruption

*(L) badge of the state police, (C) Condon's excellent book
(R) Joh Bjelke Petersen (1911-2005), premier of Queensland*

Amazingly, the badge of the Queensland Police has not one, but two, images of the British Crown. I suppose the motto on the banner "With honour we serve" should be taken to mean "With honour we serve the Crown."

Do police also serve the people? I am sure many of them do. This chapter is mostly about the ones who don't. It is a rehash of Matthew Condon's book *All Fall Down* (2015).

You could skip this chapter as it does not discuss Family Law. Still, it has value, as the main subject is the 1987 Fitzgerald Inquiry. It proves that something can be done about corruption of police and judiciary – by using law. In the end, the Police Commissioner was sentenced to 14 years in prison, and three ex-ministers did time. Per *Sunday Mail*:

"Oh-oh, the Fitzgerald Inquiry described last week as the most important thing to happen in Queensland in 100 years, has already, in the space of one short week, given a jolly good shake to the foundations of government…."

Soon enough, Premier Joh Bjelke-Petersen fell from grace, and his National Party was replaced by Labor.

Some entities mentioned in Condon's book are:
-- The Joke – insider name for a system of payoffs to cops
-- Police Special Branch, set up in 1948 for political purposes
-- "The Midnight State" a key ABC *Four Corners* show
-- The National Party, which governed Qld for 32 years
-- Australian Bureau of Crime Intelligence, the ABCI
-- The Rat Pack: Assistant Commissioner Tony Murphy,
    Commissioner Terry Lewis, and Inspector Kevin Dorries.

**Some Persons Who Helped Reveal the Corruption:**
Phil Dickie, author of exposés for the *Courier-Mail,*
Peter Vassallo, a dedicated anti-corruption cop in ABCI,
Ross Dickson ("the Sheriff of Mareeba"), got transferred
  to Townsville as he knew too much,
Chris Masters who produced "The Midnight State" for
  ABC's *Four Corners* program that engendered the Inquiry,
Lorelle Saunders, a policewoman wrongly jailed for a
  murder, to get her out of circulation,
Des Sturgess of the Office of Public Prosecutor,
Bill Gunn, Deputy Premier who called for Inquiry when
  Bjekle-Petersen was out-of-state,
Tony Fitzgerald, QC, who ran the Inquiry, and gave homilies,
Nigel Powell, Licensing Branch cop -- *and other good cops.*

**Suspicious Deaths** (a few of many):
**Hank Coblens,** p 215: "It was decided that Coblens would conduct an audit of the Queensland Day committee. This was dangerous territory. He was being asked to go through the books of the Premier's Department. Colbens interviewed Judith Callaghan and then compiled his evidence. On 4 October several colleagues noticed a change in Coblens' demeanor…. 'Hank might do himself in,' Gallagher said. The next morning he was found dead in his white Mazda: age 32."

**Shirley Brifman**, p.1: [brothel madam] Shirley had gone on national television [in 1971] and blown the whistle on corrupt police in Qld and NSW whom she had been paying off for over a decade. In a few short weeks she was to testify in a perjury trial against legendary detective Tony Murphy. Brifman was warned: commit suicide or say goodbye to your children. …Four years after Shirley suicided, [her daughter] Sonia developed peritonitis and died in agony, age 18."

**William Clarke and his wife Gravydya**, p 203: "Doctors recovered 132 pellets from his chest and 80 from Gravydya's body. The killers splashed fuel around the house, torched it. The murder was investigated by CIB under superintendent Tony Murphy." *[Later Peter Vassallo wrote:]* "Analysis shows Clarke had a drug-oriented association with Bellino group."

**Snuff Film** (p 536). "Officer Jim Slade claims to have seen a film of a child being abused and murdered. He was interviewed by investigators but was not questioned before Kimmins during the hearings. Detectives were warned that that any search warrants issued on judicial officers had to be vetted first by senior police. **The inquiry "found no evidence that police had covered up pedophilia."** *Pleeze.*

**Organized Crime**. *The Oxford Dictionary* defines *organized crime* as "criminal activities that are planned and controlled by powerful groups and carried out on a large scale." The subject of this book, *Reunion,* is the organized crime of child-trafficking, at least the part of it I label "judicial kidnap."

None of my chapters above looks at judicial kidnap as organized crime, but this chapter on Queensland crime can stand as a model of how the thing works. For one thing, as just described, **it works by bumping off its challengers – also by controlling law enforcement and government by bribery.**

Condon's book discusses many payoffs, and we know from other sources that blackmail is helpful. J Edgar Hoover famously kept a dossier on each politician's sins, making him able to keep Congress in check. So simple!

The payoffs revealed in articles by Dickie, and in the *Four Corners* program, got the public's goat. It enabled people to see what was happening. Testimony at the Inquiry named Commissioner Terry Lewis as having been "the bagman" for previous Commissioner Frank Bischof. Lewis then got the top police job and *his* bagman was Jack Herbert.

Herbert collected from hemp producers such as the Bellino brothers and from brothel owner Anne Tilley. One cop who tipped the scales was Ross Dickson. He had wanted to enforce drug laws up north but was told "Don't report on anything north of Cairns." That led to a realization that the seashore may be the receiver of illegal imports. Peter Vassallo of the ABCI tried to get Qld to help the effort to stop drugs but he ended up being in fear of his life for his trouble.

The main crime that invited corruption was "vice." In the 1980s this meant illegal gambling, prostitution, and drugs. Nowadays it's hard to get upset about such things. Prostitutes are now registered sex workers, marijuana is legalized in many places, and states run casinos. But back then, police had to be paid off to not report the crimes. Condon tells how a veneer of law enforcement was conveyed to the public:

"Licensing Branch had an occasional phoney bust. They would ring Miller and tell him to have a girl ready tomorrow night. She would be booked into a room at the Southern Cross Motel. The girl goes there and is busted and charged with soliciting. Miller would pay the fine and the girl would be paid $500 for taking the rap…. Licensing would always have a beer which was kept in a fridge for them and then leave."

In many brothels all services for cops were free.

It's my guess that there is more to "corruption" than what was revealed at the Inquiry.  I imagine there was a major plan to get the public immersed in drugs, gambling, and the commoditizing of sex in order to destabilize society.

That may be why Terry Lewis – who became *Sir* Terry Lewis - - was recruited as a young cop for the top job; he would do what distant bosses told him, perhaps robotically. Even today, after prison, he robotically says he is innocent.

I speculate that long-serving premier, Sir Joh Bjelke-Petersen, who was considered a conservative pro-Bible premier, was also under foreign instruction perhaps without realizing it. If I am right, his "conservatism" and religious sayings could have been but a good, noisy cover.

The book *All Fall Down* is not strong on explaining the chain of command. There were Ministers of Police in Parliament but did they condone the Joke? I don't know.

## Police Culture

I go further.  An outside effort, to cause bribing of police, could have been engineered simply for the purpose of making police departments corrupt. It has been said that the 18th amendment to the US Constitution that made alcohol illegal may have been done to help a mafia get started and to also help a mafia-police relationship get formed, in 1919.  (The Prohibition Amendment was later repealed in 1933.)

Since people know that if cops can be paid off, a cop who would not be paid off will find it had to "hold the fort." One of Tony Fitzgerald's homilies (given from the bench at various moments in the Inquiry), included this brilliant item:

> "It is impossible to concede how an honest policeman could rationally believe the acceptance of a situation, that involves corruption by any of his colleagues, benefits either himself or his force or is justified by his shared interest and burdens with any who are corrupt – merely because like him they are policemen."

Graeme Parker turned state's witness and testified: "I would also receive hundreds of calls every week from police who said Lewis was corrupt but were too scared to be named or provide a statement for fear of losing their jobs."

This is very good news. We wonder if hundreds of police (and social workers) want to phone someone to dob the child-stealers in. Better get those Truth Commissions going!

Don't forget, Fitzgerald's Inquiry, unlike the Wood Royal Commission in NSW, or the Mullighan Inquiry in SA, had results. Some cops were offered immunity for 'fessing up, and it worked. Many of the baddies found themselves in jail.

Nevertheless, I strongly urge that we skip official inquiries in future. They are bound to create a false belief that something is being done. Nothing is ever done. I also don't think the public should have a sort of People's Inquiry. How would we prevent an internal takeover of it? But it is not for me to advise. Let everyone think up a plan. Solving the problem piecemeal is fine. "Let a thousand flowers bloom," as the fellow once said.

And remember that laypersons have every right to try to get unethical professionals removed from their occupation. Every lawyer requires a license to practice and many do get suspended or "struck off" – even for relatively trivial infractions.

178

## 29. Which Do You Prefer – Real Law or Law of Jungle?

*(L) Sir William Blackstone, author of Commentaries on the Laws of England, (R) After the take-the-cannoli's scene in The Godfather*

This penultimate chapter asks whether law is worth saving or whether we should just agree to let it all collapse.

First, a list of the black-letter-law crimes we have discussed:

1. Kidnaping
2. Child abuse
3. Grievous bodily harm
4. Threatening a person with death or serious harm
5. Fraud
6. Perjury
7. False imprisonment (e.g., of Dr Pridgeon)
8. Perversion of the course of justice
9. Cover-up of crime
10. Impeding an investigation
11. Failure to report a crime
12. Falsifying records or destroying records
13. Harassment
14. Murder or manslaughter

Doesn't it seem strange that no matter how many of the protected criminals get outed, they still do not go to jail?

And just consider the following "notices to desist" that could be sent by official bosses, such as Attorneys General or Chief Justices, but which never happen (as far as I know):

1. Cease giving any presence in law to "parental alienation."
2. Cease ordering grandparents not talk to the grandchild.
3. Cease telling families that police cannot hear complaints while a case is before the Family Court.
4. Cease threatening a parent that if they don't sign a consent order, his/her side has no hope of prevailing.
5. Cease disbelieving the child unless he is blatantly lying.
7. Cease supervising visits unless there is identifiable danger.
8. Cease appointing Independent Children's Lawyers.
9. Cease ordering a parent to get a forensic psychiatrist assessment if there's no evidence of his/her being harmful.
10. Cease preventing the kid from having a say in this matter.
11. Cease the trick known as "parent responsibility contracts."
12. Cease forced guardianship and forced adoptions.
13. Cease pretending that Childrens Court is a court, when in fact it is an administrative arm of police, a Star Chamber.

*Cover of Keith Snow's invaluable 2015 book*

Clearly the players are all in on it. Anyone can see that the normal thing, per the values of our society, would be to apply the above "desist notices." The reason that the child abuse epidemic, worldwide, must be that it is carefully engineered. On the next two pages please find my review of Snow's book *The Worst Interests of the Child* that shows US "child protection" people to be behaving exactly like those in Australia. Exactly.

180

## Keith Snow Conducted a Thorough Search of One Case

Most of Keith Snow's book it is down-loadable under its previous title "Life Sentence." Don't miss it. His main target is Connecticut. Judges in that state outdo themselves in meanness, and doctors do worse. Boy do they need to be struck off. Plus there's a palpable "union" of the bad guys. The corruption is brazen. Doctors act as "custodial consultants" and freely slander the mother. Judges order records sealed at the drop of a hat, to conceal their own crimes as well as those of the pedos.

The amount of money in US cases is stupefying. A lawyer may submit a bill for $58,000 and the client is *forced* to pay it. A judge made one mum sign over her Teacher's Retirement fund, despite its being non-garnishable. Keith is known for human rights reporting of genocide. (He is *persona non grata* in Rwanda.)

Keith Snow holds media accountable. He tells of his efforts to get Mike Melia of the Associated Press to cover a hot story of judicial corruption.  After many tries, Snow asks Melia: "I'd like to know why you dropped the Sunny Kelley story when it was such a clear case of sexual violence."
"I can't continue this conversation." Melia hangs up.

Snow worked furiously to get at the political connections that determine outcomes in Hartford. He also looks at members of the boards of relevant charities and state committees. He has even found a case where the feds took action:

"The corruption and judicial abuse being perpetrated thru GAL [guardian ad litem] systems … has provoked federal lawsuits. In 2012, the US DoJ raided the family court offices in Lakawanna County, PA and subsequently filed a lawsuit seeking to dismantle the GAL system there."   (page 42)

Snow also analyzes the new Fathers' Rights groups and considers them to be part of the racket. He agrees (page 22) with a the writer of the Carver County Corruption blog:

"There are many honest and wonderful fathers' rights groups [but] Fathers' Manifesto Groups are corrupt groups that sell children into … severe traumatic situations …"

I ask why the strident groups of fathers aren't trying to coordinate with the mums' groups to put an end to the industry of false claims and the obvious participation of government. Huh?

The book is largely about the case of one boy. Snow quotes the mother as saying her son came home from Dad's house (page 111) singing "We wish you a Merry Christmas and a happy electrocution." At age 7 he said, during a *supervised* visit, "Electric shock is what they do to you to make you forget the bad things they do to you." Thus his remark is in the court record. Surely anyone can see that a boy didn't work out the science by himself. Snow also covers the plight of his reporter-colleague:

*Lori Handrahan, PhD*

The state of Maine has seized Handrahan's daughter and she asks all of us to help get the girl back. Shame on you, Maine!

Note: in a Youtube interview, Lori tells of some amazing help she got – not on her own case but for other cases. She involved the Internal Revenue Service in a hunt based on the crime of money-laundering. Lori says they were very helpful. Seems like you can learn something new every day!

The strongest part of Snow's book is the Preface, where he pins down the whole operation as being organized crime. "It's not a metaphor for organized crime," he says, "it *is* organized crime." It involves the state house, the media, and the judiciary as well as a well-heeled legal profession. Being an experienced overseas reporter Snow knows that the media won't cover much. Thus, US citizens continue in their traditional, optimistic belief that government is mainly good. No. Sorry. "It's organized crime."

## Comes a Time You Have To Act

A huge obstacle to our being able to oppose big forces is that we are not built to join together against *our own leader* if he is bad, or to unite as weak persons against the powerful. As that issue wasn't present in evolutionary days we didn't make behavioral adaptations for it, so today we are handicapped. All human emotions exist to meet particular needs. For example, people – especially males – are emotionally equipped to do teamwork. It comes naturally to play one's small part in a big enterprise. But it's not a trait that generalizes to all situations: we *don't regularly* join together.

Another emotion is readiness to do battle, to defend one's tribe against an enemy. Men are willing to take big physical risks, even death, for this. But what we did *not* evolve a special emotion for is attacking "the top brass."

In *Homo sapiens*, as in many other species, the leader is an individual that the group needs to follow. It's beneficial, not harmful, to have an emotional proclivity to want to do as the leader directs. We even have an emotion of anger toward persons who try to undercut the leader.

Thus, rebellion is a rarity. As it says in the founding document of the US, "all experience hath shewn, that mankind are more disposed to suffer, while evils are sufferable, than to right themselves by abolishing the forms to which they are accustomed." So it's amazing the colonists did what they did.

Lest the reader think I am urging a rebellion, quite the opposite. We've already got the government we desired to create. Americans of my generation (baby boomers) inherited the cultural values aired in the Declaration. We took it to heart that showing respect for each person -- and his freedom to be what he wants to be – is the way we should function.

**Declaration of Independence, July 4, 1776** (a statement by 13 British colonies in America, "divorcing" King George III)

When in the Course of human events, it becomes necessary for one people to dissolve the political bands which have connected them with another, and to assume among the powers of the earth, the separate and equal station to which the Laws of Nature and of Nature's God entitle them, a decent respect to the opinions of mankind requires that they should declare the causes which impel them to the separation.

We hold these truths to be self-evident, that all men are created equal, that they are endowed by their Creator with certain unalienable Rights, that among these are Life, Liberty and the pursuit of Happiness. -- That to secure these rights, Governments are instituted among Men, deriving their just powers from the consent of the governed,

--That whenever any Form of Government becomes destructive of these ends, it is the Right of the People to alter or to abolish it, and to institute new Government, laying its foundation on such principles and organizing its powers in such form, as to them shall seem most likely to effect their Safety and Happiness.

Prudence, indeed, will dictate that Governments long established should not be changed for light and transient causes; and accordingly all experience hath shewn, that mankind are more disposed to suffer, while evils are sufferable, than to right themselves by abolishing the forms to which they are accustomed.

But when a long train of abuses and usurpations, pursuing invariably the same Object evinces a design to reduce them under absolute Despotism, is their right, it is their duty, to throw off such Government, and to provide new Guards for their future security.

So how come those values don't guide our action now? We have 'bought into' the cultural change that was instituted by such entities as Tavistock and its branch office, the CIA. No debate took place. Those experts know how to make change gradually by "conditioning" us.  All humans, from birth, are disposed to pick up, and imitate, the cultural signals around them. The rational brain is not involved: we are born mimics.

This is well known to Tavi and needs to be well known by the rest of us, a.s.a.p.! I interpret the judicial kidnap gig only partly as a scheme for feeding the pedophile racket. I think it is mostly for "conditioning" – to get us, by slow drip, to take in the new reality of no justice, no dignity, no family life. But  now that people are finding out that something as egregious as ripping a kid from Mum's arms is condoned by courts, this could be an oddball opportunity to unite folks.  You should ask your neighbors simply to contribute *strength in numbers*.

Blurbing Frances Lappé and Adam Eichen, *Daring Democracy*: "Americans are distraught as tightly held economic and political power drowns out their voices and values. [BUT] an essential truth: It's not the magnitude of a challenge that crushes the human spirit. It's feeling powerless -- fearing that to stand up for [a cause] is futile. Lappé and Eichen demystify how we got here, exposing the well-orchestrated effort that has robbed Americans of power. But [they offer] solutions. Lappé and Eichen offer proof that courage is contagious …"

I ask how did our once happy society get into being callous and cruel? And to be "a little bit" callous and cruel means we are on a path to much worse. Just the lifting of the discipline that used to typify a judge's life means we will lose recourse to *any* predictable law. Soon everything will be "up for grabs."

At the 2019 Red Pill Expo, one of the lectures was entitled: "Think while it's still legal."  It's legal now, but tomorrow?

# 30. Let's Get Some Reunion Chits Going

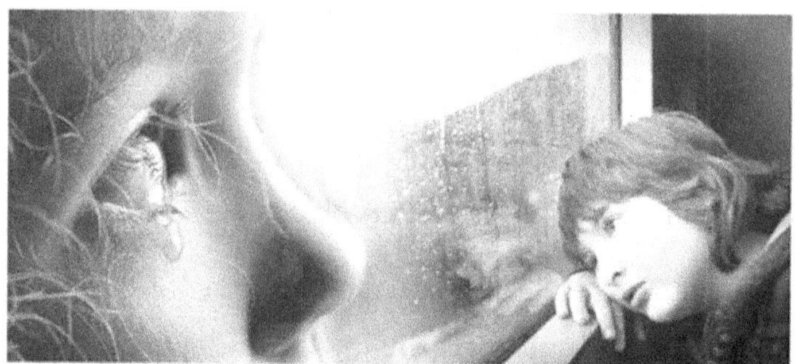

*Adapted photo: The Vibrant Heart and apworld.com*

Soon after Scott Morrison became Prime Minister, he gave a moving apology to all the victims of child sexual abuse in Australia. This included the embracing cry "We love you, we hear you, and we honour you."

Who is the "we" in that sentence? It must mean all of us. It means "We Aussies are a decent bunch, we will do the right thing now that we have learned what went on all those years – we promise, we won't let you down."

## What Is a Reunion? What Is a Chit?

The word *Reunion* in the title of this book means that we should concentrate on bringing the problem to an end by reuniting the child with its Protective parent. There are two terms in the literature similar to *reunion* – repatriation and restoration. However, I felt that the word *repatriation,* in Oz,  has a history of association with the bringing home of soldier – repats. The word *restoration* could conjure up (at least to people raised on the history of the British Empire) the 1660 Restoration of Charles II to the throne, following Cromwell's protectorate after Charles I was beheaded.

Anyway in proclaiming reunion, the idea is to  focus on the solution, not the problem.

186

As for the word *chit,* I had considered using the word *voucher,* or *certificate,* but preferred a term that is unencumbered by common usages. *The Cambridge English Dictionary* defines the little-used word "chit" as "a note that shows how much money you owe or have paid for something, or that allows you to do something. 'Before they can hail a cab, staff now need a chit signed by a senior staff member'."

The parallel would be: "Before they can fetch the kid home, a parent needs a chit signed by Review Board members."

## The Chit As a Piece of Law Currency

Think of some pieces of paper that carry weight in law: a writ of habeas corpus, a constitution, a certificate of immunity, a sworn affidavit. Those things didn't drop from the sky. Humans thought them up. The same is true of any cultural object -- a fish hook for catching fish, a clay pot for storing liquid. When something is needed, it manages to materialize.

Introducing – ta-da – the reunion chit. It's legal. Oh, how did it get to be "legal"? Recall from Chapter 1 that Kansas has a Citizen Review Board to deal with child-in-care cases.

"Volunteers meet as a group once a month and interview *families and service providers* and then deliberate in private."

I assume we have no hope of that. Our chit will be legal simply because it deals in a responsible way and does not offend anyone or any law. It *implements* law. The task is to gather some people together and focus on a few cases. Board members must be ordinary folk, *not* interested parties, OK?

Be sure to get the facts correct by looking at the documents. If your "finding" is that the child ought to be reunited with the parent, or in some cases grandparent, write a report and back it up with reasoning. **Write a chit**, and all sign it.

It should *not* contain a request for prosecution or be defamatory. Perhaps the parent who has been a perpetrator or abuser should be designated by softer terminology such as the LFG, the "less favorable guardian." Be conservative.

Note: I am not saying this is bound to succeed. At first you will almost certainly fail. Ms Rilak (see Chapter 13) has tried all sorts of proper things in her Family Law case -- at vast expense. She has appealed, has tried equity, and so forth. She is sure her daughter is being pedophile'd. She's had no luck.

But chitting is different. When the court fails us (which indicates that the holders of court positions are negligent or are impostors!), *we have to skirt around the court system.* Be sure to let the public know that the trafficking issue is well docu-mented, so they won't call it a conspiracy theory. You can use, Senator Portman's official report in Appendix B that tells how the US government traffics kids as slaves.

**Give Your Chit Some Ballast**
Now back to the production of the reunion "chit." I do not claim to know what the item must look like – it can vary, but its signatories would no doubt wish to have the chit contain authorization from society. It's easy to come up with that! Here, again, are law maxims, now cherry-picked for chitters:

***To a judge who exceeds his office or jurisdiction no obedience is due.** [Think of the three-fingers man.]

***When laws imposed by the state fail, we must act by the law of nature.** [Father criminal for saving his babies? No.]

***We must have recourse to what is extraordinary, when what is ordinary fails.** [Truth Commission, chits, etc]

***What necessity forces, it justifies**. [Read Pridgeon's letter.]

188

***What is proved by the record, ought not to be denied.**
[See the nonsense of DCP hiding evidence of child abuse.]

***The safety of the people is the supreme law.** [*Salus populi sumprema lex esto*, by Roman senator Cicero in his *De Legibus*.]

**Get Some Ballast from Statutory Law**
Per Section 286 of Queensland's Criminal Code:

> (1) It is the **duty of every person** who has the care of a child under 16 years to  (b) take the precautions that are reasonable … **to avoid danger to the child's life**, health or safety; and (c) take the action that is reasonable … to remove the child from any such danger. [Emphasis added]

South Australia *Criminal Consolidation Act*, Division 1A, Sec 5E (1)14 **provides a penalty of 15 years prison** for neglecters. So the chitters can say they're acting to protect themselves:

> "A person is guilty of the offence of criminal neglect if —
> (a) a child… suffers harm as a result of an act; and
> (b) the defendant had, at the time of the act, a duty of care to the victim; …and (d) the defendant failed to take steps that he or she could reasonably be expected to have taken … ."

SA *Children's and Young Persons Safety Act* says, in Sec 62:

> "[The Child] **must be given** a reasonable opportunity to personally present to the Court their views related to their ongoing care and protection. [and] (63) (1) the legal practitioner must, as far as is reasonably practicable, act in accordance with **any instructions** given by the child." [Emphasis added]

Your panel can interview the child. If child is not contactable, you may present any past communications from him or her.

Note: Few people know that such a law exists, mandating that the child be allowed to speak!  This is very helpful for chitters.

**Major legal protection**: Family Law Act, sec 70NAE, says you can act if it's **"necessary to protect the health or safety of a person."** No later section nullifies or even modifies that. I don't know why lawyers don't celebrate that wonderful point.

## Aboriginal Strong Grandmothers

In Central Australia there is already a banding together of grandmothers who oppose the states' over-eager use of guardianship. Indigenous peoples who have been colonized have got greater awareness than others, of course, as to what governments get up to.

Aboriginal Australians see their children being removed as a scheme to end their culture. The group, which is called "Strong Grandmothers," oversees the placement of a child into guardianship by finding him a home with relatives, or at least in the community. Like the Kansas Citizen's Review Board, it acts as a check on runaway power. It conjures up an alternative authoritative source. Is anything more authoritative than Strong Grandmothers?

**"Injunctionize" the Chit?** Once you are armed with the chit the next question is what to do with it. Time is of the essence. Your local court regularly issues emergency injunctions, such as restraining orders. You could petition for an injunction. Lawyers often provide the judge with the desired wording.

On the next page I offer a "template" for a chit.  But please don't treat it as gospel. And remember, your Board is not depending on cooperation from the judge. If no injunction is issued you still have a right to reunite the child with parent. Once again I say, the crime is not in reuniting them; the crime, a crime actually on the books, is *leaving a child in danger*.

190

### TEMPLATE FOR A REUNION CHIT

1. Name, date of birth, and address of child _______________.

2. Name, address, phone number of Protective parent ____.

3. Name and occupation of signers of this chit (many)________.

4. Who has custody? Name, address, phone number, and relationship of that person ____________________________.

5. Date of last court ruling ________. (Attach the ruling.)

6. Which court to petition for injunction regarding the chit?____.

7. Is the child presently in danger? ____. Describe___________.

10. Give reasoning why reunion is appropriate ________.

11. List of efforts already made in the case, unsuccessfully _____.

12. Indicate measures that can be taken to avoid disruption of child's life as a result of reunion __________________.

I declare under penalty of perjury that the above is true to my knowledge and belief.  Signatures of board members _________ _____and witnessing of them __________________. Date ______.

You might provide the judge with appropriate wording to use for his injunction, such as:

"It is ordered that James Bart Connelly, born June 5, 2013, be returned to his parent Mary Joan Higgins, born ________ no later than______[say, a few days hence, or immediately], and it is ordered that she become the guardian until James attains age 18. The current custodian may seek judicial review of this decision if he believes Mary Joan Higgins will not be a suitable guardian for ______.  Evidence of that may be submitted to the _____ Court within 30 days." [Make it easy for judge to agree!]

You still need assurance that your chitting work is OK? See:

*Magna Charta* – **The Great Charter   (signed in 1215 AD)**

John, by the grace of God, king of England, lord of Ireland, duke of Normandy and Aquitaine, and count of Anjou, To the archbishop, bishops, abbots, earls, barons, justiciaries, foresters, sheriffs, … and to all his bailiffs and liege subjects, greetings. Know that, having regard to God for the salvation of our soul…we have granted as underwritten… to all freemen of our kingdom, for us and our heirs forever, all the underwritten liberties, to be had and held by them and their heirs…forever.

…**No bailiff for the future shall, upon his own unsupported complaint, put anyone to his "law," without credible witnesses** brought for this purpose. … … We will appoint as justices, constables, sheriffs, or bailiffs only such as know the law of the realm and mean to observe it well. … **All fines made with us unjustly…shall be entirely remitted.**

**How about "and all kidnapped children returned."**
The barons who forced King John to sign also built in the method they would use if he dragged foot. They agreed to choose 5 barons who could report to a larger group of 25

"who shall be bound with all their might, to …cause to be observed, the peace and liberties we have granted…so that **if we [the king]** or our justiciar…**shall in anything be at fault towards anyone… the said four barons shall repair to us …and, laying the transgression before us, petition to have that transgression redressed without delay.**

"And if we shall not have corrected the transgression…within forty days…the four barons aforesaid shall refer that matter to the rest … and those five and twenty barons shall, **together with the community of the whole realm, distrain** and distress us in all possible ways, namely, by seizing our castles… saving harmless our own person and … our queen and children. – " *Magna Charta* [Emphasis added]

**More Ballast -- The Universal Approval of Rescue**
Humans have an instinct to help someone in trouble. People understand when someone is desperate, and they can recognize when a group is trying to conduct a rescue. If it's a small child, everyone understands that this should happen.

As Dr Pridgeon said on April 5, 2019:

> **"There is no law against protecting children from rape**. …Raping children is a crime. It is an abomination. Ordinary decent people regard it with horror but the AFP … do not."

I assume many teachers and many cops have *not* liked having to play the "warden" to an unwilling child and will be glad to hear that something is afoot. They'll be very keen to know what the law actually says. They may also be relieved that Peter Lewis's efforts have not ended by sheer intimidation.

*Lewis, Speaker of SA House, tried his best.*

If there are any good judges in Australia they should want to make a big fuss about the bad judges. Budding law students, too, should be happy to tackle many issues related to legal kidnap.  Recently, in 2019, Judge Sarah Derrington of Australian Law Reform Commission handed down a report critical of Family Law judges. Judge Derrington said 734 families had written their story to the ALRC.  Will they be listened to?

**Dee McLachlan** in the last year has contacted the people on the following list, who each said "It's not my responsibility":

Attorney General, Police Commissioner, Minister for Child Protection, the state's Guardian, Minister for Policing, the Ombudsman, Judicial Complaints Commissioner, the AFP, and the offices of the state Governor and the Prime Minister.

**Victories!** Still, we have only begun to fight. Here's a recap of some victories recorded in this book (shown with chapter #):

2. Don Rufty gets bad judges kicked out of one NC county.
4. Ms Cranmore uncovers the skullduggery of the "Contract."
7. Corey Feldman insists "This [Hollywood] has got to stop."
11. Annie Cossins and Freda Briggs crack down on academia.
12. McLachlan's survey reveals the perfidious role of the ICL.
14. Dr Pridgeon, "out on bail," identifies the AFP criminals.
16. Philadelphia judge Younge is transferred for intimidating.
21. A bill to investigate Holsworthy will tickle Fiona Barnett.
25. Dr Day repents, albeit fictionally, at the Adelaide Fringe.
26. Toffs "unfit to stand trial" are sent to clinic -- fictionally.
27. Qld Police Commissioner Lewis jailed -- non-fictionally.

Court rulings can brighten your day:
*Baron v Walsh* says OK to report perjury while case is running!
*Rhodes v OPO* says free speech sometimes overrides privacy.
*Vreeken v Hardwick* says perjury by social worker won't do.
*Gorman v Johnson,* 1910, verified that "An act of a judge that
   does not relate to his office, is of no force." Wonderful.
*Hazel-Atlas Glass* SCOTUS ordered: nullify the judgment "if
   the fraud procured it…. as required by settled federal law."
Still to come in Appendix E: *G's* case in UK says due process
is nonnegotiable. In Appendix J, European Court in *Johansen v
Norway* says no adopting if mum hasn't had chance to appeal.

See? The law covers everything reasonably – if it be true law. Are there bad people wrecking the courts? Well, out they go then. Show no mercy. This is a life and death matter, and not just for the litigants but for all of us.

*Dee at Gumshoe interview with Justice Kirby*

196

*A daily online news show, non-MSM*



*Arena and Justice Wood*



*Curved knife still in use*



*Savile and Thatcher*                    *photo by Djukanovic*

*In 1966: Jane 9, Grant 4, Arnna 7, children of Jim and
Nancy Beaumont -- deprived of their future.*

Some men are shy. Some men are weak.  Some men are strong.
Some men are fearless.  Meet South Australian Andrew McIntyre
— fearless. As we will see, Andrew, who is now 64, has tried
exhaustively to tell anyone who would listen that he knows who
killed the Beaumont children. Namely, his father, Max. The jig is
now up.  His story can be denied no more.

## A Terrible Day in Adelaide's History

The Beaumont kids went to Glenelg Beach on Australia Day,
January 26, 1966 and "disappeared." Allegedly no one saw them
after that afternoon, but that's not true.

Media say there are many theories to explain what happened. But
no "theories" were ever needed!  SAPOL (police of SA) always
knew. Please feel free to be a bit suspicious of anyone who pushed
any explanation of the case, as they may be been part of a cover-
up.

The fact is that POLICE KNEW ALL ALONG what had
happened. Although Andrew McIntyre had solved the case of the
murder of the Beaumont children *many* years ago, SAPOL had
sufficient prestige with the population of SA – including *moi* – to
be able to belittle all his evidence.

**The Deep State**

I assume there is a layer of "rulership" in the human race that is higher than the various national governments. We can easily trace this "cabal" back to 1913 and it may have been in place well before that. Secrecy is their mainstay. Today the label 'Deep State' is gaining popularity. The point that's relevant to the Beaumont story is that it must be **that group that lent sufficient authority to the SA police and the SA media** to turn the law upside down. They can do this almost effortlessly because they've already got their puppets appointed to all the key positions in society. Those ones "know their duty."

***Here is my interview with Andrew McIntyre, conducted by phone*** on September 13, 2018.

Mary: Thanks for trusting GumshoeNews with your information

Andrew:  It's nice to be listened to.

Mary: We published an interview with your sister Rachel Vaughan, and then I listened to her testimony at the International Tribunal for Natural Justice.  I haven't found even the slightest point on which to doubt her.

Andrew: Maybe there will be some small points that we get wrong, but we know we lived with a terrible man.

Mary: As your family is a bit complicated, let me go over this.  Max had three wives: your mother Margaret who is also the mother of Ruth and the late Clare, and then a wife named Suzanne who is Mum to Rachel and her two siblings who don't wish to speak, and then a third wife who is a lecturer at Deakin University. Is that right?

Andrew: Yes, my mother died in 1967 when I was 13.  My father accused me of murdering her in hospital. Although it's an absurd accusation it is hard to bear.

Mary: So young, she was only 34. Did the coroner of South Australia hold an inquest?

Andrew: I don't think so. Probably Max was the murderer. By the way, in addition to his story that I did it, he has said that two male nurses in hospital murdered her.

Mary: I look for connections around Australia regarding the MK-Ultra program. I got involved in that research in 2005 in America, my "hometown," but not till 2016 did I learn of the Australian connection.

Andrew: I don't know much about it, but when we were children Max used to control us by beating us and giving us minimal food.  He drugged us and kept telling me that I was retarded and that I would never amount to anything.

Mary: The starvation bit is textbook MK-Ultra, but maybe Max was a born psychopath.

Andrew: Possibly, but it is more likely he was trained into it.  By losing all human empathy and moral conscience he became valuable to those he worked for. He fulfilled quite a heavy schedule of body-disposal for the murders they committed.

Mary: How did he claim to make a living openly?

Andrew: he was a wire tapper, employed by Telecom. And he said he was a police informant. In those days, they had people tapping into telephone conversations.

Mary: Do you have any idea who his targets were?

Andrew: I know that he wire-tapped SP bookies.. Some people who were SP bookies were Robert Symonds (Mother Goose), my maternal grandfather Hurtle Horan, and Jim Beaumont .

Mary: I understand that last June, 2017, you were prevented from attending the funeral of your father.

Andrew: Because of the malicious statements that Max had spread throughout the family about my sisters Ruth and Rachel and me, I felt that people at the funeral would have turned on us. So I viewed it from a distance. I bear so much hatred towards my father for the things that he did. His associates in crime were there, however.

Mary: You believe the three Beaumont children are buried at your father's old property in Stansbury?

Andrew: Yes.

Mary: I am trying to establish some context here. A wonderful woman in Victoria, Diane DeVere, told me that Geelong and Ballarat were havens for MK-Ultra in the Fifties. Townsville was too. She said the real boss is the Tavistock psychiatrists. I think the cult run by Anne Hamilton-Byrne in Victoria is in some way connected.

Andrew: I have heard of Anne Hamilton-Byrne.

Mary: She is over 96 years old in a nursing home, I believe. One of her adopted children, Sarah Moore, MD, now deceased, wrote a book *"Unseen, Unheard, Unknown."* There was a police raid on the property that allowed the kids to escape. Her group, like the SA group, is called "The Family." That's the name of a fine movie about her.

Andrew: I have not heard of that movie. I have cousins who have adopted the name Hamilton. Marty Hamilton-Smith is one. He's a recently-retired Liberal Party leader in Adelaide.

POLICE INVOLVEMENT, AND THE TORRENS

Mary: If you prove your story I can assure you that will have a beneficial impact on the people of Adelaide. It will teach them that the South Australian Police has known all long, yet we have been insulted for 52 years by being told of the "mystery" of the Beaumont kids' disappearance.

Andrew: It is not a mystery.

Mary: In Victoria there is an 83-year-old former police detective, Denis Ryan, who wrote a book, *Unholy Trinity,* about the way he was not believed or was told to shut up when he reported on pedophile priests. The recent Royal Commission helped him get a payment of compensation.

Andrew:  They should pay Mick O'Shea. As an Adelaide cop and he dobbed other cops in. See his 2009 interview with Graham Archer on the subject of police corruption.

Mary: I know Mick O'Shea's name because he whistle-blew the murder of law lecturer George Duncan.

Andrew: Yes, Mick said the cops all went for a few beers that night, then they threw some guys into the Torrens. …

Mary: I read at *Wikipedia* that two Vice-squad cops were put on trial for manslaughter but were not convicted — Francis Cawley and Michael Clayton. I believe George Duncan's death wouldn't have been investigated at all but for my dear law teacher, Professor Horst Leucke insisting on it.

Andrew: Mick O'Shea said that the cops knew, before they started, that the night was going to end badly. They knew George Duncan couldn't swim and that he had only one lung. You can ask Mick — if he is still alive. He had to go into hiding as he had ratted on the Brothers.

Mary: Thank God whistle blowers pop up every-where.  Some people have a drive for truth.

Andrew: My sisters and I have been acting on our truth drive for many years.

Mary:  My 2018 Fringe play was about "false memory syndrome." My MK-Ultra friends all claim that the FMS attack on them in the 1990s was worse than the suffering they had early in life – and that's saying something.

Andrew: Being rebuffed by SAPOL is no joke either.

Mary: How do you think your father became a bad man?

Andrew:  I don't know.  He had only a Grade 7 education but he was very smart. He was an all-rounder for talent.

**Second Interview, September 25, 2018**.  Mary: I'd like to ask you about the Beaumont children and about your dear sister Clare. I noticed that Rachel said Ruth was taken by your father to see some of his crimes actually happen. Can you explain why?

Andrew: Ruth told me that she would be taken along to witness things. Max would use his children as witnesses to the dismantling, disposal, burial of bodies. No one else was murdering children at the time, it was our father doing it, along with (Tony) Munro, who is now in prison.

Mary: What about the supposed sightings of the Beaumont children after they went missing?

Andrew: I believe they died immediately. If any children were found at the Castalloy site, they'd be the 3 wards of the state.  Max took 3 kids from Goodwood Orphanage who resembled the Beaumonts. He dressed them and cut their hair to look like them, then paraded them around Adelaide so people would report sightings of them.

Mary: You mean he was so powerful that he could snatch children from a public institution and not get questioned?

Andrew: Max then murdered those orphans. Amazingly my sister Ruth was later taken to a police station and told to make an admission that it was she who pushed them off a cliff. But she refused to say that. She knew about kids being used as "substitutes."

By the way, as I told the *Sunrise* journalist, there were approximately 600 children that went missing from grouop homes.  That was reported in the 2008 Mullighan Inquiry.

Mary:  I am so sorry that you lost your sister Clare and so sorry for her that she lost her life.  Was there an inquest?

Andrew: I don't know. I was asked to file a written report, which I did. I say she was murdered and as usual I think it was Max who did it. She was found in the back garden with a broken neck. It was called a suicide.

Mary: And your mother's death, too, was ruled a suicide.

*Margaret McIntyre (1932-1966)*

Andrew:  My mother had admitted herself to hospital early on New Years Eve in 1966. Max had given my sister Ruth a letter to hand to my mother telling her he was kicking us all out and selling the family home.  He suggested that we could all live with our grandfather. This is why my mother admitted herself to hospital as she was so distressed and had become very anxious.

Mary: How old was Clare when the Beaumont kids died?

Andrew: Clare was 15. The dates of birth for the first three kids of Max (real name Allan McIntyre born 1929) are: Clare, 1951; Andrew, 1953; Ruth born 1955.  When my father left, my mother, Margaret, had to continue to work her full-time job to pay the mortgage.

Mary: Did you report to the recent Royal Commission?

Andrew:  It was statements made to the RC by myself and another victim that led to the 2017 prosecution of Munro, as he had been a Scout leader. He was convicted of rape.

-- End of interview with Andrew McIntyre. Please help him avoid the fate of his mother and his sister Clare.  Won't you?

Each year, tens of thousands of children enter the US, unaccompanied. Congress has tasked the Department of Health and Human Services (HHS) with the task of placing each with a suitable adult sponsor -- someone who can care for them and ensure their appearance at their immigration hearings.

Over a period of four months in 2014, HHS allegedly **placed a number of UACs in the hands of a ring of human traffickers** who forced them to work on egg farms in and around Marion, Ohio. According to the **indictment,** the minor victims were forced to work six or seven days a week, twelve hours per day. The traffickers repeatedly threatened the victims and their families with harm, even death, if they did not work.

The indictment alleges that the **defendants "used a combination of threats, humiliation, deprivation, financial coercion, debt manipulation, and monitoring to create a climate of fear and helplessness** that would compel [the victims'] compliance."   [Does that sound familiar?]

Specifically, the files reveal that, from June through September 2014, HHS failed to run background checks on the adults in the sponsors' households as well as secondary caregivers, failed to visit any of the sponsors' homes; and failed to realize that **a group of sponsors was accumulating multiple unrelated children.** ... HHS policy was that *no* **criminal conviction could disqualify a sponsor**, no matter how serious [!].

In August 2014, **HHS permitted a sponsor to block a child-welfare case worker from visiting with one of the victims,** even after the case worker discovered the child was not living at the address on file... HHS allows sponsors to refuse post-release services offered to the child.  [Emphasis added]

*Stolen: Cecil Bowden, Manuel Ebsworth, Michael Welsh.*  nma.gov.au:

The 1915 amendments to the *Aborigines Protection Act 1909* gave the (NSW) Aborigines Protection Board the power to remove any Indigenous child… It led to thousands of children being taken from their parents. "The Board may assume full control and custody of the child of any aborigine, if after due inquiry it is satisfied that such a course is in the interest of the moral and physical welfare of such child. The Board may thereupon remove such child to such control and care as it thinks best." The 1909 Act provided for all reserves and stations and all buildings to be vested in the Board. It had the power to: move Aboriginal people out of towns; set up managers, local committees and local guardians (police) … and to stop whites from associating with Aboriginals.

The Board had sought the power to remove children, but the 1909 Act only gave it the same powers that applied to neglected white children. The 1915 amendments gave it the power to remove any child at any time and for any reason. Babies were sent to the United Aborigines Mission Home in Bomaderry; girls were sent to Cootamundra Girls Home, boys to Kinchela Aboriginal Boys Training Home. While the Board asserted that children received care and education at these institutions, oral histories from the children themselves show the homes to be harsh and desolate places, offering a limited future. The children were brought up to reject their Aboriginal heritage.

Note: Ms Rilak appeared in Chapter 13, in regard to her diligent efforts to make the courts behave properly. On this occasion in 2017 she was in Civil Court so was not prevented from speaking out. The following is thus a rare performance by a litigant mum.

**HIS HONOUR**: Please be seated. Now, Ms Rilak, I have affidavits that you have affirmed on 17 April 2018, another on 9 April 2018, [etc]. The latter of those was in support of the show cause application… I have read them and will take as read, are there any other affidavits that you seek to rely upon?

**MS RILAK**: There are not, thank you.

HIS HONOUR: I have also read your very helpful submissions. This is an opportunity in this oral hearing for you to make any submissions that you wish to make orally.

MS RILAK: I am seeking the High Court intervening to provide the appropriate direction to the Honourable Chief Justice of the Family Court because I have very little confidence that the things how they progressed even last four or five years, and especially two and a half years that I have not seen my child …

I have little confidence that the things will progress justly and fairly if the matter is still before him. I have been treated in [that] hearing as an alienating parent and it is a legal principle in the Family Court. When there is disclosure of sexual abuse the child is automatically taken away from the protective parent and given to the abuser. There is no inquiry how the child is doing, nobody is looking after the welfare of the child ….

HIS HONOUR: Yes, I have read the Family Court's decision and the decision of the Full Court including in relation to those matters. The difficulties or obstacles at this stage that you face with the show cause application and with your summons are that this Court will very rarely entertain a fresh application when appeals have already been brought … in relation to a number of the matters that you seek to reagitate today…. It would be very rare for this Court to remove those matters while they are still in progress where a particular constitutional issue is not raised.

MS RILAK: Your Honour, if the High Court does not provide an appropriate direction, we have been in a court at eight years…. We lost a lot of money. We lost a lot of time and the best interest, it is paramount in a Family Court, has not been upheld by any of the judges and I might say that there was a consistently and systematic perversion of justice, not only by one judge or one registrar but it is systematic. … My child has been sexually abused. That has been thrown away from the primary justice because apparently there was no prima facie.

HIS HONOUR: Ms Rilak, sorry to interrupt you, I just want to make it clear I have read the primary judgment and the Full Court's judgment very carefully ….

MS RILAK: Your Honour, if the judge made a mistake in the judgment that he will deliver, …there is no way that that can be addressed until the matter goes before the appeal. I have been in appeal proceedings for several times and every time when I bring matter, the colleagues of the judge make the decision, the colleagues that sit in the same building, they meet in the same corridors, they have lunch together. So, your Honour, there is a collusions in a Family Court matters and if the High Court cannot intervene to provide appropriate directions, I have very little confidence that something will happen in the Family Court.

HIS HONOUR: On 4 June the hearing is concerned not just with your interim application to see your daughter on her birth-day, but also your application to, in effect, vary the orders that were made where – to provide for telephone contact and access where you now seek to have, effectively, the primary access.

MS RILAK: …My initiating application to proceed is, I believe, on hold while the contravention orders that the father contravened 400 orders to date, that is still on foot.

HIS HONOUR: Those contraventions concerned the [father's] failure to abide by the access regime whereby you are supposed to have supervised access and telephone contact with your daughter?    MS RILAK: That is correct. That is correct.

HIS HONOUR: What orders is that appealing from?

MS RILAK: That is the order from the contravention order that I filed 2016 … then the barrister was seeking over $33,000 for a one-day hearing. Then it was decided that he cannot seek indemnity costs, so then he settled about $22,000 and then the justice, made the order that within 2 weeks I made … submissions why I should not pay $22,000.

As I mentioned, the Family Court goes by the parenting alienating syndrome which is a legal principle in a Family Court and when there is a disclosure of sexual nature – abuse, then the parent is not able to protect the child but the child is cruelly taken away from the protective parent and given to the perpetrator.

Then it is exactly the same as I would witness a crime in a park and I go to the police and I report that crime and I will be sentenced and I will be jailed because I reported that crime. My daughter has disclosed sexual assault. It was my duty to go to the police - - -

HIS HONOUR: Ms Rilak, …I will hear what you have to say – the submissions that you have to make -- now.

MS RILAK: …For example, my daughter was interviewed by the police in English and her primary language at that time was [not English]. She would not even understand a question put before her. I have never slapped my child and the evidence put before the court was hearsay by the father, for example. The Family Court does not abide by the Evidence Act. They take the evidence on a face value without any evidence really because none of my witnesses were able to give their part of the story – their side of the story. The biggest problem is that the court is heavily relying on the expert witness. In my case, the report writer is not specialised in her field…. She does not publish any peer review. She is not even a clinician.

I think she said she is 30 years in a Family Court. She probably purely just writes the reports and within one hour she can predict the father has no mental illness and the mother has a borderline personality disorder. ….one psychologist and psychiatrist both stated that there is absolutely no traces of any mental disorder. I might suffer from post-traumatic stress disorder because what happened, the trauma and the grief that I have been put through ….

So, I have absolutely no access to my daughter, not even school photos. I cannot even order the school photos that I have paid for because the principal believes, incorrectly pointing to the court order, that I have no access to the school, ignoring that I am supposed to have face-to-face contact with my daughter ….

So the problem is so systematic that I might say they – it actually borderlines criminal negligence. The evidence is fabricated in the Family Court because they do not have to abide by the Evidence Act and whoever pays more money wins; you can buy the justice in a Family Court.

The protective parents have no means of protecting the child – we are forbidden to protect the child. Once the child is taken away there is no one who can care for the child in what state is the child. School will not look after the child. The court does not look after the best interests of the child once the primary orders are done. Not the police, not the judge, the Child Protection Agency, no one looks after the wellbeing of the child while the child is taken away from a good loving and protective mother…

The PAS, which is a legal principle, parenting alienation syndrome, was first coined by the doctor, Richard Gardner, and it was refuted on many occasions, but the Family Court in America as well as in Australia follow this legal principle which says Dr Richard Gardner was of the view that when there is allegation of sexual abuse in a court that the mother wants to take advantage…. And the child is taken away and given to the perpetrator to cure the alienating syndrome which he calls as mental illness. Now, Richard Gardner's theory came to Australia in probably the 1990s by Kenneth Byrne, a Melbourne psychiatrist, have – can I have a drink of water, please?

HIS HONOUR: Certainly.

MS RILAK: Thank you. When Kenneth Byrne presented this to the judges and so the judges do not believe that sexual assault happens in a family setting - - -

HIS HONOUR: Well, Ms Rilak,… I have read the findings by the Family Court and upheld by the Full Court and there was no finding of sexual assault. This Court does not make any primary findings and is not concerned.

MS RILAK: I understand, your Honour, I understand that the balance of probabilities are much lower in a civil court case than in a criminal court case. So, of course, you cannot put a four or five-years-old child in a witness box that will make evidence against the perpetrator. …and that is under section 118 of the Constitution as well ….The task of the Child Protection Agency is to protect the child. Family Court does not have this task. The Family Court is not concerned about protecting the child. The Family Court decides who the child live with and spend time with. – End of excerpt from RILAK's case.

*(L) EO Britannica.com     (R) Lord Justice Peter Jackson*

Law wins. I've always known it. You can laugh at me, call me naïve. But I'm not naïve -- I know what law really is. It is biological. It's an exoskeleton in the species *H sapiens*. It holds the structure of society together despite the fact that, being mammals, we are individually selfish.

People obey authority; they are genetically predisposed to do that. Sure, that can lead to some persons or groups taking over the symbols of law and exerting brute force. Sure. Happens a lot, and happened in the Family Law situation that I am about to describe in the UK (which is virtually identical to the Family Law situation we have been screaming about).

But in addition to "physical" law there is intellectual law. Here the members of *H sapiens* have exercised another of their genetic traits, the tendency to carry thought to its highest reasoned point. For centuries, some of the great minds have worked at the subject of law, extolling justice. "Justice" which is merely a concept, is the antidote to naturally-formed situations of oppression and cruelty.

I am sure there will never be a time when "forces" will cause people to stop thinking about justice, as we are built that way.

As EO Wilson pointed out in 1978 in his book *On Human Nature,* the concept of human rights is plainly and simply an outcome of human selfishness.  We all want what we want -- and *this* inevitably leads to the production of law that focuses on justice.  Yay!

**The Sheffield Case: Interim Order for Children in Care**
A mother in Sheffield, England had the care of her two children. She and the father were separated and he had the kids for a holiday abroad. Upon return he sent only the younger kid back to the mother. She and "others" went to his house and reclaimed the older kid.

As a result she was arrested, the kids were taken into police's protective custody and placed in foster care. At a hearing where she wanted to challenge this, a female judge, Annabel Carr, beat her down.

You don't need to know details about the two parents, as the triumph of law to be celebrated here has only to do with legal *procedure.* Long story short, an Appeals Court judge, in February 2019, ruled that during the aforementioned hearing, **the behavior of the judge was so unacceptable that her ruling cannot stand.**

Maybe her ruling will eventually be found to be the right decision in the case (a re-hearing has been scheduled). No matter, she can't treat a litigant like that.

Law calls for exact correct procedure. There are many, many features built into English law (and therefore the law of US, Australia, Canada, etc) that have to do with setting up the "niceties" of law. They are not silly niceties. They were invented to counteract injustice. The authors of the niceties paid attention to *moral hazard* – e.g., court personnel might misuse their power or litigants might cheat each other. The law can anticipate that and try to stave it off.  All right, I'll get to the point that all Protective parents are waiting to hear: Justice Jackson held, on appeal, in *G (Children: Fair Hearing):*

**Justice Peter Jackson Knows His Onions.**
--1. It is not OK for a judge to walk into the courtroom with her mind already made up without having given the parties a chance to speak. (as we see *routinely* in Family Law Australia). Judge Annabel Carr had said: **"the preposterous proposition you're putting to me, it'll fall on deaf ears"**.

--2. It is not OK for a judge to state that a litigant has no chance of winning, no matter what. (This is usually "taken care of" in Australia's Family Law by the *solicitor*, who has already told his client that the deck is completely stacked against a Protective parent.) Judge Annabel Carr had said **"I'm not making any findings against [the father] because he's accepted the inevitable"**.

--3. It is not OK for a judge to get the person to sign a consent order unless there is real consent, given freely. (Many of the mothers reported to Gumshoe say they were 100% coerced, by a threat of "never seeing the child again.")

Justice Peter Jackson said the consent order in this case was **"secured by oppressive behaviour on the part of the judge in the form of inappropriate warnings and inducements."** He said the ruling could not stand as "there has been a serious procedural irregularity" and "what occurred in this case **fell well outside the proper exercise of the court's powers"**. [Emphasis added]

Interestingly, one of the dirty tactics identified in the case consisted of "isolating" the mother by telling her that all the other players are in agreement. (In Australia, this would mean the court reporters, the Independent Children's Lawyer, the State Guardian, the psychologists and the social workers. Maybe God, too.)
So what happened? Lord Justice Jackson's decision at the appeal level was to set aside Carr's decision. He did make one

change in the actual orders, by altering them to "short-term interim care orders" until the next hearing can take place. Frankly that is not quite good enough. Anything can happen to a child in the meantime. All the thousands of kids who were wrongly sent to a parent need to be looked at again, pronto. It's urgent because a kid's brain is still forming.

In the UK case it seems that the kid had not been *awarded* to the father, but that the father violated the term of the holiday. I know of three cases in Australia where the mum has long since obtained orders in her favor, yet the father does not return the kid (and the judiciary, police, et al say "Ho hum, who cares"). So our work is not over yet.

But for my money, the appellate decision in the UK case is sensational. I say – and Justice Peter Jackson virtually says -- justice *of procedure* is indispensable for everyone's sake and for the sake of law's survival.

He did not go so far as to say that Judge Annabel Carr needs to be in jail. She committed Blackstonian crimes galore and the world needs to become aware of this. I say Lock her up. It was no mistake – she knew better.

## Precedent and Further Development

Australian litigants, you've now got a precedent! Yay! Surely it's great cause for rejoicing. Too bad it didn't happen locally, but the locals, in every state—Tas, Vic, SA, NSW, Qld and WA -- can now vie with one another to forge ahead quickly and make more developments, thrilling developments.

Hey, this is better than Abe Lincoln – the legal profession can free the slaves.  In doing so they can free all of us from the child-trafficking mafia that has been destroying our judiciary. Even now, that mafia remains self-assured of their right to treat all humans as their plaything.

Gonna be findin' out otherwise.

Woo-hoo.

## Validation for Protective Parents from the UK Case

Natasha, at the website ReserchingReform.co.uk, carried Justice Peter Jackson's ruling and asked for comments. She got 139 in a few days. I list some to show, as Chapter 9 showed for the US, that Australia's situation is part of a global plan to hurt families. It couldn't be a matter of judges being sloppy or tired.
I'll omit the names of the commenters:

* I was treated badly throughout my court case. First Judge had obviously come to a decision about me before I entered the court. Greeted all except me, then went on to threaten change of custody because of something I did as a child 26 years ago.

*It is time for the absurd  'At risk of future emotional harm' -- as a cut and paste method to force a parent into silence when faced with flawed and un-evidenced accusations.

*The rest of the case had been heard by DJ Cooper, who was completely fair and held very different views from DJ [edited] who shouted over me, would constantly interrupt when I was answering a question, tapped his fingers impatiently on the table and sighed and huffed throughout my time on the stand.

*My McKenzie friend talks about the hostile environment of the family court as he was threatened with imprisonment and even told he was guilty of contempt, for asking the right questions.

*At my recent court hearing, the judge who had only been at one hearing over a year ago, gave me or my barrister no time to defend myself against a comment made by Cafcass that I had highly influenced my daughter. We were brought into court for 'housekeeping' whereby I was threatened with my children going into care or my daughter to live with abuser.

*Family Courts and judges are an absolute disgrace. They actually said in court that the child was young and attractive enough to be adopted. That wording doesn't sit right with normal people. I'm ashamed to be British.

*It's important to note that the Court of Appeal was correcting malpractice, rather than an error of law, and yet there will be no personal consequences for Judge Carr at all.

* The public should demand this Judge be struck off by the Bar.

*In December 2016, Judge [edited] granted an interim care order on my children in Hull combined courts, after social worker [edited] lied under oath. My defence fell on deaf ears. Judge [edited] had already made up his mind and my kids spent 6 months in care before East Riding of Yorkshire social services were forced to withdraw applications for full care orders. My kids and myself are still being maliciously targeted to this day.

*As you say, this happens frequently in the Family Courts – because it can. It would be interesting to know who took the step of going to the Court of Appeal on the judge, I've not heard of this being done after a Family Court hearing before.

*This is not unusual but it isn't just confined to parents. Other family members can be threatened with jail – and often sent to jail – for minor misdemeanours or even nothing at all when 'not playing ball' with Social Services and bending over backwards to appease them. It is the most corrupt system. When is it going to change, when anyone is going to do anything about it?

*MP John Hemming seems to care. Many judges are in cahoots with 'professionals' who lie to assist them in winning care or adoption orders or are getting backhanders or similar to remove as many children as possible from loving parents.

*My imprisonment is due to breaching of injunction forbidding me to criticise social worker. I got 6 month suspended for criticism of public servants. This judge's wife owns children's home.

*(R) Dame Quentin Bryce, Governor General*
*(L) Dame Marie Bashir, b 1930, psychiatrist, violinist, Patron NSW police*

Australian Mother of the Year (1971)
Director of the Rivendell Child, Adolescent and Family Service

Chair of the University of New South Wales Third World Health Group (1995–2000)

Consultative role of senior psychiatrist to the Aboriginal Medical Service (1991–1999).  Consultative psychiatrist Juvenile Justice Facilities (1993–2000)

Appointed Governor of NSW on the recommendation of Premier Bob Carr, 2001
Patron of the Australia-Vietnam Medical Trust (2002)

Patron of Opera Australia, the Sydney Symphony Orchestra [Bashir is a violinist]

Australian Living Treasure;  Companion of the Order of Australia

Grand Officer of the National Order of the Cedar by President of Lebanon

Chancellor of the University of Sydney (Appointed 2007)

Honorary Member UN Development Fund for Women (2004)

Chevalier of the Ordre National de la Légion d'Honneur by President Sarkozy (2009)

218

**Fifteen Questions for an Interview with Dame Marie:**

Do you believe the things Fiona Barnett is saying at her web-site PedophilesDownUnder.com?

What do you think is the extent of pedophilia in NSW?

Did it surprise you that the NSW Police asked you to be their patron after you left office as Governor?

When you worked with troubled adolescents, did you see any signs of mind-control or dissociation?

Did any of your patients show evidence of being tortured?

What did you think of the cult run by Anne Hamilton-Byrne?

Have you ever filed a mandatory report of child sexual abuse?

Do you agree that NSW's Wood Royal Commission white-washed police corruption?

How serious do you think the problem of police corruption is today in NSW?

Do you believe Fiona Barnett's claim that a "thug" harassed her after she reported a pedophile?

If that proves true, what do you recommend we do about it?

Do you think NSW has any cops who might be eligible for compensation like that given to Detective Denis Ryan of VIC who was blocked in his efforts to deal with pedophile priests?

Had you heard of ritual sacrifice in the Great Hall at Sydney University while you were Chancellor?

Did you know the late Anne Conlon of St Sophia College?

On 1 June 2019 the DCP of NZ, which is called the OT, went to Hawke's Bay Hospital to take a newborn boy. This led to a confrontation in which the hospital seemed to side with the DCP, de-activating the swipe card of the midwife so she could not be with her patient. A Maori group learned that 3 Maori babies per week are "uplifted" from their homes. Causes listed: poverty, drugs, lack of parenting skills.

Ms Jacoby Poulain of the Health Board objected to baby-uplifting. Her boss criticized her for commenting to media. She replied that her **legal obligations under the Public** Health and Disability Act 2000, among other laws, **override those of the board's Code of Conduct and Ethics…."** She also said "A big part of this picture is that **society still doesn't know that huge injustices are occurring in this space.** In other words, you've got one side of the community yelling out injustice and state abuse and the other side saying 'sit down be quiet'."

The Hawke's Bay mum gave birth by Caesarian. Her rellies in the parking lot had to use a megaphone to talk to her. The media coverage may lead to a No Confidence vote of NZ Prime Minister Jacinta Ardern. *I hereby call for a vote* of no confidence against every holder of a position related to this child stealing.

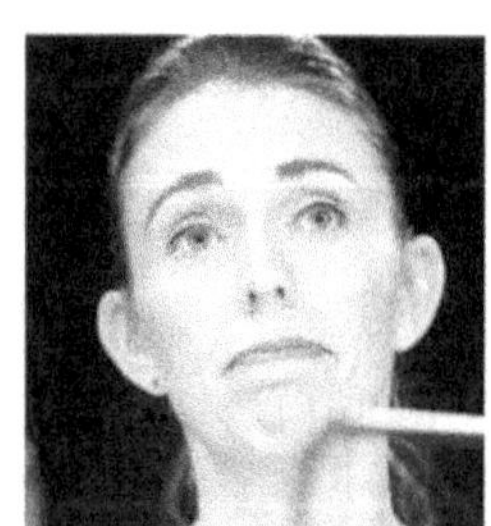 *PM Ardern.*  *J Poulain*

Let's have a competition in the Antipodes to see which country can overcome the crazed racket soonest. It is noteworthy that the indigenous people of NZ are the ones that have had the brains to unify. Recall that an aboriginal group of Strong Grandmothers has stepped up to the plate in Oz to do something about forced adoptions.

I ran a survey by hiring a company, SurveyHero, to post it on the Net from October to December 2018.  It got 79 responses.  On the opening screen I said it was about FAILURES of the Family Court. I assume the responders are persons who have complaints. Hence it is not a scientific survey of all Family Court litigants.

**Introduction**

1. The first question identified who responded to the Survey. They were 70 Protective Mothers, 4 Protective Fathers, 7 Grandparents (or Aunt/Uncle), and 2 Victims over eighteen. [That question was answered 83 times, which I have attributed to re-starts. – DM] "Percentages" are % of persons answering the particular question.

2. How old was your child when you realised that SEXUAL ABUSE (or a serious injury) occurred? Number of responses: [79 responded to this question]
    Less than 2 years: 11x chosen (13.92%)
    2 – 4 years: 33x chosen (41.77%)
    5 – 8 years: 27x chosen (34.18%)
    9 – 12 years: 7x chosen (8.86%)
    Older than 12 years: 1x chosen (1.27%)

3. Who was the first person the child disclosed sexual abuse to? Number of responses: [75]
    Mother or Father: 60x chosen (80.00%)
    Grandparent: 5x chosen (6.67%)
    Teacher, school counselor, etc: 3x chosen (4.00%)
    Someone else: 7x chosen (9.33%)

4. Who did you contact once you realised there had been abuse? Number of responses: [77, These were multiple choice questions, and the responder was invited to tick more than one box, e.g., MC]
    Family (40)
    The police (41)
    My doctor, the hospital (34)
    Child Protection Services (48)    Other (27)

5. When you confronted the perpetrator about the abuse, did they
do any of the following? [77, MC]
   Deny the allegations (60)
   Threaten with violence (24)
   Advance proceedings into Family Court (34)
   Call me delusional, resulting in me having to undergo mental
   health assessments (37)   Other (17)

**Believing the Child**

6. How many people [the number] has your child disclosed to so far?
In most cases the child had disclosed to many people. [These are
their raw answers. It was a fill-in question]:

11, 8, 2, 3, 4 or 5, 1, 20, 13, Only me, 2, 1, 3, 5, 2, 1, 10+, Minimum
dozen people, 6, dozens, approx 20 re sexual abuse and 30 plus re
physical abuse, 4, 6, 4-5, 8, 5, 6+, Four, 5, 10, 10, Three, 3, 4, more
than 10, 3, 3 generations family + doctor, [Because child would not
go into formal interview room alone with JIRT staff, case was
closed, child was 3yrs old.] 5, Three, 6, At least 10 people, 6, 7, 7,
11, 5, Grandmother and me, to school friends also, 5, 2, 15, 9, I don't
know apart 2, 9, 6, 10, fourteen people, 10, To many to count, 3,
Grandchild disclosed witnessing the oral sex to more than 10 people
and assaults to 23+, 7, 1, Qld police child protection, 3, 4, 10, At
least 15, 7+, 6.

7. Who DID believe your child?  Did someone (even one person)
from the categories below believe your child? [71] [MC]
   Members of my family (58)
   Anyone in the police, detective etc (21)
   Child Protective Service Officers (15)
   Social workers, supervised visit personnel (12)
   A doctor, nurse, medical personnel (29)
   Court reporters, supervision services (3)
   ICL, independent child lawyer (2)
   Your psychologist/psychiatrist (41)
   Court appointed experts (6)
   Court appointed psychiatrist (3)
   The judge (the court) (2)      Other (20)

222

8. Who did NOT believe your child?   Did someone (even one person) from the categories below not believe your child? [71] MC
    Members of my family (11)
    Anyone in the police, detective etc (38)
    Child Protective Service Officers (38)
    Social workers, supervised visit personnel (21)
    A doctor, nurse, medical personnel (6)
    Court reporters, supervision services (40)
    ICL, independent child lawyer (47)
    Your psychologist/psychiatrist (2)
    Court appointed experts (40)
    Court appointed psychiatrist (23)
    The judge (the court) (49)     Other (12)

9. Who DID BELIEVE your child — but was/were PREVENTED from speaking or testifying in any way? [63]  [MC]
    Members of my family (43)
    Anyone in the police, detective etc (7)
    Child Protective Service Officers (8)
    Social workers, supervised visit personnel (10)
    A doctor, nurse, medical personnel (19)
    Court reporters, supervision services (0)
    ICL, independent child lawyer (1)
    Your psychologist/psychiatrist (22)
    Court appointed experts (0)
    Court appointed psychiatrist (1)     Other (16)

10. Who DID BELIEVE your child — but did NOTHING TO ASSIST? [53]  [MC]
    Members of my family (12)
    Anyone in the police, detective etc (23)
    Child Protective Service Officers (20)
    Social workers, supervised visit personnel (10)
    A doctor, nurse, medical personnel (12)
    Court reporters, supervision services (6)
    ICL, independent child lawyer (7)
    Your psychologist/psychiatrist (7)
    Court appointed experts (9)    Court appointed psychiatrist (4)
    The judge (the court) (9)     Other (10)

**General Questions**

11. In what State do you live, and where did this happen?
    NSW – 28          SA – 6   VIC – 11   WA -- 8
    QLD – 20          TAS – 3          NT – 0


And it was spread across the country. There were no clusters. Examples; Coffs Harbor, Wyong, Weston, Maroochydore, Mandurah, Northern Beaches, Lindfield, Bendigo, Mandurah, Hillston, Nerang, near Mullumbimby, Bunbury, Buderim, Nulkaba, Lismore, Rockhampton, Cairns, Wynyard, Newcastle.


13. How many children are involved in the family court issue? [73]
    1 child 34x chosen (46.58%)
    2 children 22x chosen (30.14%)
    3 or more: 17x chosen (23.29%)


14. How many years have you been 'involved' in family court proceedings? [72]
    Less than 1 year: 4x chosen (5.56%)
    1 – 3 years: 25x chosen (34.72%)
    4 – 8 years: 25x chosen (34.72%)
    More than 8 years: 18x chosen (25.00%)


15. How much MONEY have you lost (or spent) trying to achieve (or manage) your outcome in the family court, so far? (TOTAL of solicitor fees, transcripts, supervised visits, court fees, etc) [71]
    0 – $50,000: 28x chosen (39.44%)
    $51,000 – 150,000: 16x chosen (22.54%)
    $151,000 – 350,000: 16x chosen (22.54%)
    $351,000 — 750,000: 7x chosen (9.86%)
    More than $750,000: 4x chosen (5.63%)


16. As a result, have you… [67]
    Lost ownership of a house? (32)
    Lost a job, or business? (38)
    Lost support or partial support from friends and/or family? (50)
    This has put me in debt (50)

**How Evidence Got Handled**

17. Do you believe crucial evidence of abuse or injury was disregarded in your case? [69]
    Yes: 67x chosen (97.10%)      No: 2x chosen (2.90%)


18. Which of these people / departments DISREGARDED evidence of abuse/injury? [67]  [MC]
    Members of my family (7)
    Doctor, medical personnel (13)
    The police (46)
    Your psychologist / psychiatrist (7)
    Social workers, supervised visit personnel (29)
    Child Protective Services (44)
    ICL, Independent child lawyer (52)
    Court reporters, pre-court services (43)
    Court appointed psychiatrist (29)
    Court appointed experts (45)
    The judge (the court)  (58)   Other (9)


19. Was evidence DESTROYED?    (I do not want to lead the witness.) [64]
    Yes: 36x chosen (56.25%)     No: 28x chosen (43.75%)


20. Which of these people / departments DESTROYED evidence of abuse? [51]  [MC]
    Members of my family (3)
    Doctor, medical personnel (2)
    The police (18)
    Your psychologist / psychiatrist (1)
    Social workers, supervised visit personnel (11)
    Child Protective Services (11)
    ICL, Independent child lawyer (14)
    Court reporters, pre-court services (9)
    Court appointed psychiatrist (7)
    Court appointed experts (10)    Other (20)


21. Did the Judge destroy evidence, or order that evidence be destroyed? [55]
    Yes: 17x chosen (30.91%)    No: 38x chosen (69.09%)

22. What kind of evidence was DISREGARDED by Police, CPS or
the Family Court, etc? [48] [MC]
    Video evidence (16)
    Audio evidence (16)
    Photographic evidence  (22)
    Medical reports (25)
    Blood evidence, and/or DNA (2)
    Child disclosures reported to me (38)
    Child disclosures to various authorities (police, CPS etc) (36)
    Psychology or psychiatric reports (27)
    Any Expert (8)
    Reports of serious behavioural problems, fears etc, (31)
    Reports that my child ran away from  police, or from a
    home (9)     Other (6)

23. What evidence was DESTROYED, Trashed, or was ordered to
be destroyed? [48] [MC]
    Video evidence (6) audio evidence (8) Photographic evidence (9)
    Medical reports (6)
    Blood evidence, and/or DNA (1)
    Child disclosures reported to me (12)
    Child disclosures to various authorities (police, CPS etc) (11)
    Psychology or psychiatric reports (5)    Any Expert (1)
    Reports of serious behavioural problems, fears etc (12)
    Reports that my child ran away from the police, or from
    a home (1)   Other (5)

24. Do you have physical proof (documents, injunctions, emails, etc)
of the deliberate destruction of evidence? [56]
    Yes: 21x chosen (37.50%)   No: 35x chosen (62.50%)

**Family Court Judges**

25. Who was the Judge in your case? [59]
Carmody, Murphy, Bell, Justice Tree, Judy Turner, Magistrate
Kaeser, Scarlett, Boyle, Paul Howard, Johnston, Stewart, Deputy
Chief Justice Faulks, Amanda Tonkin, Shane Gill, Justice Rees,
Cronin, Judge John Coker, Judge Baker, Judge Kelly, Howard,
Vasta, Justice Kirsty McMillan, Andrews, Justice Berman, John

Geral Barlow, Catherine Carew, Justice Johnson, Croker, Loughnan, Forrest, Rees, Cleary, Stephen Scarlet, Middleton, Meyers, Magistrate Joe Harman, Judge Coates, Stuart Austin, Justice Tree, Young, Demack, Duncanson, Piter, Tree, Harmon, Justice Philip Butchardt, Justice Steven Strickland, Austin, Cronin, Multiple Judges, Robert Benjamin, David Monaghan, Judge Ryan, Magistrate Berman, Pascoe, Aldridge, Ryan, Coates, Justice Barry, Jarrett, Justain Curtain, Murphy, Kent, Federal Magistrates Jarret and De Mack, Justice Kent, Justice Forrest, Justice Hogan, Judge Cassidy, Justice Forrest, Justice Katherine Carew, Loughnan.

**Experts and Lawyers**

26. Who was/were the Expert/s in your case? [58]
(A few names did keep surfacing. One was Dr Rikard-Bell)

27. Anyone that you believe OBSTRUCTED JUSTICE for your child? [57]
(Respondents named countless names and organisations — across the board. Not shown here.)

28. Did a court EXPERT, i.e., PSYCHIATRIST, claim that you were "coaching" — i.e. that you were trying to sway or enhance your child's version? [66]
    Yes: 53x chosen (80.30%)   No: 13x chosen (19.70%)

29. Who was the Psychiatrist / Expert? [54 replied with names.]

30. Do you believe someone in the authority tried to "COACH" your child — and sway your child's version to him/her admitting to less or no abuse? [62]
    Yes: 42x chosen (67.74%)    No: 20x chosen (32.26%)

31. Who do you believe "COACHED" your child — or altered their original disclosures, or outlook? (The next question is about changing reports etc) [48]  [MC]
    Members of my family (9)
    Doctor, medical personnel (3)
    The police (13)

Your psychologist / psychiatrist (7)
Social workers, supervised visit personnel (8)
Child Protective Services (14)
ICL, Independent child lawyer (19)
Court reporters, pre-court services (16)
Court appointed psychiatrist (10)
Court appointed experts (13)
The judge (the court) (4)     Other (20)

32. Who do you believe CHANGED, or FALSIFIED REPORTS
— or COMMITTED PERJURY?  [53]
    Members of my family (7)
    Doctor, medical personnel (5)    The police (17)
    Your psychologist / psychiatrist (9)
    Social workers, supervised visit personnel (12)
    Child Protective Services (26)
    ICL, Independent child lawyer (28)
    Court reporters, pre-court services (25)
    Court appointed psychiatrist (16)
    Court appointed experts (15)
    The judge (the court) (21)     Other (19)

33. Do you have physical evidence of this corruption, falsifying
reports and people committing perjury? [59]
    Yes: 34x chosen (57.63%)    No: 25x chosen (42.37%)

34. Explain briefly who, what and how evidence was falsified — if
applicable. [36 responded. Not shown here.]

35. Have you presented this proof to authorities? [53]
    Yes: 22x chosen (41.51%)   No: 31x chosen (58.49%)

36. Were you told by your legal representative NOT to report abuse
— as you could be at risk of losing custody? [63]
    Yes: 49x chosen (77.78%)   No: 14x chosen (22.22%)

37. Did the police, at any time, REFUSE to investigate abuse claims
because the matter was before the Family court? [62]
    Yes: 50x chosen (80.65%)   No: 12x chosen (19.35%)

38. During or after court proceedings, did anyone warn you to NOT REPORT any further abuse — or any further claims? [54] [MC]
    Doctor, medical personnel (4)    The police (17)
    Social workers, supervised visit personnel (8)
    Child Protective Services (16)
    ICL, Independent child lawyer (17)
    Court reporters, pre-court services (8)
    Court appointed psychiatrist (6)
    The Judge (the court) (18)        Other (30)

39. What "punishment" would be put on you, if you did bring forward more accounts or evidence of abuse? [55]
Nearly all were threatened that they'd never see their kids again.

40. SUPERVISED VISITATION: Have you in the past, or are you presently in an arrangement of supervised visitation'? [64]
    Yes: 35x chosen (54.69%)    No: 29x chosen (45.31%)

41. Were THREATS ever made by supervision personnel that you could lose visitation rights, or your child altogether? [56]
    Yes: 26x chosen (46.43%)   No: 30x chosen (53.57%)

42. Anything to add for advice and threats? [36 responded]

43. Was your child asked to reveal their disclosures in an interview — with their abuser present?: [59]
    Yes: 26x chosen (44.07%)   No: 33x chosen (55.93%)

44. Did the court ever PREVENT you from seeking medical or psychological assistance for your child? [64]
    Yes: 42x chosen (65.63%)
    No: 12x chosen (18.75%)    Other: 10x chosen (15.63%)

45. Did the ICL (Independent Children's lawyer) speak with the child they were representing or rely on information given to them? [62] [Sorry, this question is confusing]    Yes: 10x chosen (16.13%)
No: 31x chosen (50.00%)   Other: 21x chosen (33.87%)

**Mental Health Issues**

46. Did your child undergo 'therapy' ordered by the Judge to 'make them understand that the abuse
NEVER happened'? [64]
   Yes: 12x chosen (18.75%)
    No: 38x chosen (59.38%)   Other: 14x chosen (21.88%)

47. Did you have to undergo MENTAL HEALTH assessments?
[65]   Yes: 35x chosen (53.85%)     No: 19x chosen (29.23%)
        Other: 11x chosen (16.92%)

48. At any point, was your child removed from you, because your were/are labelled an "ANXIOUS PARENT"? [64]
   Yes: 12x chosen (18.75%)
   No: 36x chosen (56.25%)   Other: 16x chosen (25.00%)

49. (Sorry to ask) What abuse do you believe occurred — or was disclosed in some way?   [64] [MC]
    They don't want to say (7 kids)
    Touching, Fiddling, (38)
    "Milking the cow" (1)
     "Doodle vomit" (another example) (13)
    Photographic or video sessions (camera flashes) (12)
    Penetration (18)
    Bleeding rectum etc (9)
    Injuries, scars (29)
    Rashes, swelling, other medical issues (26)
    Descriptions of sex toys (7)
    Rituals (7)
    Urolagnia, other fetishes (6)     Other (39)

50. In general, what is or has been the emotional state of your child — on the whole? [65] [MC]
    Okay, managing (8)
    Appears to be dissociating (33)
    Behavioural problems (anger, etc) (48)
    Has run away (16)
    Suicidal, or talked about that (32)
    In fear of his/her life (25)        Other (25)

51. Was the abuser, the alleged pedophile, investigated? [60]
    Yes: 15x chosen (25.00%)    No: 45x chosen (75.00%)

52. Was the abuser, the alleged pedophile, prosecuted? [61]
    Yes: 3x chosen (4.92%)    No: 58x chosen (95.08%)

53. Did anyone go to jail? [63]
    Yes: 2x chosen (3.17%)     No: 61x chosen (96.83%)

54. Did the court order that your child/ren live with their abuser after evidence of abuse was presented?  [61]
    Yes: 40x chosen (65.57%)    No: 21x chosen (34.43%)

**Justice**

55. If you only had ONE choice what OUTCOME would you vote for? [65]
    A Royal Commission into Family Court: 28x chosen (43.08%)
    A  Special Unit, with the power to prosecute, to investigate criminality in the Family Court, CPS etc — with the promise to jail anyone that broke the law: 35x chosen (53.85%)
    Financial Compensation: 2x chosen (3.08%)

**Postscript to Survey**: By Dee McLachlan.   I was born in Africa. To the African peoples, Motherhood is sacred, and is a powerful spiritual component of a woman's life. There is something special about how Motherhood is viewed, and the empowering aspects of it.  Somehow in Australia, we have drastically lost our way with regard to "family."  Are we also becoming unable to gauge pain, grief, and love?

*European Court of Human Rights, Strasbourg*

This case was decided at the European Court of Human Rights in Strasbourg, France.  Any citizen of the 47-member countries can bring a case after he or she has exhausted domestic remedies.  In *Johansen v Norway* (1997), a child had been taken from the mother at birth.  The mum made the case that this violated her rights under Article 8 of the European Convention on Human Rights, on the right to respect for private and family life.  The judges were 8 to 1 in favor.  The European Convention on Human Rights reads:

"1. Everyone has the right to respect for his private and family life, his home and his correspondence. 2. There shall be no interference by a public authority with the exercise of this right except such as is in accordance with the law and is necessary in a democratic society in the interests of national security, public safety or the economic well-being of the country, for the prevention of disorder or crime, for the protection of health or morals, or for the protection of the rights and freedoms of others." [sort of like the US Fourth Amendment]

I will describe the family only as is shown in the court transcript. Earlier, Ms Johansen had a baby boy – we must call him "C" – in 1977 when she was 17. She sought help from welfare and lived with a man who mistreated her and C, eventually spending 2 years in jail for his drug issues.

"Friction arose" between mum and the child welfare authorities. The son, C, began to receive psychiatric treatment and in 1989

was sent to a special school. In November he was taken into care by Barnevernet on the basis of danger to his development."
The court notes:
"The police assisted the child welfare authorities in enforcing the decision. After spending the period from November 1989 to early January 1990 at the Child Psychiatric Dep't Haukeland Hospital, C. was placed in a children's home...."

I can't make a judgment on the rightness or wrongness of that. Anyway, the case is not about the son, it is about Ms Johansen's daughter, codenamed "S" who was born in December 1989. On December 13, the Chairperson took S provisionally into care.
The grounds for this was the physical and mental state of the mother from which was assumed her inability to care for baby.
The baby was placed in a short-term foster home at which mum was allowed to visit her twice a week. "She did not challenge this access arrangement, which was not based on any formal decision." [Good heavens how would she know how to go about challenging it!] One of the expert opinions stated
"I regret that, as the expert in this case, I am not hopeful about her future ability to take care of her children, although she undoubtedly loves them and is attached to them."

Turning to the rights of the *child* it was stated: "It is of decisive importance for S's personal development that she now gets the opportunity to attach herself to persons whom he may regard during her adolescence as stable and secure parents." At that point, Mum asked for a second opinion but the state would not allow it so she got one herself from a Mrs Lise Valla. That psychologist's opinion, filed when S was 4 months old, said:

"I cannot find that there are sufficient reasons for depriving [the applicant] of the care of her [two] children.

**Adoption.** I will jump over more of the discussion to point out that what is being discussed here is official termination of the parent's right. The justification went like this:

"Adoption had the advantage of clarifying the situation and of creating security and stability for the child and the adoptive parents. Moreover… in order to secure the child's development and its relationship with the persons who would permanently assume the care, it would be appropriate for the authorities to deprive the applicant of all her parental responsibilities. …"

So it took years to get to the Human Rights Court. In 1991 the City Court had a 40-day hearing presided over by one specially appointed judge. The Ministry was the defendant. There were two *appointed* experts. They upheld the decision to take the girl:

"According to the Child Welfare Act, the starting-point is that a child should grow up with his or her natural parents. [But] the general rule as it cannot be interpreted so as to allow the child to be subjected to considerable harm."

Note: I personally do not advocate "parental win at all costs in every case." I think there is much to be said for protecting a child from harm. Even as we speak, there are plenty of children who are in terror every day of the week. Still, it was not listed at Strasbourg that the girl, then a year old, was being harmed.

Professor Freda Briggs in her 2014 submission to the Royal Commission told harrowing tales of children who were very happy with their *foster* family, being spirited away (not to the natural parent but to other foster placements, including against the will of the loving foster carer!)

So, by now, you are wondering if parents, generally speaking, have a high-priority right to raise their child. The Europeans do have such a right. The Article 8 of their convention says:

"1.Everyone has the right to respect for his private and family life… 2. There shall be no interference by a public authority except … for the protection of the rights … of others."

"Therefore the Court reaches the conclusion that the national authorities overstepped their margin of appreciation, thereby violating the applicant's rights under Article 8 of the Convention. …". Victory! A symbolic victory as the kid was already adopted, but the mother won the principle of her rights.

Ten million people stand up to this at same time around the world!!!! People cannot do this alone!!! God bless her!!!

Everyone should join in and start exposing the CPS.

Now that's a Backbone!!!! Would love to buy her a lunch!!!

BRAVE AND COURAGEOUS -- WELL DONE YOU ARE A NATIONAL HERO -- BRING FORTH TRIALS

What a brave, together lady. Wish there were more like her.

I am also an EX Social worker in Edinburgh. I agree with everything! There needs to be more of us talking about it.

Lots of social workers in the UK, why is only one speaking? out? Maybe if more did there would be strength in numbers.

They adopted my 6 year old daughter!!!!! I hate them!!!!

Finally we get it from a Worker who has been in the system; the Social Services are driven by corruption and money.

Her integrity and professionalism – I'm deeply grateful.

Brian Gerrish -- what a diamond he is.

Nothing new here, this has been going on, part of English Culture within all local authorities to take away children and vulnerable people from their perfectly safe and caring homes and put them where they are abused and damaged.

The DoJ and DEA have also been allowed to rain Unholy Terror on legitimate ethical doctors. See Doctors of Courage

Cherry Blair and that whole gang were just evil.

You couldn't invent a movie of this. Well done, UK Column

Document fraud is so common in social care as is ignoring and arranging the exit of whistle blowers.

You informed us about Cherie Blair at a time 2000 when Tony Blair set adoption targets to ensure more were taken.

*Aussie babies have rights!*

I suggest a voluntary *Covenant* of Rights.  It skips the middleman – government. Each Australian who wishes to join this covenant may do so, and can then expect both to benefit from it directly and to participate in protecting other covenanters.

We the covenanters agree that we have the following rights and will support others in obtaining them:

1.  the right to survive and to find food

2.  the right to live with unpolluted Nature

3.  the right to bodily integrity and to be left alone

4.  the right to a home and to privacy

5.  the right to freedom of thought and speech

6.  the right to make enforceable agreements

7.  the right to be helped in an emergency

8.  the right to be appreciated for our work

9.  the right to have possessions

10. the right to determine who will govern us

11. the right to defend against violators

12. the right to be different

In 1997, as a member of the NSW upper house, known as The Legislative Council, Ms Arena France intimated that three persons were conspiring, in regard to the Wood Royal Commission, to protect NSW police. Colleagues were unhappy that she spoke and created an Inquiry. It reported:

STANDING COMMITTEE ON PARLIAMENTARY PRIVILEGE AND ETHICS INQUIRY [bolding added]:

If a **Member uses offensive words** against another Member, makes **imputations of improper motives** or personally reflects on another Member. If Members fail to withdraw, and in appropriate cases, apologise, **they may be suspended** from the House under the Standing Orders for disorderly conduct. 6.3.12 Should Mrs Arena fail to withdraw and apologise the **need to protect the dignity of the House and its Members will, in the Committee's view, be best served by requiring Mrs Arena to be suspended** and remain suspended from the House until she has made the necessary formal apology and withdrawal ….

As the protective sanction determined by the House should be aimed at **remedying the damage caused by Mrs Arena's wrongful conduct**, the House should not leave the decision as to the terms of the apology and withdrawal to Mrs Arena's discretion. **The danger exists that if Mrs Arena is to choose the words** in which to express any apology and withdrawal, she may do so in a manner which **leaves the community in doubt** as to what she is withdrawing, and … is truly apologising.

6.3.13 If Mrs Arena merely makes a token apology **in grudging or qualified terms,** suggesting that the real problem has been misinterpretation by the House rather than Mrs Arena's own conduct, the **damage done to the**

**House and its reputation** ...will persist....[That is exactly what is happening; let's put an end to it!]

The Committee therefore recommends: That Mrs Arena be called on to withdraw the allegations made in her speech which involved imputations against (a) the Premier, Mr Carr (b) the Leader of the Opposition, Mr Collins(c) the Royal Commissioner, Mr Justice Wood.

[In her defense]:

--Mrs Arena says she has been vindicated by the fact that after the NSW Police Service began to investigate the documents tabled by her in the House, she was advised by Senior Police Officer that certain persons whose conduct was being investigated, based on the material she had provided, may face prosecution. -- The publicity created by her speech on 17 September 1997, and the subsequent tabling of documents, **has encouraged more alleged victims to make complaints**, and provided the impetus for increased inves-tigations, and ultimately prosecutions to be undertaken.-- She had already **suffered extreme emotional distress and significant financial expense** in the aftermath of her speech.

Committee has given careful consideration to Mrs Arena's submission that there is **no material in the speech of 17 September 1997 or in the evidence placed before the Committee justifying a conclusion that she is likely to commit further contempts of the House.**
Mrs Arena's submission to the Committee dated 30 January 1998 and her supplementary submission dated 16 February 1998 both referred to and annexed documents containing **very serious allegations made to her** that various persons who occupy, or have previously occupied, high positions in public life **have engaged in sexual misconduct towards children.** [These] have **been demonstrated to be totally without foundation.**
**Fiona Barnett's Chat with the Royal Commission**

Victims of child abuse were invited to appear at private meeting with Australia's Royal Commissioners. Fiona Barnett participated in a two-hour interview. She later wrote:

"At my hearing, I asked the commissioners what they planned to do differently in order to avoid the pitfalls of the last royal commission into institutional responses to child sexual abuse in New South Wales — The Royal Commission into the New South Wales Police Service [better known as the *Wood* RC].

"It was sparked by complaints of a paedophile ring in 'high places' in Sydney, including established Christian churches, the Department of Children's Services [holy cow!], and the NSW Education Department [holy double cow!]. It was alleged that this paedophile ring was being protected by the NSW Police Service [No holy cow there – that's de rigueur.]

"[However], based on the subjective opinions of a pro-paedophilia organisation, Commissioner Wood's 1997 report dismissed the existence of high end paedophile networks. It concluded that child abuse memories could be artificially created as a result of third person suggestion [False Memory].

**This Is the Time for an Apology to Franca Arena**

Now that the Royal Commission has published its findings, in 2018, we know that 17,000 Australians said they suffered child sexual abuse. Franca Arena deserves an apology. More that that, she deserves great thanks and admiration for having tried to do what ultimately the big RC did.

A formal apology to Mrs Arena would teach citizens that there is such  a thing as parliamentary privilege.  I wish parliamentary privilege would be used voluminously.  Second, it would start a debate about *secrecy*.

240

# Appendix N. Rachel Vaughan's Effort To Tell Police about Murders. Vital!  Help!

The first person I contacted in my search for information about the Adelaide pedo-rings was Rachel Vaughan, based on a comment she made about scrapie (long story) at Fiona Barnett's website pedophilesdownunder.com. Then I came to see that Ms Vaughan is Olympic medal material for the high jump, or the "most letters sent to SA police since the First Fleet."

On the next page is a sample of her efforts.  Why not have it laminated and wear it on your back on Rundle Mall in Adelaide?

People will also be amazed to hear that Rachel knows about the death of Louise Bell. Per the *official* story, an abductor reached in the window of the room where two sisters were asleep and carried Louise out. As an Adelaidean in 1983, before I had the slightest knowledge of conspiracies, I was surprised that such a story could be said to match the published picture.

*Bell's bedroom* *in Hackam*

But thus far, Rachel is unable to get any cop to hear her story just as her brother Andrew McIntyre (see Appendix A) is always ignored as to the true fate of the Beaumont children in 1966.

What's this doing in a book about reunion of Protective parents with their child? It is to demonstrate the almost unbearable fact that the police upper echelon do not work for us. They are enslaved, I believe, to the pedo-rings -- and are proud of it!

Here's the laminate-able and magnifiable page of Rachel's work:

## EFFORTS TO GET ATTENTION of SA POLICE

*April 2006:* *STATUTORY DECLARATION* to SAPOL re:
1) Max's assault on me with knife, at 30 months of age; 2) in 1977 saw a mutilated child in Macklin Street bathroom.

*June 2007:* Letter to many MPs re lack of investigation by SAPOL, naming Max as the body boy for 'the Family,' also to Doug Barr, Major Crime and Det. Supt. Phillip Hoff.

*8 Aug 2007:* *RESPONSE:* letter from Paul Holloway, then Minister for Police. Declares that Major Crime Detectives "show there is no evidence linking [Max] McIntyre" to this.

*21 Aug 2007:* *INTERVIEW* with Annette Burden and Scott Barker, SCIB, detailing abuse of me and witness child's dismembered body as well as a man's right foot, 1977.

*5 Sept 2007:* Second letter to politicians re SAPOL, to MPs: Paul Holloway, Jane Lomax-Smith, Michael Atkinson, Jay Weatherill, Carmel Zollo, Nick Xenophon, Kris Hannah.

*20 Sept 2007:* *RESPONSE* from Wainwright, Police Complaint Authority: *"cannot justify commitment of personnel and resources."*

*8 Feb 2008:* 4th letter sent to officials re 1) SAPOL refusal to act on our allegations; 2. Beaumont kids seen deceased in boot of car by my siblings in 1966.

*23 Sept 2009:* I rang Paul Llewandowski SCIB to say that a child (age 11) is living on same property as Max, and is in danger. Llewandowski tells me he won't take the report.

*Sept 2009:* My Stat Dec that I saw a young girl being killed under my house in 1983, and that Max filmed us together.

*19 Jan 2012:* Told Crimestoppers' David Sheridan: 2) Max is the body boy for a group who have conducted murders of kids for decades; 3) Louise Bell is buried at 8 Macklin St., Edwardstown, under a slab of concrete.

*23 Feb 2012:* My letter to SCIB asks why my deceased sister Clare's psychiatrist wasn't questioned re her allegations.

Then in 2012 Rachel Vaughan gave up. That lasted for three years but in 2015 it came to her attention that others were trying so she re-started.  Even that continued to prove futile, so she took a new step in 2019 by giving testimony to the International Tribunal for Natural Justice. It has already had 118,000 views!

**Fraudulent Convictions**

Note that Rachel was not just trying to tell SAPOL about past murders but current and even likely *future* murders. In the video'd testimony to ITNJ she states that she was an eyewitness to the murder of her age-mate Louise Bell and that the person who killed Louise was Rachel's father, Max McIntyre. It was thus not the man convicted of it, Dieter Pfennig.

*Dieter Pfennig, in prison in SA for life*

Although Louise's death took pace in 1983, Pfennig wasn't tried till 2016! I imagine his trial was a way for the pedo-rings to protect Max, their bodyman, who was still alive when his daughter Rachel was beginning to get some listeners. (Max died in 2017).
I'll mention a few things from the trial of Pfennig to show how the media make fools of us. Remember this all came up 33 years after the murder. (Originally Raymond Geesing was convicted but then freed in 1985). There was a pyjama top left on the grass of a nearby home, and it was found to have DNA that pointed at Pfennig. The cloth had been dunked in the Onkaparinga River "to which Pfennig had attachments!" Oh please. I have attachment to the entire Atlantic Ocean.

Another "clue" was a phone call made by someone with a "European accent" telling how to find Louise's earrings under a rock. Pfennig, a German, had the requisite accent. He was also said to have made boast-like remarks about the child to various people. (*Note:* Would any murderer be so foolish?)

The Chief Inspector in the murder of Louise was Graham Bennett Fraser. In 1987 he was accused by two girls of having abused them, one of whom was the same age as Ms Bell. What did SAPOL (South Australian Police) do to punish Fraser? They demoted him from Chief Inspector to Inspector. At the time, a statute of limitations prevented his being prosecuted but when the Rann government changed the law in 2007 he was tried.

> Judge David Smith said: "The crimes occurred in his home, his shed and a swimming pool belonging to a friend … From any position, this offending was loathsome... You were a senior police officer, and these girls had no one to turn to…."

Hang on a minute! Girls today, and their Protective parents **have no one to turn to**. Trust me. We have checked out many cases. Anyway, I am not trying to solve the Bell homicide, I prefer to call attention to the list of Rachel's unrequited efforts. We must wonder, Is every one of her addressees *in* on the game?  -- the game being "Make every protected pedo stay safe." Is this SAPOL's motto? *Non fiat jusitia, ruat caelum–* "Don't let there be justice, though the heavens fall"?

Another point to add. Social media now makes it possible for whistle blowers to reach a big audience. But the nature of social media also makes it possible for a whistle blower to be harassed more or less anonymously. Rachel Vaughan has suffered about as much from Facebook as she did from the father's abuse. OK that's an exaggeration. But there is something especially painful about being accused of things you did not do, and of having your relatives suffer from all the dirt flying around. Note: I believe some employees of "the system" are at it fulltime to smear, intimidate, and scare. They, too, are victims.

I do not want the world to think less of Adelaide because of all this. It is a beautiful coastal city. The citizens are as ignorant as I was of the behind-the-scenes evil. They need to get with the program and capture the many devils. There's no other way.

There are some very incriminating items in Dee McLachlan's survey. Regarding 9 of them, when the child grows up he is likely to say "How did no one intervene to help me?"

(These are  percentage of 79 persons who took the survey):

**40%  say that their child speaks of suicide.**

**30%  say the child is in fear of his/her life.**

**63%  say the police refused to act, "as *the case is sub judice.***

**57%  say  the reported abuse was not investigated.**

**53%  say "The Court prevented me from seeking medical**
         **or psychological help."**

**73% say the abuser did not get prosecuted.**

**53% say "I believe someone in authority coached the**
         **child to say that the abuse did *not* happen."**

**50% say the judge ordered child to live with the abuser.**

**11% say the child "had a bleeding rectum, etc".**

My definition of judicial kidnap is:  court-ordered removal of a child *from* a Protective parent when there has been an allegation of sexual abuse.  I feel sure there is malice involved – by the court, no matter how much we want to shy away from that fact.
Still, I offer here a lesser condemnation. I say the judge himself is mentally ill. Let me concentrate on the item that says 11% of the 79 responding parents said a child had *"bleeding rectum, etc."*

If your child had a bleeding rectum you would rush him or her to get medical help. Let's overlook the fact that this could land you in jail (wrongly designated as the abuser). Or at least "written up" as a parent who is over-anxious and is out to blame your ex. Yes this does happen a lot. But I will not rehash that story.
We are talking about the *child's* urgent need. He or she wants adults to come to his/her rescue.
We know of an adult in Australia who has a report from a physician, who is willing to state under oath, that her injury is

caused by a curved knife up the rectum. Indeed I know of another child who at this minute is suffering the same harm but no one will assist. The mum is turned away, always.

Dee McLachlan has been pursuing this subject for a year. Dee has approached all who could possibly relieve the problem – from parliamentarians to  the "Office of Public Integrity."  No help is forthcoming and it may not change soon. It's the judiciary that makes the custody order, knowing what is going on. Have we lost our humanity?  Can we really stray that far?

As I said, I see the judge as ill. The diagnosis I offer is BRS. (Yes I mean it as a rejoinder to PAS parental alienation syndrome and FMS, false memory.) BRS stands for Bleeding Rectum Syndrome. Next time you meet a judge ask them if they suffer BRS. It has nothing to do with the judge's rectum, it's his/her *brain*.

Glance again at the list of percentages. The judge knows that the court's removal of the caring parent from the child may cause suicide. (It has done so.) We've got a sick system here. The time has come to put a stop to it, whatever that takes.

The person ultimately responsible is you. And me. And your neighbor. We can't ask a mentally ill judge to clean it up.  It has gone on for ages – with no abatement and certainly no punishment.  It is never going to just correct itself. As far as I can deduce, the system is run by thugs who get the judges to underwrite the sex-trafficking of kids. (There's also the claim that the judges belong to a club and prize the whole disgusting practice of hurting people.)

We have got to stop being so "considerate" of the thugs, and the obeisant judges, and also stop being so hands-offish about them. They are in want of the old *caput gerat lupinum* routine. They are outlaws if the paid personnel won't capture them.

*Necessitas non habet legem.* Do what you must do. It's normal. It's legal. Think about it. Debate it. Approach the so-called officials.

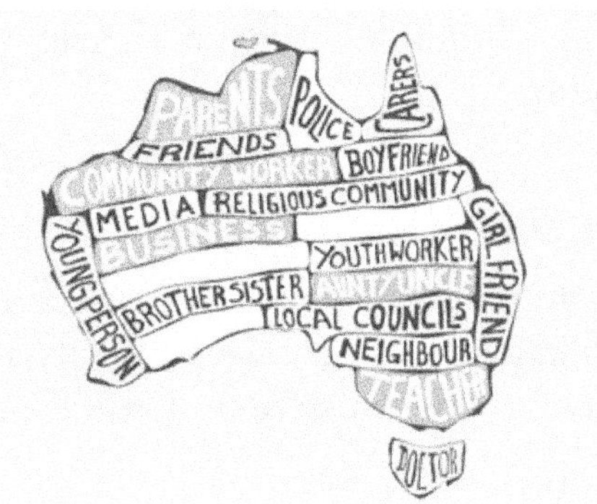


*NSW poster: "Protecting Children Is Everybody's Business" [Too right!]*

At the website Humansarefree.com, Fiona Barnett has presented a 9600-word article to explain the pedophile crisis. Note: all of the following is the theory of Fiona, quoted and abridged, by Mary Maxwell. Passages related to child-trafficking are bolded.

## Immigration

*The International Refugee Organization was instrumental in bringing here many Slavs, Ukranians, Serbs, and East Europeans after 1945.

*These people, when in their home country — Poland, Lithuania, etc — were already Luciferians and the Nazi party attracted them into working for the Nazi's.

*After Yalta, when many countries became Soviet satellites, some of these people would have been in trouble under the Russians because of their collaboration with Germany.

*Fiona's supposed grandfather, Peter Holoczak, was one of the people allowed to sneak in to Australia. He claimed to be the husband of her grandmother, Helen. Barnett later found out that he was not Grandma's spouse, and she was glad of that. Peter abused Helen's son (Fiona's father) and her brothers. Fiona's family lived in Engadine, NSW. She mentions a corridor of Nazi immigrants (not Germans) settling all the way south from Sydney to Wollongong.

*One of her tormenters was Leon Petrauskas, also known as Dr Mark. She describes him as a Jesuit Luciferian, who ran religious services in Engadine.

*Luciferianism has roots in ancient Babylon and Egypt. **It turns right and wrong upside down**. [That seems the key point.]

*Over time, the immigrant descendants of the Luciferian pedophile refugees collaborated with existing Luciferian dynasties and **infiltrated** Australian **government** and influenced law.

**Fiona's Childhood**

*Fiona's father, who has complex PTSD and DID, once told the relatives: "Everything Fiona says about the Satanists is true, but we just don't tell her, for her own good."

*Fiona (maiden name Rylco, after her real maternal grandfather) was child-sex-trafficked to California in a cargo plane, having been gassed and **stuffed in a wooden crate like an animal.** She was trafficked to the annual summer camp at Bohemian Grove attended by notable politicians, businessmen, and VIPs.

*At Bohemian Grove, she was one of a group of children dressed as teddy bears and **hunted for sport by men** to the theme song Teddy Bears Picnic and witnessed a ritual murder.

*Kim Beazley, Sr, a **parliamentary leader in the Labor Party, was the head of the trafficking operation.**

*The trafficking is a **coordinated worldwide affair run by the CIA with ASIO** as its Australian administrator. Jim Rothstein, a New York Police detective, told Fiona that the CIA were behind a blackmail operation in which **child prostitutes were used to honey-trap and compromise politicians,** military brass, top businessmen, and key government officials.

**Luceiferianism** *Luciferianism is arranged according to a hierarchical structure which vaguely resembles a caste system. At the very top sit 13 dynasties including Rothschilds and royals..

*Below this group sit the commoners who can never attain higher status because they lack the desired bloodline. These are your random covens based on nationality (e.g., there's a strong Scottish coven in Bundaberg), sexual orientation (e.g., Bond University has a lesbian coven), gang membership (bikie gangs).

***It is from these lines that the cult obtains 'breeders' – women who are forced to breed unregistered babies for sacrifice and sex trafficking.** Their behaviour is usually barbaric and requires constant management to stop them exposing the cult.

***Child rape, torture, and murder are routinely practised within Luciferianism for various reasons.** These acts are established traditions thought to appease their god Lucifer. Some members get off on raping and murdering kids, but not all. **It is believed to bestow power on the practitioner. Sodomy is called the 'fountain of youth' and is thought to transfer the child's youth to the abusing adult.**

*Luciferianism is a cult. Cult indoctrination alone is a strong enough influence on human behaviour. But the impact of indoctrination is reinforced by fear of the consequences of betraying or exposing the cult. **The number one rule of Luciferianism is – there is no such thing as Luciferianism.**

*Mind control is a Luciferian tradition stemming back thousands of years. Luciferian offspring are trained in witchcraft, and psychic manipulation of the physical elements.

***Children are tested at age 3 for whether they should be raised with conscious or dissociated awareness of their cult involvement.** [Mothers may well panic over that statement.]
[Note: I now switch to **using the first personal pronoun** for Fiona. This article entirely a direct quote from her article – MM]

*Children with a strong ethical objection to cult practises are never made aware of their involvement. These children are forced to dissociate through trauma, and their minds fragmented. My husband and I were two such children.

**Eastern Star**

*This was an OTO themed ritual murder, with Kidman and four others dressed in rather camp, theatrical coloured robes based on the Eastern Star pentagram which dominates the Alistair Crowley **Thelema** offshoots **including Freemasonry.**

*I bring your attention to a document titled, Ordo Templis Orientis, INTERNATIONAL CAMP, OASIS AND LODGE MASTER'S HANDBOOK, Revised Spring Equinox, 2002. Page 33 of this document lists the name **Kylie McKiernan as treasurer of the OTO**. Kylie was in a **senior administrative position within the ABC broadcasting network in 2015**, when the ABC TV show Media Watch publicly attacked me.

*Catherine Hand took me aside for a little chat. "Fiona, have you seen my ring?" she asked me. She showed off her ring which was an Eastern Star pentagram with coloured gemstones.

*This was linked to a South-East Queensland DOCS pedophile ring that police raided in the year 2000. **DOCS [Department of Child Safety!!] staff were intentionally placing foster children with pedophiles** who were prostituting the kids out.


**Influence on Government**

*The Luciferian pedophiles have infiltrated all areas of Australian government, education, health and human services. **They have control over the police, media, universities, defence forces, parliament, schools, health services, churches of all denominations, psychiatric hospitals, and fake child abuse advocacy organisations like Bravehearts.**


*I came forward to Bathurst police detectives after Tor Nielsen reported to police that **he saw 60 children ritually raped in the same hall by NSW Police and Catholic priests** who worked at nearby St Stanislaus College. Multiple St Stanislaus pedophiles have since been convicted for ritual abuse crimes.

*So, I found a strong link between Antony Kidman and Hillsong church. Hillsong church was founded by a **pedophile for the** sole purpose of procuring child trafficking victims and produce kiddie porn snuff films.

## MK-Ultra

*My recruitment as a MK-Ultra lab rat began with my abuser Leonas Petrausaks who was an expert in sea creature poisons. He attended the Australian School of Pacific Administration, a cover for MK-Ultra activity, weaponised anthropology, and MK-Naomi bio-weapons research conducted in Papua New Guinea. he worked alongside notable MK-Ultra recruits Margaret Mead, and Hitler's bio-weapons scientist, Erich Traub.

*After Whitlam threatened to expose Australia's CIA agents, and shut down the CIA facility at Pine Gap, the CIA orchestrated a coup against Whitlam. Whitlam was forced into compliance since the CIA had him compromised as a pedophile.

*Antony Kidman and Leonas Petrauskas were close associates of Dr **Harry Bailey** who was trained in **deep sleep** methods by MK-Ultra perpetrator Ewan Cameron. The CIA funded Bailey's MK-Ultra deep sleep project at Chelmsford Private Hospital. I was subjected to MK-Ultra procedures by Harry Bailey, in the presence of Kidman and Petrauskas, at Chelmsford in Sydney.

*Antony Kidman returned to Australia in 1972 after years of work at St. Elizabeth's Hospital, Washington DC. John Gittinger was the CIA's head psychologist. He developed the test battery to assess potential CIA case managers and agents.
***All top Australian military brass were Luciferians. Most Sydney University staff were**, too. Child victims were **sourced from Luciferian** covens, various cults, BoysTown, juvenile detention centres, **child protective services,** foster care…

***The CIA continue to make money out of child trafficking** by laundering it through banks and funnelling it **into CIA terror organisations that have decimated Syria** and other nations.

*Note: Validation of Barnett's claims can be sought in books by Kathleen A Sullivan, Cheryl Hersha, and in Wendy Hoffman's "Enslaved Queen."*

# Appendix R. Andrew Wakefield's Book, Waging War on the Autistic Child – Parents Accuse of Munchausen

*A camp at St Croix*

The poster above is an ad for a children's camp in Virgin Islands. The reference is to the New Testament, Galatians 5:22:

"But the fruit of the Spirit is love, joy, peace, forbearance, kindness, goodness, faithfulness, gentleness and self-control. Against such things there is no law."

Cherilyn is a missionary there, bringing God's love. I learned about her when reading a book by Andrew Wakefield, MD, entitled *Waging War on the Autistic Child.* Believe it or not, it is the story of parents in Arizona whose 5 autistic children were grabbed by the state on the basis that both parents had "Munchausen syndrome by Proxy." It involves a court, a CPS agency, and surprisingly some doctors who I can only think of as vicious. Cherilyn says at her blogspot:

"On July 15, 2010, I got a phone call from my parents telling me that the government had taken my 5 autistic siblings away. They had been taken without any notice or warning and been placed into three different foster homes. That call tore my heart into shreds. I have never had such a physical reaction to any words the way I did when my mom told me they had taken the kids. I felt like I had been stabbed through the heart, I couldn't breathe, and I was shaking …All of the charges are 10,000% false. My parents have never done anything but love and follow God, and teach their children to do the same. They have invested their lives into their children so this was insane and has thrown my family into Chaos.

"Please God, You are the only one that can make this nightmare end. You can take it and turn it into a 'Happily ever after.' Please God, let your mercy reign over them and your justice fall on their accusers.  Bring truth to the situation and peace over their hearts."
~Cherilyn Derusha

**Parental "Guilt"?**    Andrew Wakefield's book is about his researching the gut problems of the kids in this family to prove that the parents were not "making it up." He writes:

"Following an analysis of the family's prospect for reunification by the Foster Care Review Board, part of the Judicial Branch of the Arizona Supreme Court, on May 23, 2011, the findings were prepared or submission to the new judge – Judge Brutinel's successor – Judge Ethan Wolfinger.

"The board's clear view was that the children's biological parents should forfeit all right and that the children should be placed in permanent foster care…. The biological parents had not shown meaningful progress, which included a signed confession of their guilt…. guilt of medical, emotional and psychological abuse of their children.

**Judge Wolfinger, showing wisdom**…ordered that the children be returned home to their parents. The mother likened the scene to the wining players' Superbowl celebration seconds after the final whistle.

"The children asked for and were granted permission to bounce on their beds. At this stage the beds were just mattresses and box springs on the floor.  To have erected the children's beds before this day would have been tempting fate."
-- Andrew Wakefield, MD

I (Mary) add a word about the prestige of physicians. Dear Docs, If others around you behave unethically, either punish or ignore them – don't imitate them! We need all the pillars of the community we can get. We give you authority, so please deploy it. I consider Dr Kieran Le Plastrier's letter (in the Afterword) to be of highest value in this regard. It stunned me when I saw it.

Here is a poem I wrote for the website ageofautism.com, in anger over the unconstitutional vaccine court. It stakes my position against Louis Pasteur and the first vaccinist, Dr Jenner.

**If for Doctors**   (in the style of Rudyard Kipling's *If for Boys*)

If you should learn who gave us this Vaccine Court,
And realize your participation in a crime,
If you can wonder how it be sport
For more babies to be allowed to lose their mind,

If you can hear that Pasteur was a cheat,
And know that Edward Jenner hoaxed us all,
Start to see two centuries of science in defeat,
And determine to ask for a complete recall,

If you can brave the remarks that other men may send you
And not turn back, but keep a forward gaze
And be the kind of friend you
Would wish for, with or without "professional" praise,

To end this tragedy before it brings more terror,
To help society put dishonesty on the wane,
And turn around colossal error,
No matter whose the loss, or whose the gain,

Then the families will transmit a grateful roar,
And joy will swiftly break out 'round the earth,
Truth'll make a good old court appearance, and what's more,
The title "Doctor" will resume its former worth.

*San Francisco 49ers "taking a knee" -- refusing to stand during the national anthem   --  Photo: AP*

An Adelaide mum, whom we will codename Barbara, is opting to boycott, sidestep, or otherwise protest the corruption of the Family Court by not showing up at the upcoming trial of her case. Isn't that marvelous!

Lest anyone think I put her up to it, no.  I would never have thought of it and was amazed to hear that Barbara feels so strongly that she will "risk all" by not showing up.

It is well within a judge's discretion to issue a bench warrant for the arrest of someone who refuses to appear at trial, even a civil trial, as it is a contempt of court to do so.

**South Africa, pre the 1990 Referendum**

Gumshoe's editor, Dee McLachlan, has already told us about her father, a doctor in South Africa, who attended a military parade but sat out the national anthem. He did this in the super-apartheid city of Pretoria in the early 1960s.

I don't know the words to the then-anthem but presumably McLachlan could not agree with them or just had to find some way of saying "I do not go along with this system of treating Blacks like dirt."

It takes courage to protest. Cops had their truncheons at the ready. South African poet Breyten Breytenbach once said that when he noticed the police approaching him (for civil disobedience) he looked down and saw that his legs were wobbling. Archbishop Tutu of Cape Town also once said, when someone congratulated him for marching against apartheid, "You should have been closer. You would have heard my knees knocking."

**Barbara's Dilemma**

Barbara is of course worried that if she blows it, she may get more than a prison sentence. She may "lose the case." Even though the authorities have not one shred of cause for removing her child – they don't even pretend to have a cause – it could still happen.  In fact it does happen a lot. And she does not want to do this to her kid who has already suffered plenty of physical attacks.

But she asks – isn't it even *more* contemptuous of court to attend a farce of a trial?  And wouldn't attending make her a participant, a contributor to the now-standard miscarriage of justice that goes on in Family Courts when a protective parent has alleged sexual abuse of a child?  (I think yes.)

**Knee-Takers**

In the 2016-2017 season, footballer Colin Kaepernick did not feel right about the US national anthem, which states that his country is "the land of the free."  Colin did all of us a favor by not mouthing words he could not agree with.  How could he agree when he had seen police brutality on the streets?  Kaepernick's action was much criticized, but others started to imitate him.   I don't know how much this did to change police brutality but it was better than nothing. Rosa Parks' caper of not moving to the back of the bus led directly to the end of "segregated transport."

**Tragedy of Our Courts**

Readers of Gumshoe know that I consider the court sacred. It is proper for the court to demand respect, and punish those who disrespect it. But you CANNOT respect a court that has been taken over by "outside forces." And you SHOULD NOT.

256

As with other mothers that we have written about, Barbara is not provided with due process.  Her valid evidence gets thrown out, while evidence from the other side, such as hearsay, is accepted even though it should be inadmissible.  She is not allowed to question her accusers (an 800-year-old right), as she can't find out who her accusers are!

**SOLIDARITY.** Pleases show solidarity with Barbara howsoever you can.  On the football field, one alternative to "taking a knee" consists of forming a line in which everyone locks arms with the next guy. I think we all ought to do that, bigtime.
Regarding the Family Courts' (and Childrens Courts') mockery of the family and deprivation of the rights of the child, I say *enough is enough.* Go Barbara!  Oops, I mean *don't* go, Barbara!
Or to put it neutrally:  Ms Barbara, kindly do whatever you can to obstruct the forces that are determined to take away our great weapon, the law.  If that means boycotting your trial, we support you. If that means you get imprisoned, we thank you.

***

Note: Here is the offending 1998 High Court precedent *M v M:*

> "…the **resolution** of an allegation of sexual abuse against a parent is subservient and ancillary to the court's determination of what is in the best interests of the child. The Family Court's consideration of the paramount issue which it is enjoined to decide cannot be diverted by the supposed need **to arrive at a definitive conclusion on the allegation of sexual abuse.**
>
> "The Family Court's wide-ranging discretion to decide what is in the child's best interests cannot be qualified by requiring the court **to try the case** as if it were no more than a contest between the parents to be decided solely by reference to the **acceptance or rejection of the allegation of sexual** abuse on the balance of probabilities."

Mason CJ, Brennan, Dawson, Gaudron, and Toohey JJ agreed.

# RECAP OF LEGAL ANGLES YOU CAN USE

1. Identify the wrongdoer – who kidnapped your child?

2. Try to get him/her prosecuted. Kidnap is a crime, the officials who kidnap never have immunity regarding crime.

3. But wasn't it ordered by a judge?  Ditto #2.

4. Will the DPP or AG balk at the prospect of prosecuting? Then of course that is a Blackstonian crime against justice.

5. Did a judge rely on Gardner's parental alienation theme? That is unjust; there is no support for that CIA trick.

6. Were you lured into a Parental Responsibility Contract? A contract is not enforceable if there was fraud or coercion.

7. Were you threatened to sign a Consent Order? Ditto #7.

8. Have you been gagged? Was it to conceal court's crimes? Go get a megaphone and tell all, but use pseudonyms.

9. Were you unfairly jailed for contempt? Ditto #8.

10. Are you accused of coaching? They must show evidence, including evidence of how this actually harmed that child.

11. Have government-appointed people hurt the child? Sue them for assault, deceit, IED, malicious prosecution, etc.

12. Did they harm you, the Protective parent? Ditto #11.

13. Is there a situation that needs urgent action? Ask civil court for injunction to do something or stop something.

14. Did lawyers or doctors cheat?  Get them defrocked.

15. Have cops harmed you? See # 2, 4, 11, and 12 above.

16. Should you go after big fry or small? Either is fine.

17. Can you ask civil judge to rule as a Court of Equity? Yes.

18. Identify ministers or pollies who criminally neglect duty.

19. Can you present good legislation to Parliament? Yes.

20. If judge acted wrongly, petition for Error Coram Nobis.

21. Can you run for office? Yes, or recruit good candidates.

22. Did someone slander you? Sue for defamation.

23. What of criminals steadfastly protected? Outlaw them.

24. Can you start a Truth Commission? It's a sin not to!

25. Can you perform citizen's arrest? It is common practice.

# AFTERWORD
## by Kieran Le Plastrier, MBBS (Hons), MP, PhD

*Dr Le Plastrier, a GP with expertise in psychiatry, wrote this letter to a Mum. His keen eye for law and ethics is great and we feel it has liberated all of us. With his permission, it is the Afterword. All family names and one social worker's name (Smith) are pseudonyms. A doctor and a psychologist are "initialed."*

Dear Brenda [Ella's mother], Please understand that I am not offering this as an opinion regarding the facts of the various allegations. Instead, my primary concerns arise from what I see are dangerous consequences of decision-making based on inappropriate application of principles of law and the professional requirements to act in a child's best interests. If even a sliver of what has been alleged is found to be likely beyond a reasonable doubt then a travesty of miscarriage of justice has occurred. I hold significant concerns about a series of major issues with the quality, timing, and underlying professional reasoning that is used throughout the case. I wanted to note some of these for you.

1. The most cogent and reliable departmental correspondence in all the information we have shared is, ironically, the [Departmental] document dated 2016 and addressed to Barry [the father]. In reviewing all the documents it is the most contemporaneous with the initial allegations and investigations and therefore should be heavily relied upon for its direct and unequivocal summation of the grounds for Ella's removal from her father for 'sexual acts and exploitation'. I note there is reference to Brenda [mother] having been assessed by a psychi-atrist at the time and to be found without mental health issues.

2. The timeline of investigations and professional reviews is also critical. In respect of whether or not allegations of 'coaching' were made out, I note that Dr JB an independent forensic psychiatrist appears to have addressed this directly and found no basis for the allegation. The full report from this assessment

would be useful to review. I see also that a second competent psychologist came to the same conclusion around the same time. This appears to be part of the initial 2016 investigation so its proximity to the original disclosures is important as a matter of law and to the question of fact.

Your summary suggests the Protective Services had not formed a view of psychological risk of abuse by you towards Ella and it was only after the father alleged a Notice of Risk. This notification would have required a very high level of scrutiny as it is a standard defense ploy for any person charged with sexual abuse or other abuse of a child to allege that the child's other care givers are deliberately fabricating a story of abuse. This counter-notification is made in order to introduce the element of doubt at a future trial of the alleged perpetrator's own charges.

3. I remain alarmed by the failure to investigate the new cut to Ella's limb in 2018 when I have heard firsthand that Ella alleged her father inflicted the wound with a knife. This is professional misconduct of the highest order given the 2016 and 2017 allegations and would easily reach the threshold for professional misconduct requiring urgent Ministerial investigation. Anything less than a Ministerial complaint and formal response would be a gross dereliction of ministerial duties under the relevant child protection Act given that Ella was an active client of Protective Services at the time, and hence ultimately the responsibility of the Minister at the time.

Hiding behind a procedural issue of delegated responsibility to a CEO or other entity cannot satisfy the *prima facie* responsibility of a Minister of the Crown to ensure their portfolio and responsibilities are enacted with due regard to the lives of the people whom they serve, especially when the allegations are of such a profound criminal threshold -- aggravated assault occasioning grievous bodily harm.

4. I am concerned by the cursory and incomplete annotations of interactions between the psychologist SN and Ella in which the person writing the report (Ms Smith) makes contradictory and

non sequitur statements.  Specifically, she reports that Ella has 'not retracted' (p 26) her earlier allegations and without any substantive statements (in the notes and reports I have seen) the psychologist appears to continue therapeutic interventions under the assumption that said allegations are false or coached.

I am alarmed that the psychologist appears to be acting on the instruction of the department when her professional and ethical duty can ONLY be to the child.  Page 24 of the report you showed me has in it in the last paragraph a statement that 'the department' holds grave concerns for Ella's safety in the care of her father given the historical allegations of abuse "which are believed to be false".  False according to whom? False according to which professional assessments and contemporaneous investigatory notes? False according to which inconsistent and implausible statements by the child?
But wait, in the same report Smith states "Ella has shared many highly detailed accounts of being abused. Irrespective of inconsistencies regarding timelines, specific events etc. the department cannot discount the possibility that Ella could have experienced sexual physical harm and be at risk of experiencing this in the future with in the care of Barry." SN goes on to report that Ella "denied that her mother had ever encouraged her to say things that were not true".  This last statement was made in 2019. This indicates that departmental personnel have concluded that a witness, a child of 6, 7, 8 and 9 years of age over all that time, has been lying for three years.

It is profoundly unprofessional to continue to allege such perjury and not bring charges against the child and mother for the myriad 'false' statements they must have made under oath in that time, if the department has proof that the allegations are false and coached.  As such, I am highly suspicious that the reason such charges have not been laid is that this would entail a test of the truthfulness and veracity of any evidence upon which the department is basing its own allegations of perjury.

5. I would like to know why a criminal investigation has not apparently been conducted into the allegations of sexual abuse and alleged grievous bodily harm in a criminal court. Is this the case? As such, the department relying on a family court judge for the finding of facts regarding allegations of abuse of this highly serious and criminal nature, and with such obviously credible witnesses, is also a matter of grave concern.

Smith points to a Family Court judgment as the Department's justification for sustaining a belief (not a fact) that the abuse is unsubstantiated. This is grossly negligent should it be the case. Instead, if the DPP or some other independent authority of law had deduced that there was insufficient evidence to charge Barry there might be grounds for a position of uncertainty -- although I would point out that to deny the allegations is to suggest a 6-year-old child is a liar and perjurer over three years.

Unless I am wholly misled about the nature of justice in [your State], these allegations require an appropriate test as potential criminal acts and it would most certainly not be the purview of a child protection department to determine the facts of such serious allegations. In a breathtaking contradiction in the 3rd paragraph of p24 of the Smith report, the author states that despite having evidently concluded the 'facts' of the case without appropriate jurisprudence – i.e., that the abuse was "unlikely" – "the department cannot discount the possibility that Ella may have been exploited or abused at some point by Barry".

6. In a final comment on the report signed by Smith, to conclude that family repatriation with the alleged paternal abuser, when the alleged abuse is obviously of an extreme nature, without the satisfaction of an appropriate jurisprudence determination of facts, and flying in the face of three years of consistent reporting by a child, who also clearly says she does not want contact with Barry, is the grossest level of negligence by a government department I have ever had the misfortune of bearing witness to in any child related matter. It beggars belief that the authors of

this report could conclude that a repatriation or family contact process is anything less than a perpetuation of abuse -- an abuse they are paid and allegedly supposedly trained to protect children from.

7. With respect to some notes I have reviewed regarding the work of the psychologist SN, I think she may have previously published in the area of child sexual abuse, though I cannot be 100% sure that it is the one and same person. I draw your attention to a paper she may have co-authored that concludes it is natural for a child to have some confusion about details.

It appears that some of the serious errors by the department are based on a false conclusion that a child who reports some inconsistencies with respect to dates and actions of abuse should be considered to be lying. It seems highly unusual that a professional who has published peer-reviewed work on such a specific issue would then apparently view that a child who consistently reports abuse and is believed by investigators, but who after three years may have reported some 'inconsistencies', is to be considered a liar.

I am deeply concerned that in the report dated 2019, SN states that Ella "agreed that her mother worried a lot about her getting hurt," which is then conjuncted with a comment from herself that Ella's mother thought Ella was deliberately hurt when it was an accident. This conjunction is highly misleading in that it artificially interpolates a suggestion from the therapist into a statement from the child. This is sloppy recording of facts and calls into question the reliability of any other statements in these reports as to whether or not they are the actual words of the patient or interpretations, leading statements, or misdirections by the therapist.

-- End of Afterword by Dr Kieran Le Plastrier

# ACKNOWLEDGEMENTS

I thank, in no particular order, the huge number of people who have assisted me. I thank Robert the Bruce for saving Scotland so that I could meet my husband. I thank Chaucer and the Bard for helping the English language. I thank my landlord Ted for installing air conditioning (I said this was in no particular order).

I thank all the Protective parents and empathize with their incredible suffering. I thank Dad for all the songs he taught me. I thank old Blackstone for having one eye on the pillory. I thank Boss Dee for many adapted photos and for not fussing over the niceties of, say, "minimum wage."

I thank [redacted] for persevering against all those bad judges, and may God forgive them. I thank Ed Wilson for 1970s mentoring. I thank the species that went before us and made possible the eye, the hand, and so forth (no, seriously). I thank my mother for being selfless and I mean selfless. I thank the whistle blowers and the survivors of MK-Ultra, total game-changers, they. I thank Trish for insisting on positive first (not that I wouldn't have anyway). I thank Fiona Barnett for not knowing when to quit. I thank George Maxwell for everything.

I thank the dear commenters at GumshoeNews for midnight companionship. I thank every ghost gum that ever lived. I thank the good cops and those who are hoping to "come out." (Don't wait too long, guys.) I thank Deb for caring about pedo stuff even to the point of door-knocking.

I thank the chillums who try to protect their Protective parents -- wouldn't that put everybody to shame. I thank my lawyer Paul for "bail," and Riley for brains. I thank Youtube for letting me think I am Edith Piaf and Paul Robeson all rolled into one. I thank the Adelaide Fringe. I thank Prema for giving me a miniaturized Bible. Diane has provided more inspiration than she knows. I thank my travel agent Teresa who helps me do my running away, and the great lady who wrote the Foreword. I thank any politician, doctor, or judge who gave succour *sub rosa*.

There are some people whom I do not thank, but we won't go into that just now. They know whom they are.

266

**BOOKS BY MARY W MAXWELL**

Human Evolution (1984)

Morality among Nations (1990)

The Sociobiological Imagination, editor (1990)

Moral Inertia (1991)

Prosecution for Treason (2011)

Teen Etiquette with Feelings  (2012)

Consider the Lilies (2013)

A Balm in Gilead (2014)

Fraud Upon the Court (2015)

Truth in Journalism (2015) co-author Dee McLachlan

Port Arthur: Enough Is Enough (2015) co-author DM

Inquest: Siege in Sydney (2017)

Deliverance! (2018)

The Soul of Boston and the Marathon Bombing (2019)

Reunion: Judging the Family Court

(Those last six are free downloads at GumshoeNews.com)

**Plays by Mary Maxwell at Adelaide Fringe Festival**

Puppetry of the Watermelons (2015)

A Pardoners Tale for Our Era (2016)

A Moot Court Trial for Martin Bryant (2017)

My Best False Memories (2018)

Crikey! Australian Conspiracy Theories (2019)